A TEXT BOOK OF
ANIMAL DIVERSITY - I

FOR
B.Sc. Zoology, Paper - I (Semester - I)

*As Per New Revised Syllabus of Shivaji University,
Kolhapur and Solapur University, Solapur*

Prin. Dr. KISHORE R. PAWAR
M.Sc., Ph.D.
Karmveer Shantarambapu Kondaji Wavare,
Arts, Sci. & Com. College, CIDCO,
Nashik – 422008.

Dr. ASHOK E. DESAI
M.Sc., Ph.D.
Reader in Zoology, P.G. Deptt. of Zoology,
K.T.H.M. College,
Nashik – 422002.

Dr. DAMA L. B.
M.Sc., Ph.D.
D.B.F. Dayanand College of Arts and
Science, Solapur
Dist. Solapur

Dr. PATIL R.N.
M.Sc., Ph.D.
Head, P.G. Department of Zoology and
Chairman BOS, Shivaji University
SGM College Karad, Dist. Satara

ANIMAL DIVERSITY - I   ISBN 978-93-5164-288-6
First Edition : **September 2015**
© : **Authors**

The text of this publication, or any part thereof, should not be reproduced or transmitted in any form or stored in any computer storage system or device for distribution including photocopy, recording, taping or information retrieval system or reproduced on any disc, tape, perforated media or other information storage device etc., without the written permission of Authors with whom the rights are reserved. Breach of this condition is liable for legal action.

Every effort has been made to avoid errors or omissions in this publication. In spite of this, errors may have crept in. Any mistake, error or discrepancy so noted and shall be brought to our notice shall be taken care of in the next edition. It is notified that neither the publisher nor the authors or seller shall be responsible for any damage or loss of action to any one, of any kind, in any manner, therefrom.

Published By :
NIRALI PRAKASHAN
Abhyudaya Pragati, 1312 Shivaji Nagar,
Off J.M. Road, PUNE - 411005
Tel - (020) 25512336/37/39. Fax - 25511379
Email : niralipune@pragationline.com

Printed By :
Repro Knowledgecast Limited,
Thane

DISTRIBUTION CENTERS

PUNE
Nirali Prakashan
119, Budhwar Peth, Jogeshwari Mandir Lane,
Pune - 411002, Maharashtra.
Tel : (020) 24452044, 66022708
Fax : (020) 2445 1538
Email : bookorder@pragationline.com

MUMBAI
Nirali Prakashan
385, S.V.P. Road, Rasdhara Co-op. Hsg.
Society, Girgaum,
Mumbai - 400004, Maharashtra
Tel : (022) 2385 6339 / 2386 9976,
Fax : (022) 2386 9976
Email : niralimumbai@pragationline.com

RETAIL SHOPS

PUNE
Pragati Book Centre
157, Budhwar Peth, Opp. Ratan Talkies,
Pune – 411002, Maharashtra
Tel : 2445 8887 / 6602 2707

Pragati Book Centre
676/B, Budhwar Peth,
Opp. Jogeshwari Mandir,
Pune – 411002, Maharashtra
Tel. : (020) 6601 7784, 2445 2254

PUNE
Pragati Book Centre
152, Budhwar Peth,
Near Jogeshwari Mandir,
Pune – 411002, Maharashtra
Tel : (020) 6609 2463 / 2445 2254

PUNE
Pragati Book Centre
Amber Chamber, 28/A, Budhwar Peth,
Appa Balwant Chowk
Pune : 411002, Maharashtra
Tel : (020) 20240335 / 66281669
Email : pbcpune@pragationline.com
Pragati Book Centre
917/22, Sai Complex,
F.C. Road, Shivaji Nagar,
Pune – 411004, Maharashtra
Tel. : (020) 2566 / 6602 2728

MUMBAI
Pragati Book Corner
Indira Niwas,
111-A Bhavani Shankar Road,
Dadar (W), **Mumbai** – 400028
Tel : (022) 2422 3525 / 6662 5254
Email : pbcmumbai@pragationline.com

DISTRIBUTION BRANCHES

NAGPUR
Pratibha Book Distributors
Above Maratha Mandir, Shop No. 3, First Floor, Rani Zanshi Square, Sitabuldi,
Nagpur 440012, Maharashtra, Tel : (0712) 254 7129

JALGAON
34, V. V. Golani Market, Navi Peth, Jalgaon 425001, Maharashtra,
Tel : (0257) 222 0395, Mob : 94234 91860

KOLHAPUR
New Mahadvar Road, Kedar Plaza, 1st Floor Opp. IDBI Bank
Kolhapur 416 012, Maharashtra. Mob : 9855046155

www.pragationline.com   info@pragationline.com

PREFACE

The authors are indeed very happy to present this book **'Animal Diversity - I'** for the students of B.Sc. Part I Zoology Paper I, Semester I of Shivaji and Solapur University.

The book has been written according to the new revised syllabus. Board of Studies of Zoology has thoroughly revised the syllabus which has been designed with the topic of Animal Diversity - I.

There was a long felt need of the students as well as teachers community for a text book which covers the entire syllabus prescribed by Board of studies. The present book is an outcome of our sincere efforts. We tried our level best to present the subject matter in easy style and in a comprehensive manner. The text book is profusely illustrated with number of clear line drawings.

No doubt, there are several textbooks written by Indian and foreign authors on the subject, but they are costly and number of copies are very limited in the college libraries. The students can not get the matter on prescribed syllabus in one book and they also cannot afford the costly books. Therefore, we have presented all the topics in one book in a low price. We sincerely feel that this book will fulfill the requirements of students and teachers.

We are thankful to Shri. Dineshbhai Furia, Shri. Jignesh Furia, Shri. M.P. Munde and the entire staff of Nirali Prakashan for taking keen interest in publishing this book and bringing out in time.

Constructive suggestions for improvement of the book are most welcome.

Authors

– **Authors**

SYLLABUS

(SHIVAJI UNIVERSITY)
B.Sc. Part - I, Semester - I : Paper I: Animal Diversity - I

Unit I
1. Principles of Classification (Five Kingdom Method) Salient features and classification up to classes with suitable examples of Kingdom Protista and Kingdom Animalia with reference to Phylum - Porifera, Coelenterata, Platyhelminthes, Nemathelminthes and Annelida. **(5)**
2. **Protista - *Paramoecium*** **(7)**
   - (a) Morphology
   - (b) Locomotion
   - (c) Nutrition
   - (d) Osmoregulation
   - (e) Reproduction (Binary fission and conjugation)

UNIT II
1. **Porifera - Sycon** **(6)**
   - (a) Morphology
   - (b) Cell types
   - (c) Canal System and its significance
2. **Coelenterata - Hydra** **(6)**
   - (a) Morphology
   - (b) Locomotion
   - (c) Nutrition
   - (d) Reproduction

UNIT III
1. **Platyhelminthes - Tape worm** **(3)**
   - (a) Morphology
   - (b) Parasitic Adaptations
2. **Nemathelminthes - Ascaris** **(3)**
   - (a) Morphology
   - (b) Parasitic adaptations

UNIT IV
1. **Annelida - Earthworm** **(10)**
   - (a) Digestive System
   - (b) Circulatory system
   - (c) Excretory system
   - (d) Nervous system
   - (e) Reproductive System and Cocoon Formation

***

(SOLAPUR UNIVERSITY)
Semester - I: Animal Diversity - I

1. Five Kingdom Classification: Salient Features and Classification upto classes of following kingdoms with suitable examples.
   - (A) Kingdom: Protista, (B) Kingdom: Animalia with reference to Phyla. Porifera, Coelenterata, Platyhelminthes, Nemathelminthes and Annelida. **[5]**
   (This topic may be taught in practical classes)
2. Protista – Type Study – Paramecium: Morphology, Locomotion, Nutrition Osmoregulation, Reproduction (Binary Fission and Conjugation) **[6]**
3. Porifera – Type Study – Sycon – Cell types and Canal system **[4]**
4. Coelenterata – Type Study – Hydra: Morphology (including Cell Types), Locomotion, Nutrition and Reproduction **[5]**
5. Platyhelminthes – Type Study – Tape worm: Morphology, Life Cycle and Parasitic Adaptations **[3]**
6. Annelida – Type Study – Earthworm (*Pheretima posthuma*): Morphology, Body Wall, Coelom, Digestive System, Circulatory System, Excretory System, Reproductive System (Copulation, Fertilization and Cocoon Formation) and Nervous System - Brain. **[12]**

***

CONTENTS

1. **Principles of Classification and *Protista - Paramoecium***
   1.1 - 1.136

2. **Porifera and Coelenterata**   **2.1 - 2.60**

3. **Platyhelminthes and Nemathelminthes**   **3.1 - 3.30**

4. **Annelida - Earthworm**   **4.1 - 4.56**

***

Chapter 1...

Principles of Classification and Protista - *Paramoecium*

(A) PRINCIPLES OF CLASSIFICATION

1.1 Systematics - Linnaean Hierarchy
    1.1.1 Systems of Classification

1.2 Nomenclature
    1.2.1 Binomial Nomenclature
    1.2.2 Trinomial Nomenclature
    1.2.3 Taxonomic Hierarchy
    1.2.4 Taxonomic Categories

1.3 The Five Kingdom Classification
    1.3.1 Monera
    1.3.2 Protista
    1.3.3 Plantae
    1.3.4 Fungi
    1.3.5 Animalia
- Summary
- Review Questions
- University Questions

1.4 Protozoa
- Summary
- Review Questions
- University Question

1.5 Porifera
- Summary
- Review Questions
- University Questions

1.6 Classification of Coelenterata
- ✍ Summary
- ✍ Review Questions
- ✍ University Questions

1.7 Platyhelminthes
- ✍ Summary
- ✍ Review Questions

1.8 Aschelminthes
- ✍ Summary
- ✍ Review Questions

1.9 Annelida
- ✍ Summary
- ✍ Review Questions
- ✍ University Questions

Introduction

- The living world of our planet earth consists of a great number of living organisms. The living organisms of the world again show great diversity and variations.
- There are unicellular micro-organisms like bacteria, *Paramoecia* which are seen only under a microscope as well as there are giant animals like elephants and whales.
- Among the living organisms there is great variety and number of animals and plants.
- Moreover, these tremendous variations in plants and animals which have again created problem to human being for their study. How to recognise and study the plants and animals with their similarities and differences was a difficult task for man.
- Therefore, from the beginning of human civilisation it was necessary to arrange them not only just by studying their external morphology but also their anatomy.
- With the available knowledge and methods, many biologists tried their level best and placed those organisms which show common characteristics in one category or group and so on. In other words they classified the organisms.

- For example, all green organisms which have no power of locomotion were grouped in the plant kingdom, while other non-green organisms capable of locomotion were placed in animal kingdom.
- But with the development of world civilisation and new scientific discoveries, creation of new sophisticated instruments and devices for analysis of subcellular and subatomic particles have again created another problem in the methods of systematic arrangement of plants and animals.
- Now, the old concepts which were taken into consideration for the systematic arrangement of plants and animals have been changed.
- Now, several aspects are to be considered for their arrangement, which include their anatomy, histology, embryology, cytology, physiology, cytochemistry, genetics, ecology, palaeontology, geography and evolution etc.
- If living things were not classified, it would be impossible to deal with their enormous diversity.
- It would be like dealing with a large library where books have not been classified and arranged according to title, subject or author.
- In such a library neither a title could be added in a meaningful way nor particular book located without a tedious search. In a similar manner biological classification allows us to identify organisms later. It also allows us to recognise those already classified.
- Classification is however, different from identification and should not be confused with it. In identification, we determine the correct place of an organism in a previously established plan or classification.
- Biological classification has two functions. The first, is to recognise and describe as completely as possible the basic taxonomic units or species. The second, is to device a way of grouping these units on the basis of their resemblances and relationships.
- Another importance of classification is that no scientific, ecological survey can be carried out without identification of all the species of ecological significance.

- We can readily appreciate that no purpose is served if a scientific study of an organism is made without knowing what the organism is. Even the experimental biologist needs sound taxonomy.
- A knowledge of systematics is complementary to all branches of basic and applied biology. It is needed for the identification of any organism of interest to us whether it would be economically useful, harmful, dangerous, disease-producing, a pest or a parasite.
- Systematics provides the basic information needed in many disciplines of agriculture, medical and verterinary science. So far, there are more than one million species of animals and more than half million species of plants are described. Still there are large number of organisms yet to be described.
- Therefore, for the discovery of new species of plants and animals knowledge of systematics is essential. Moreover, it is necessary to know much about the organisms of our surroundings. Hence, classification is of great importance for human beings.

1.1 Systematics - Linnaean Hierarchy
(Phylum, Class, Order, Family, Genus and Species)

- The term, systematics is derived from Latinised Greek word *Systema* as applied to the systems of classification and it is developed by early naturalist **Carlous Linnaeus** (1704-1778).
- **Systematics** may be defined as the science of diversity of organisms. A systematist determines by comparison, what are the unique properties of every species and groups of species at every level of classification.
- Taxonomy and systematics are complementary disciplines. Because of this, these terms are often used interchangeably.
- According to **Simpson**, *'Systematics is the scientific study of kinds and diversity of organisms and of any and all relationships among them'*.
- Systematic includes taxonomy, identification, classification and nomenclature and all other aspects of dealing with different kinds of organisms and data about them.

Fig. 1.1: Carlous Linnaeus (1704–1778)

- The origin and development of systematics and human civilisation began simultaneously. As the knowledge developed people started naming the plants and animals, according to their own choice.

- In *Vedas* and *Upanishads* (1500 B.C. to 600 B.C.), we get clues for earlier classification. In which several technical terms are used for description of plants. The ancient Indian scholar and ayurvedic physicians **Charak** and **Susruta** contributed lot to our knowledge of diversity and utility of organisms. **Parasara**, described plant life in *Vrikshayurveda* which formed the basis of botanical and medical studies in ancient India.

- Then Greek scientist **Aristotle** prepared a plan of classifying 500 different kinds of plants and animals that were known to him. In this *Historia plantarum*, he classified and described the plants but this classification was strictly artificial. Later on **Otto Burnfels** (1464-1554), **Jerome Bock** (1498-1554) and **Andrea Ceasalpino** (1519-1603) classified the plants.

- **Gaspard Bauhin** (1560-1624) who classified the plants on the basis of texture and form. **Carolus Linnaeus** (1707-1778) did the remarkable work in the field of taxonomy and therefore, he is often referred to as the 'Father of Taxonomy'. He gave the scheme of classification in his famous book 'Systema Naturae' in 1753. He introduced the binomial system of nomenclature. The work of **Linnaeus** became the foundation of systematics.

- **Lamarck** (1744-1829) had also described concepts of natural classification in his book. **Charles Darwin** (1809-1882) explained the origin of species through natural selection. **Huxley** (1940) introduced the new term "*New systematics*" in which he modified the older ideas of classical systematics.

1.1.1 Systems of Classification

Taxonomists have proposed three different systems of classification. They are: (1) Artificial system, (2) Natural system and (3) Phylogenetic.

1. **Artificial System of Classification:**
   - This system of classification was first adopted by **Pliny**, in the first century A.D. for animals.
   - He classified the animals on the basis of their flying ability or presence or absence of wings. The flying animals like butterflies, birds, bats were placed together.
   - This classification is based on comparison of one or a few characteristics or characters of convenience without relation to phylogenetic significance.
   - The characters erroneously presented to indicate phylogenetic relationship. Artificial classification is based on a single arbitrarily chosen criterion, instead of an evolution of the totality of characters.
   - Plants were also classified on the basis of habitat into herbs, shrubs and trees. The basis of classification adopted although very simple and easy to follow are arbitrary and do not reflect any natural relationship among the organisms.
   - Artificial classification, leads to heterogeneous assemblage of unrelated organisms under one common character which does not do justice to the totality of characteristics of an organism.
   - **Carolus Linnaeus** also adopted artificial system of classification for plants in which he considered number and the arrangement of stamens and carpels. Thus, this system conveys little information and cannot differentiate closely related species of organisms. But they are kept apart in this system.

2. **Natural System of Classification:**
   - This system compares many characteristics, which increases the amount of information available from groupings.

- This classification is based on the characters which indicate natural relationships and similarities.
- The organisms show close resemblance or similarities because they are descendents of one common ancestor.
- Zoologists and Botanists have different opinions regarding natural system of classification.
- According to Zoologists, this system includes the phylogenetic and evolutionary trends. But Botanists separate phylogenetic system to include the evolutionary trends in plants.
- **Bentham** and **Hooker** proposed the natural system of classification for plants.

3. **Phylogenetic System of Classification:**
   - This system is based on the evolutionary and genetic relationship of the organisms.
   - It gives clues to trace out the ancestors. However, our knowledge of phylogenic classification is inadequate.
   - The present phylogenetic systems are formed by the combination of natural and phylogenetic evidences. **Engler**, **Prantl** and **Hutchinson** first adopted this system for the classification of plants.

1.2 Nomenclature

- The common name of a species often varies with the language. Onion in English, Pyaz in Hindi and Bengali, Vengayam in Tamil and Irulli in Kannada and so on.
- Common names do not serve the purpose because a particular animal is known by different names in different parts of the world. For example, the bird house sparrow is known as gauraiya in India and Pakistan but it is known by different names in other countries. It is called Pardal in Spain, house sparrow in England, Suzune in Japan and Musch in Holland and so on.
- Many times the common name is also used for different kinds of animals. For example, the name Kenchua is used both for the earthworm and *Ascaris*. Thus, in classification naming is very important, which is called nomenclature.
- Nomenclature is the system of naming of plants or animals or groups of plants and animals.

- Taxonomists use the scientific names for organisms. When taxonomist identifies and describes the natural group of animals or plants, he gives appropriate scientific names to these groups.
- The scientific name is internationally accepted or universally used for a particular species or particular group of animals.

1.2.1 Binomial Nomenclature

- In naming an organism, the name of the species is composed of two words in Latin. Hence, the nomenclature is called *binomial nomenclature*.
- The first word is called generic name and it identifies the genus to which the species belongs. The second word called specific name which identifies the species itself. It is also known as two naming system.
- The genus (pleural-genera) is a group of related species which have several characteristics in common. The name of the taxonomist who first described the species name in a scientific journal is added at the end.
- As an example, *Homo sapiens* Linnaeus (or L. for short) is the complete scientific or technical name for the modern human species. Here *Homo* is the genus to which the species belongs and *sapiens* the specific name which identifies the species.
- In this case, **Linnaeus** was the first author to have published species named *Homo sapiens*. It is also important to note that the generic name always begins with a capital letter whereas the specific name does not. The scientific name should be printed in italics and underlined when typed or handwritten. Thus, it is *Homo sapiens* and not *homo sapiens*, *Homo Sapiens* or HOMO SAPIENS.
- Actually, binomial system is very old. **Cato** used two names for plants. Later on different ideas were developed with the evolution of the idea of nomenclature. In one idea Greek nouns were used for genera into Latin. This resulted into two words in the generic name. These were called binary generic names. The another idea was to use descriptive phases for specific names. This resulted into a polynomial system of nomenclature.
- Later on in 16th century, a number of binary generic names were changed to single ones. **Dodonaeus** and **Banhin** later followed in

general the binomial system but it is usually credited to **Linnaeus**. Thus, in binomial nomenclature long names were cut short so that they could be used with greater convenience.
- When the binomial system nomenclature was first used by **Linnaeus**, the appropriate Latin or Greek common names were used. For example, homo (= man in latin) became *Homo* and ficus (= fig, in latin) became *Ficus*. Technical names continued to be given in Latin. When words in a language other than Greek or Latin are used they are latinised with suitable ending.
- For example, banyan is *Ficus bengalensis*. Here *bengalensis* means from Bengal where the banyan is commonly found. In some organisms (fossil and most organisms) are known by their technical names only. In some cases, the generic and common names are same. Thus, *Gorilla* is gorilla and *Eucalyptus* is eucalyptus.
- To avoid confusion, no two generic names in any kingdom can be the same. Specific names can however, be repeated as they often qualify the generic name. For example, the specific name of both mango (*Mangifera indica*) and tamarind (*Tamarindus indicus*) are the same and mean of India. Being in Latin the gender of the specific name follows the gender of the generic name and hence, the difference in word-ending.
- Often specific names of animals and plants are given in honour of some persons. If the person honoured is a man the specific name ends in 'i'. For example, the earthworm *Lumbricus friendi* is named after Rev. H. Friend. If the person honoured is a woman, the specific name ends 'ae'. Sometimes the specific name indicates a locality (e.g. indica for India) or colour (e.g. niger for black).
- It is customary to write the name of taxonomist after specific name. If the species, after its publication, is transferred to any other genus or the generic name is changed the first authors name is written in brackets (parenthesis) For example, *Panthera leo* (Linnaeus) means that species leo was originally assigned by **Linnaeus** to some other genus (Felis).

2.2.2 Trinomial Nomenclature
- When nomenclature consists of three names called trinomial nomenclature. The three names are genus, species and

subspecies itself. Thus, use of subspecies is the third name in this method of naming.
- The subspecies name is also a Latin or Latinised word and follows the name of species to which it belongs.
- For example, the house crow *Corvus splendens* is found in India, Pakistan, Burma and Ceylon. There is slight morphological difference in the house crow of India and Pakistan, Burma and Ceylon.
- Therefore, they are separated as distinct subspecies.
- The Indian and Pakistani house crow has subspecific name *Corvus splendens splendens*, the Burmese house crow *Corvus splendens insolens* and Ceylonese house crow *Corvus splendens protegatus*. This type of naming is trinomial nomenclature. Botanist do not recognise a subspecies category.
- There is an International Commission on Zoological nomenclature and commission set up by International Congress of Zoology in 1898.
- This body has framed the rules which would be binding for all scientific journals dealing with taxonomical work.
- The aim of this organisation is to make the stability in naming the taxa, avoiding the use of names which may cause error, ambiguity or confusion. The International Zoological Congress is responsible for standardization and legislation of nomenclature.

Following are the common rules and recommendations which are considered as essential for nomenclature:

(i) The naming system adopted is binomial nomenclature to indicate the specific name and trinomial nomenclature for subspecific name.

(ii) The generic name is single and always begins with the capital letter. The specific name begins with small letter.

(iii) The name of the taxonomist, who first described the species name in a scientific journal is added at the end. It should be abbreviated and is printed in Roman type.

(iv) The scientific (technical) names of plants and animals must be different.

(v) The scientific names should be printed in italics and they must be in Latin or Latinised form.

(vi) Care should be taken that within plant and animal kingdom no two genera can have the same name as well as within a genus no two species can have the same name.

(vii) If the species, after its publication, is transferred to any other genus or the generic names changed the first author's name is written in bracket.

(viii) A name may be based on any part of an animal's life cycle.

Recommendations:

Following suggestions should be considered while giving new names:

(i) A name should be in Latin or it should be Latinised with suitable endings.

(ii) In the new name there should not be less than three and more than twelve letters.

(iii) It should be easy to pronounce.

(iv) The name should describe some important characteristics of the organism.

(v) A name should be derived from single language.

(vi) A name should be important.

Taxon and Category:

Taxon:

- The term taxon (plural: taxa) is used to refer to the concrete biological objects. The taxa are the groups of animals generally groups of species. For example, fishes, birds, reptiles and mammals are the groups of organisms in animals and algae, fungi, ferns, mosses etc. are the groups of plant organisms. Thus, these are the concrete objects of classification. Any such group of such population is called taxon.

- According to **Simpson** "*A taxon is a group of real organisms recognised as a formal unit at any level of hierarchic classification*". Like tigers are real animals belonging to the species category *Panthera tigris*.

- In this example, all tigers form the species taxon *Panthera tigris*. All cat like species of animals constitute the family taxon Felidae. All mammals constitute the class taxon Mammalia. All vertebrate animals constitute the subphylum taxon Vertebrata.

Category:

- The group of animals are taxa. Each taxon is placed at some level in hierarchy.

- A category designates level or rank in a hierarchic classification.
- The categories are species, family, order or class is an abstract term representing a rank of a level.
- But what is placed in a category are real or concrete biological objects. A category may be higher or lower. They have the names like kingdom, phylum, class and so on.

1.2.3 Taxonomic Hierarchy

- There are large number of plants and animals species in the living world. It is impossible to know them individually by their names or to refer them in the literature. Therefore, it is necessary to arrange them into categories and taxa of different grade.
- The categories and taxa are arranged in an ascending order to that the higher category includes one or more lower categories and higher taxa include one or more lower taxa.
- **Carlous Linnaeus** was the first taxonomist who established a definite hierarchy of taxonomic category in animal kingdom. There are species, genus, family, order, class, phylum and kingdom designate seven obligate categories or ranks in the hierarchy. Similar species are grouped into genus based on common characteristics, similar genera are grouped into a phylum. (Botanists use the term division instead of phylum). Finally, similar phyla are placed in a kingdom, the highest grouping.
- Such a classification is called a hierarchical classification. Hierarchy means a group of things ranked one above another.
- **Linnaeus** also used varieties as an optional category of various types of intraspecific variants, which was replaced by the species. Initially, few categories were used as the number of plants and animals was less.
- As the number of known species increased the original category names were used with prefixes super or sub. Thus, now in hierarchy there are super order, super family, sub order, sub family etc.
- Now the most frequently used additional new category called 'tribe' is used in between genus and family. There is another category called 'Cohort' used in between order and class and it was included by vertebrate palaeontologists.

- Some taxonomist also used some additional terms or categories like cladus, legio and sectio. Some used infraclass below subclass and infraorder below the suborder. Following are the universally accepted categories arranged in hierarchy.

  Kingdom
    Phylum
      Subphylum
        Super Class
          Class
            Subclass
              Infraclass
                Cohort
                  Superorder
                    Order
                      Suborder
                        Infraorder
                          Super family (– oidea)
                            Family (– idae)
                              Sub family (– inae)
                                Tribe (– ini)
                                  Subtribe
                                    Genus
                                      Subgenus
                                        Species
                                          Subspecies

- In the bracket or parenthesis, there are standardized ending for the names of tribes sub families and super families.
- The taxonomic hierarchy which is considered by some scientists as an unscientic system of classification. Therefore, some people have proposed alternate method called numerical scheme. But this scheme has not gained any support from taxonomists.

1.2.4 Taxonomic Categories

There are different categories in the taxonomic hierarchy which are described in brief as follows:

1. **Species:**
   - It is the most important category in the taxonomic hierarchy and it is considered as a basic unit in classification and in the process of evolution. Several taxonomists have defined the term species.

- Species refers to a group of organisms, that closely resemble each other either because they freely interbreed in nature, or because they have descended from common ancestors from a not too distant past.
- They are called Biological species. They are genetically special which are groups of interbreeding populations and are reproductively isolated from each other. They are thus, the same as Biological species.
- For example, in *Homo sapiens*, the *sapiens* is the species of *Homo*. The species inhabiting different geographical areas are called allopatric species. Whereas those species which occupy the same geographical areas called sympatric species.
- Some species only show morphological similarities known as morpho species. Sibling species include groups of very similar and closely related species.
- When there are two or more subspecies they are called polytypic species. Monotypic species consists of a single subspecies.
- Taxonomic species are given specific name under the International Rules of Nomenclature.

2. **Genus:**
   - The first higher category above the species level is the genus (*plural: genera*) which is a group of related species. The genus has a position of special importance in the classification.
   - By the rules of binomial nomenclature, a species cannot be named unless it is assigned to a genus.
   - Which species are then to be grouped together to form the various genera? In general, species in a genus usually have many features in common.
   - Such groups of common features are called correlated characters. Some of the correlated characters may appear small or inconspicuous, like the number or position of bristles on the wing of an insect. Others may be of great importance to the organism.
   - The significant point is species in which such characters occur together, are more closely related. Such species are taken to belong to the same genus.
   - Sometimes, a genus may consist of only one existing species, for example, modern man in the genus *Homo*.

3. **Family:**
   - This is a taxonomic category containing one or more related genera and which is separated from other related families by important and characteristic differences.
   - The family Felidae includes the tiger, the lion and all types of cats belonging to different genera. Felidae family is distinctly different from Canidae which includes dogs and foxes.

4. **Order:**
   - It is the basic taxonomic category which includes similar families, suborders, infraorders, super families and infra-classes. In some phyla, orders are well known groups, but in some they are less well known than classes.
   - For example, the order Carnivora includes families Felidae and Canidae.

5. **Class:**
   - Class is the basic category called the class group in which super classes, infraclasses are included. The classes are the best known taxa in animal kingdom.
   - The class is the subdivision of a phylum. For example, the order Carnivora includes the lion, the cat, are included in the class Mammalia.

6. **Phylum:**
   - The taxa included in the phylum category are the phyla which are nothing but the subdivisions of the kingdom.
   - The superphyla or subphyla are also included into phyla.
   - The phylum Porifera includes three classes such as Calcarea, Hexactinellida and Demospongia.

7. **Kingdom:**
   - Kingdom is the highest taxonomic category.
   - All types of animals are included in the animal kingdom and all plants are included in the plant kingdom.

1.3 The Five Kingdom Classification

Two Kingdom Classification:
- Until the early 1970s, it was customary to allocate all living organisms into two kingdoms namely animal kingdom and plant kingdom.
- We readily distinguish a living animal from a living plant in our environment.

- The plants are fixed in a place and have a spreadout appearance with green parts like leaves.
- Plants prepare their own food in the leaves by the process of photosynthesis.
- Whether it is a tall tree, a bush, a vine or a low creeper in the group we identify them as plants.
- The coloured seaweeds, green moss on a wet rock or a green filamentous tangle from a pond are plants.
- The animals are mobile and do not show photosynthesis. They have compact body.

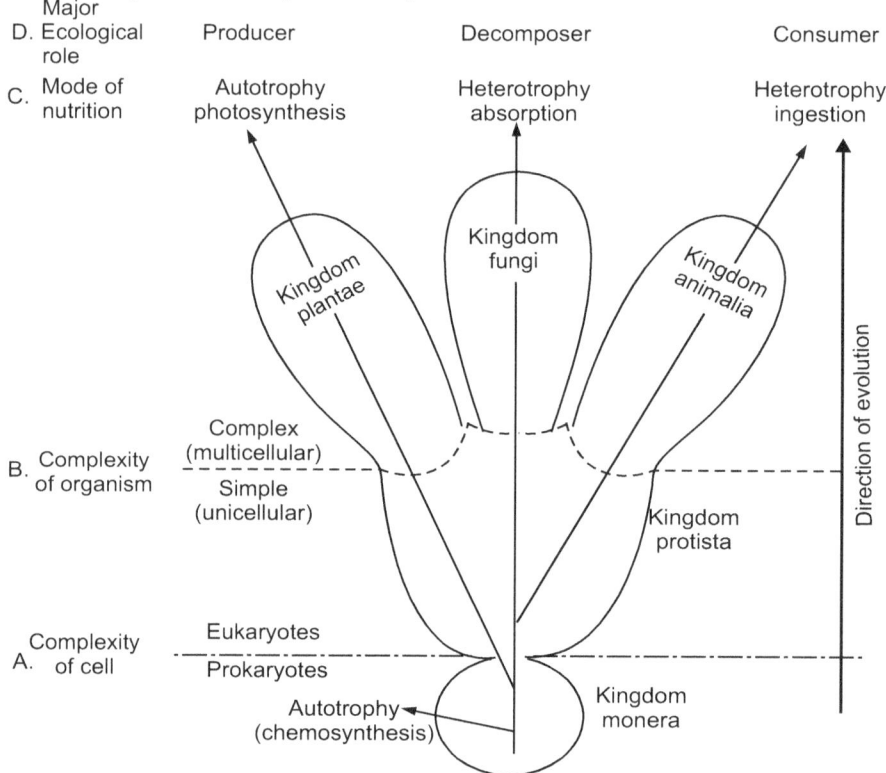

Fig. 1.2: The five Kingdoms of Life. The kingdoms are arranged to show the probable phylogenetic relationships among the kingdoms based on fossil and other evidences.
Such an arrangement allows us to visualise increase of complexity with evolutionary time and divergence of the three modes of nutrition in the three multicellular kingdoms (plants, fungi, animals)

- But, where shall we place the colourless cotton-like fungi growing on things like stale bread or mushroom growing out of a rotten log or a decomposing heap of straw?
- They live on decomposing and absorbing organic matter but do not prepare their food like plants. But given the option between plants and animals, we may still call them plants because of their immobility and their spreadout appearance. What about lichens growing on a rock or on a bark of a tree?
- If we examine a drop of water from pond, lake, ditch or sea under microscope, we can see numerous living things, some moving vigorously, some slowly and others hardly at all. Many of them are unicellular organisms of various shapes. Some are coloured green, yellow, brown or red.
- These are photosynthetic like green plants. Others are colourless. Where shall we place them among animals or plants?
- There are large number of different types of bacteria, the smallest living organisms, first observed in 1675 by the Dutch physician and microscopist **Leuwenhock**. Do we call these minute organisms plants or animals?
- Following the system of classification introduced by **Linnaeus**, all organisms were placed in either one of the two large kingdoms, the plant kingdom (or kingdom plantae) and the animal kingdom (or kingdom animalia).
- The animal kingdom included the multicellular forms and unicellular organisms called Protozoa (first animals). All other organisms, green plants, mosses and multicellular sea weeds, moulds and mushroom (fungi) lichen, minute coloured or colourless unicellular organisms and bacteria were put together in the plant kingdom.
- The grouping of such diverse organisms into only two kingdoms has appeared unsatisfactory to many biologists. It puts together eukaryotes (organisms with true nucleus in cells) with prokaryotes (organisms without true nucleus).
- It also lumps together non-photosynthetic fungi with photosynthetic green plants.
- Whether an organism was prokaryotic or eukaryotic or whether unicellular or multicellular, were not considerations, relevant to this fundamental division of life.

- Within this classification, the multicellular plants then formed one group the Metaphyta while unicellular photosynthetic were called Algae or Protophyta.
- Comparably the multicellular animals comprises the Metazoa and single celled animals Protozoa.

Such a two kingdom system clearly suffers from a number of drawbacks, of which two are major drawbacks.

(a) First, it does not reflect any real phylogenetic dichotomy: There is no evidence at all to suggest that the cyanobacteria, diatoms, red sea weeds, toadstools and conifers, for example: all belong to one natural group (plant kingdom) in contrast to the amoebae, gut flagellates sponges and echinoderms which all belong to a second (animal kingdom). Such artificiality need not be a significant problem, however, if the aim of the classification is purely pragmatic - the kingdoms might still provide an unambiguous, convenient but arbitrary pair of mutually exclusive divisions of living organisms.

(b) Second drawback is, that the two categories of plants and animals are not really distinguishable. Within a group of apparently closely related organisms, for example, the euglenoid flagellates, some species within a given genus are apparently plants, others can be considered animals and yet further species can be both at the same time. Some dinoflagellates also obtain some 5% of their requirements from photosynthesis and 95% from heterotrophic digestion of consumed materials. Moreover, a number of flagellates could even change the kingdom to which they were assigned by remaining in the dark for 24 hours.

The two kingdom system is thus neither a reflection of phylogenetic relationships nor it is a practical working scheme, in large measure because although many organisms are 'animals' and many are 'plants', many are neither plants nor animals.

During the last 15 years or so, an alternative basic classification, which seeks both to reflect phylogeny more accurately and to be unambiguous, has gradually been gaining adherents and is now that in most widespread use.

Five Kindgom Classification

A new five kingdom arrangement of organisms was proposed by **Whittaker** in 1969 to replace the old two kingdom classification.

In this classification, the separation into five kingdom is made on the following three criteria:
  (i) Complexity of cell structure.
  (ii) Complexity of the organisms body and
  (iii) Mode of obtaining nutrition.

In the five kingdom arrangement, the subdivisions of the old two kingdom classification are not altered. Instead, they are redistributed among additional kingdoms. Such an arrangement reflects the phylogeny of different life styles better.

The five kingdoms are (Fig. 1.2):
  (i) Monera   (ii) Protista   (iii) Plantae (plants)
  (iv) Fungi and (v) Animalia (Animals)

1.3.1 Monera: Kingdom of Prokaryotes

- Monera (monos = single) includes all prokaryotic (organisms without true nucleus) organisms viz. bacteria, actinomycetes a filamentous bacteria and photosynthetic cyanobacteria.
- Moneran cells are microscopic (1 to a few microns in length) and do not contain a nucleus or other membrane bounded organelles. Most moneran cells have a rigid cell wall.
- The moneran nutrition is varied. Many monerans decompose and absorb organic matter in solution. Their wall prevents ingestion of particulate organic matter. Some are heterotrophs, others are autotrophs.
- They prepare their own food by reducing carbon dioxide, using either light energy (photoautotrophs) or energy derived from chemical reactions (chemoautotroph). Many fix atmospheric nitrogen into ammonia, enriching the soil. Some monerans thrive symbiotically with higher forms of life, others are parasitic.
- Some monerans are able to thrive under extreme environmental conditions, such as absence of oxygen, high salt concentration or high temperature (80°C) or acidic pH. These are called Archae-bacteria (ancient bacteria), because they are probably early forms of life.
- They continue to live under conditions which resemble the conditions that prevailed on primitive earth.
- Monerans are the important decomposers and mineralisers in the biosphere.

1.3.2 Protista: The Kingdom of Unicellular Eukaryotes

Diagnostic and Special Features:
  (i) The protista (protiso - primary) includes diverse kinds of mostly unicellular and primarily aquatic eukaryotes (organisms with true nucleus in cells).
  (ii) They contain typical eukaryotic cell organelles such as nucleus, mitochondria, endoplasmic reticulum, golgi bodies and plastids (photosynthetic).
  (iii) They often bear flagella or cilia with 9 + 2 internal microtubular structure.
  (iv) Protists display diverse ways of life. Many are photosynthetic: autotrophs and are the chief producers in oceans and in fresh water environments.
  (v) They include coloured unicellular algae and diatoms are called phytoplanktons.
  (vi) Some protists are predatory feeding on other protists. They are called protozoa (first animals).
  (vii) Protozoa show holozoic or animal like nutrition.
  (viii) Some protozoans are parasitic in other animals.
  (ix) Some protozoans live in the digestive tract of other animals.
  (x) Some help in decompostion of organic matter like cellulose of plant cell walls, as found in termites and wood eating cockroaches.

1.3.3 Plantae: The Kingdom of Multicellular Plants

Diagnostic and Special Features:
  (i) Kingdom Plantae includes all the coloured, multicellular photosynthetic plants found on land, sea shores, in lakes and streams.
  (ii) These include red, brown and green algae, mosses, liverworts, ferns and seed bearing plants with or without flowers.
  (iii) Plant cell walls are rigid and made up of cellulose and hence, do not show contraction and relaxation like animal cell.
  (iv) Plants are immobile and do not show locomotion like unicellular protists and animals.

(v) They are producers because they show photosynthesis with the help of carbon dioxide, chlorophyll and solar energy. Plants synthesize their organic food.

(vi) A few flowering plants have evolved into totally heterotrophic forms, living as partial parasites or full parasites on other plants.

(vii) Some insectivorous plants have developed devices to trap and digest extracellularly small animals like insects and absorb their nitrogenous matter.

(viii) Some have developed symbiotic relationship with certain nitrogen fixing bacteria or with fungi to augment their nitrogen or mineral nutrition.

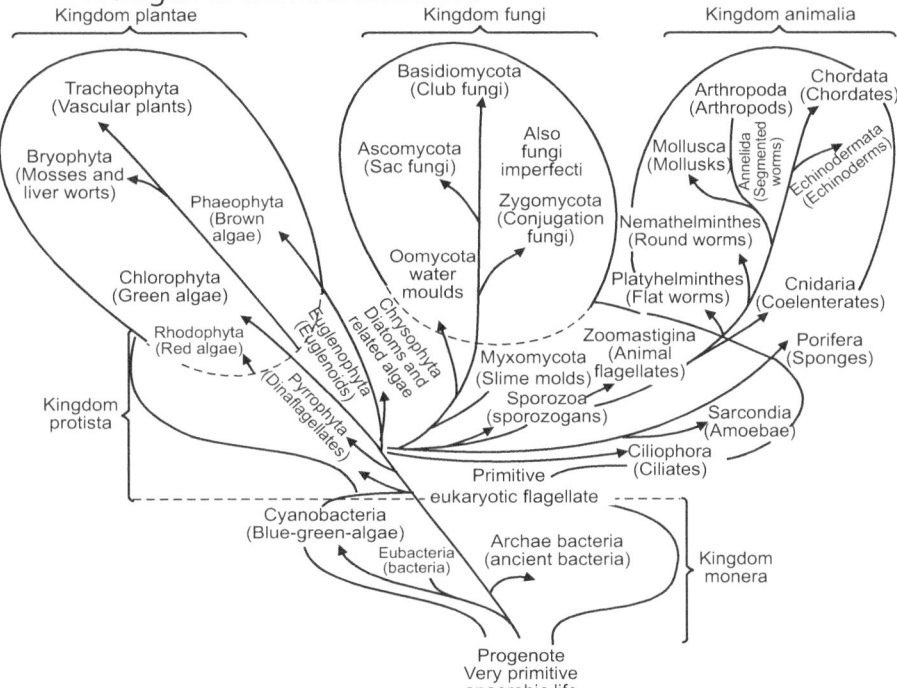

Fig. 1.3: The five kingdoms of life showing the major phyla and their probable evolutionary relationships (lines and arrows). The dotted line separates the prokaryotic kingdom (Monera) from the eukaryotics (Protista, Plantae, Fungi and Animalia). The arrangement of the multicellular kingdoms (Plants, Fungi, Animals) indicates how they may have evolved from the primarily unicellular kingdom Protista.

1.3.4 Fungi: The Kingdom of Multicellular Decomposers

Diagnostic and Special Features:
(i) Fungi include diverse kinds of eukaryotic, predominantly: multicellular heterotrophic organisms.
(ii) Their nutrition is by absorption of organic matter made soluable by decomposition or decay.
(iii) They are called saprobes when they live on decaying plant or animal matter.
(iv) Some fungi are called parasites when they assimilate tissues of living plants or animals.
(v) Fungi liberate digestive enzymes through their cell wall which makes complex organic matter soluble and is absorbed in solution.
(vi) Moulds, mushrooms, puff balls are the reproductive structures. These develop from tangle of filamentous vegetative assimilative body of the fungus which grow within the tissues of wood.
(vii) Parasitic fungi cause diseases like mildews, rusts, smuts, soft or dry rots, wilts and leaf spots in the host plants.
(viii) Yeasts are a group of exceptional fungi involved in fermentation. They have single celled body. Although they resemble protists in being unicellular, the mode of sexual reproduction indicates their relationship with multicellular fungi.

1.3.5 Animalia: The Kingdom of Multicellular Animals

Diagnostic and Special Features:
(i) Member of animalia are multicellular holozoic eukaryotes. They are also called as Metazoa.
(ii) Mode of nutrition is by ingestion of food.
(iii) The cells have ability to contract (muscle cells) or to transmit impulses (nerve cells). Sponges are exception because they lack nerve cells.
(iv) Some animal groups are parasitic which live on or within the tissues of other metazoans or plants. Some show symbiotic association with photosynthetic protists.

(v) The animal kingdom shows great diversity. These include sponges, cnidarians; flat, round or segmented worms, snails and other molluscs; arthropods, starfishes, and vertebrates such as fishes, amphibians, reptiles, birds and mammals.

Outline of Classification of Kingdom Animalia:

Kingdom Animalia is now divided into two subkingdoms Parazoa and Metazoa. The Parazoa includes only one phylum, Porifera (sponges). All the other phyla are included in the subkingdom Metazoa.

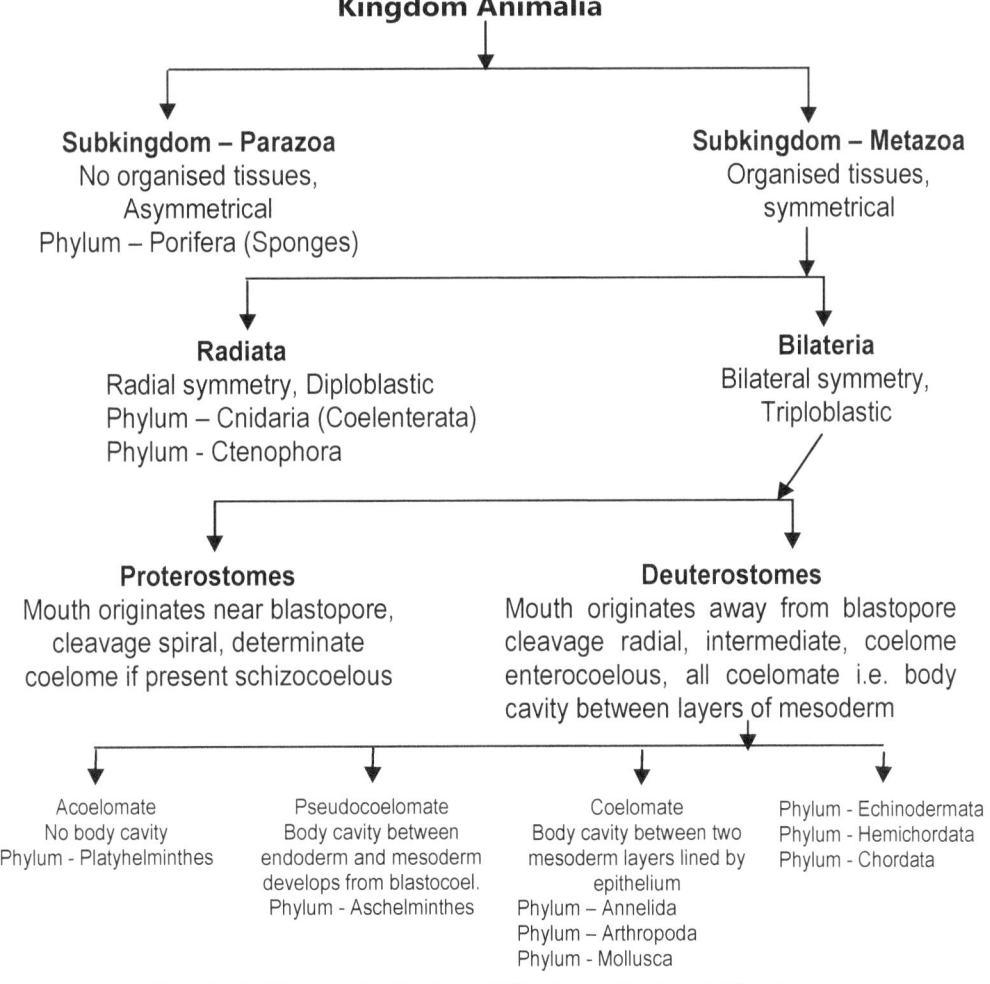

Fig. 1.4: Characteristics of Various Animal Phyla

Summary

- Classification of living organism is called Taxonomy and it is essential for scientific study.
- Systematics is scientific study of kinds and diversity of organisms and relationships among them.
- There are three methods of classification, namely artificial, natural and phylogenic systems.
- The name of the species is composed of two words called binomial nomenclature.
- If three names are there called trinomial nomenclature.
- **Carlous Linnaeus** was the great taxonomist who established taxonomic hierarchy.
- There are species, genius, family, order, class, phylum and kingdom designate seven categories or ranks in the hierarchy. They are called taxonomic categories.
- In two kingdom classification includes animal kingdom and plant kingdom.
- The five kingdom classification includes Monera, Protista, Plantae, Fungi and Animalia kingdoms.

Review Questions

1. Why is the two kingdom classification inadequate?
2. What are the aims and rules of International Code of Nomenclature?
3. Give an account of the system of classification suggested by Carlous Linnaeus.
4. What is systematics? What do you know about the origin and development of this branch of biology?
5. What is nomenclature? Give an account of binomial nomenclature.
6. Describe the different taxonomic categories.
7. What is species? Given an account of concept of species in taxonomy.
8. Make an outline of five kingdom classification. What are advantages and disadvantages of this classification?
9. Give the recent outline of classification of kingdom Animalia with suitable common examples.

10. Mention the diagnostic features of animalia.
11. Write short notes on:
    (i) Carlous Linnaeus
    (ii) Binomial Nomenclature
    (iii) Trinomial Nomenclature
    (iv) Taxonomic Hierarchy
    (v) Artificial and Natural classification
    (vi) Monera

University Questions

1. Define and explain:
   (a) Taxon (b) Systematics
   (e) Monera (f) Species
   (g) Genus, Cytostome, Food vacuole (h) Binomial nomenclature
2. Mention the distinguishing characters and classification of Phylum Protista. Give suitable examples and characters of any three subphyla.
3. Give general characters of Animalia.
4. Give general characters of Protista.
5. Write notes:
   (a) Diagnostic features of Plantae
   (b) Diagnostic features of Animalia.

1.4 Protozoa

Introduction

- The name protozoa means 'first animals' and this name has been derived from Greek word 'Protos' = first and zoon = animal. Thus they are regarded as most primitive animals, which appeared first in the evolutionary history.
- Protozoon consists of a single 'cell-like unit' or cell which is morphologically and functionally complete.
- These organisms exhibit all types of symmetry, a great range of complexicity and adaptations for all kinds of environmental conditions.

- Protozoa was first observed by **Leeuwenhock** (1677). The name protozoa was first given by **Goldfuss** in 1818. In the field of Protozology number of pioneers like **Joblott** (1718), **Linnaeus** (1758), **Hackle** (1862), **Ronald Ross** (1898), **Grassi** (1952), **Kudo** (1954) and **Allen** (1962) etc. have made the valuable contributions.

Definition

Protozoa may be defined as 'microscopic, unicellular organisms living singly or in colonies, without tissues and organs, having one or more nuclei. The colonial forms differ from Metazoa in having all the individuals alike except those engaged in reproduction.

General Characters

1. The protozoans are small and microscopic, ordinarily not visible without a microscope.
2. They are simplest and most primitive of all animals with protoplasmic grade of organisation.
3. They are unicellular animals without tissues and organs.
4. Body consists of mass of protoplasm with one or many nuclei which are monomorphic or dimorphic.
5. Protoplasm is differentiated into two parts, an outer thin; agranular and transparent ectoplasm and inner granular endoplasm.
6. Body may be naked or covered by an elastic pellicle or rigid dead cuticle or cellulose but in some forms body is covered with shells called an exoskeleton.
7. Although most protozoans are solitary individuals but there are numerous colonial forms. (In colonial forms, the individuals are alike and independent). Both solitary and colonial forms may be either free moving or sessile.
8. Body symmetry is non-radial, spherical or bilateral.
9. The shape of the body is usually constant but in some cases, it is unstable and in other it may change with environment and age.
10. Protozoans exhibit variable body shape; it may be oval, spherical, elongated or flattened.
11. Locomotory organelles are finger-like pseudopodia or whip like flagella or hair like cilia or none.

12. Nutrition is generally holozoic (animal like), holophytic (plant like), sporozoic or parasitic. The organelles of ingestion or egestion may be present or absent. Digestion occur intracellularly inside the food vacuoles.
13. Respiration occurs by diffusion through general body surface.
14. Excretion also occurs through general body surface but some times carried with the help of contractile vacuole. In some forms, temporary opening in ectoplasm is formed which helps in excretion or it is carried through a permanent pore called the cytopyge.
15. Contractile vacuoles perform the function of osmoregulation in freshwater forms.
16. All protozoa reproduce by asexual and sexual reproduction. Asexual reproduction occurs by binary fission or multiple fission and budding or sporulation and sexual reproduction occurs by conjugation of the adults (hologamy) or by fussion of gametes (syngamy).
17. Life cycle is often complicated with alternation of generation, i.e., it includes asexual and sexual phases.
18. Encystment commonly occurs to help in dispersal as well as to overcome unfavourable conditions of food, temperature and moisture.
19. Free living protozoans are mostly aquatic inhabiting fresh and sea waters and damp places. Parasitic and commensal protozoa live as ectoparasites or endoparasites.
20. The single celled body of protazoa is not distinctly differentiated into somatoplasm and germplasm, hence natural death does not take place in them.
21. All the vital activities of the life are performed by the single celled body of the protozoa and therefore, no physiological division of labour is exhibited by them.

The Phylum-Protozoa is classified into four subphyla.
Classification of Phylum Protozoa

There is dispute among the protozologists on the classification of Protozoa. **Barnes** (1980) considered four major groups i.e. Mastigophora Sarcodina, Sporozoa and Ciliophora as independent phyla. The following classification is adopted from the "Committee on Taxonomy and Taxonomic problems of the protozoologists" (Homiberge et al. 1964). According to this committee the phylum protozoa have been classified into four subphyla.

- Subphylum I: Sarcomastigophora
- Subphylum II: Sporozoa
- Subphylum III: Chidophora
- Subphylum IV: Ciliophora.

Subphylum I: Sarcomastigophora

1. Locomotory organs are pseudopodia or flagella.
2. Nucleus is monomorphic (single type).
3. Nutrition is holozoic or holophtic.
4. Asexual reproduction is by binary or multiple fission.
5. Sexual reproduction is by syngamy, no spore formation.

Class 1: Phytomastigophora

1. Most free living, freshwater or marine.
2. Plant like flagellates with or without chromoplast.
3. Usually one or two flagella, the nucleus is vesicular.
4. Reserve food as starch or paramylon.
5. Nutrition mostly holophytic or plant like by photosynthesis.
6. Sexual reproduction (syngamy) generally takes place.
7. Asexual reproduction by longitudinal binary fission or multiple fission.
8. Stigma and a contractile vacuole present anteriorily.
9. Anterior end with a gullet or cytopharynx.
10. Animals are large, slender with thick and stout pellicle.
11. Some are phosphorescent, they glow in dark.
12. Some forms are small solitary or colonial, some with rigid cellulose covering.
13. Under adverse conditions they form cysts.

Examples: *Euglena, Volvox, Noctiluca*.

Class 2: Zoomastigophorea (Zoomastigina)

1. Flagellates with neither chromoplasts nor leucoplasts.
2. One to many flagella, in most cases with basal granule complex.
3. Chromatopheres are absent.
4. Nutrition holozoic or sporozoic or parasitic.

5. These animals are free living or parasitic, commensals, or symbionts.
6. Sexual reproduction is rare.
7. Reserve food in the form of glycogen.
8. Some forms are parasitic in reproductive passages of man and other vertebrates.
9. Some forms are gut parasites or symbionts of wood-eating insects.

Examples: *Trypanosoma, Giardia, Trichomonas, Trichonympha*

Superclass B: Opalinata

1. They have numerous cilia in longitudinal oblique rows which uniformly cover the entire body surface.
2. Cytostome absent, nutrition saprozoic.
3. Two or more monomorphic nuclei are present.
4. Contractile vacuoles are absent.
5. Asexual reproduction by symmetrigenic binary fission.
6. Sexual reproduction (syngamy) by fusion of flagellated anisogametes.
7. There is no conjugation.
8. Encystment is common during host's breeding season.
9. They are endoparasites or gut commensals of cold blooded vertebrates, especially anurans.
10. Body is covered by thin and tough pellicle.
11. Mouth, gullet, cytopyge, food vacuoles and contractile vacuoles are absent.
12. The ectoplasm is clear and contains longitudinal contractile fibres, the myonemes.

Examples: *Opalina, Protoopalina*.

Superclass C: Sarcodina

1. Body is naked or with a hard internal shell or external test formed from various materials.
2. Locomotion and food ingestion by one or more processes of body called pseudopodia which may be short and blunt or long and delicate.
3. The amoeboid form is predominant.
4. Cytoplasm usually differentiated into an outer ectoplasm and inner endoplasm.

5. Contractile vacuoles are present except in marine forms.
6. Nucleus is single.
7. Asexual reproduction mostly by binary fission.
8. Sexual reproduction with flagellate or amoeboid gametes.
9. Formation of gametes and flagellated young ones are common.

Class 1: Rhizopodea
1. The locomotory organelles are *lobopodia, filopodia,* or *reticulopodia* but never *axopodia*.
2. Generally creeping forms.

Examples: *Amoeba, Entamoeba histolytica, Arcella, Polystomella, Actinophrys.*

Class 2: Actinopodea
1. The delicate axopodia with axial filament are the locomotory organelles.
2. They are primarily sessile or floating forms.
3. Test may be present or absent.
4. Reproduction by both asexual and sexual method.
5. Some are freshwater and some forms are exclusively marine.
6. Body is spherical with skeleton of mostly siliceous spicules.
7. Cytoplasm is divided into outer vacuolated and inner dense zone without central capsule.

Examples: *Actinophrys, Thallassicolas, Collozoum.*

Class 3: Piroplasmea
1. These animals are small, round, rod-shaped or amoeboid.
2. They are parasites in red blood cells of vertebrates.
3. They do not produce spores.

Example: *Babesia.*

Subphylum II: Sporozoa
1. They are all endoparasites and infect animals of all the phyla.
2. The sporozoa have simple body without locomotory organelles.
3. They lack mouth, gullet and food vacuoles.
4. Nutrition is saprozoic but occasionally holozoic also.
5. Life cycle is complicated and includes two reproductive phases: asexual or schizogony and sexual or syngamy.
6. Infective bodies or sporozoites are formed in syngamy hence they are called sporozoa.

7. Alternation of generations are accompanied by alternation of hosts.
8. Cilia or flagella may be present in gametes.

Class 1: Telosporea
1. Pseudopodia are absent and locomotion is by gliding or body flexion.
2. Spores without capsules or filaments, naked or encysted.
3. Adult trophozoites with one nucleus.
4. Reproduction is both by asexual or sexual method.
5. These are parasites of gut and body cavity of invertebrates.
6. They are parasites in epithelial and blood cells of invertebrates and vertebrates.
7. Body is covered with thick pellicle.
8. Nutrition sporozoic.
9. Sexual reproduction by spore formation.

Examples: *Monocystis, Plasmodium.*

Class 2: Taxoplasmea
1. Spore formation is absent.
2. Reproduction is only by asexual binary fission method.
3. There are no flagella or pseudopodia.
4. Cysts are formed which have many naked sporozoites.
5. They are parasites in vertebrates.

Examples: *Toxoplasma, Sarcocystis.*

Class 3: Haplosporea
1. Spores are present.
2. Pseudopodia may be present but flagella are absent.
3. They show only sexual reproduction.
4. These animals are the parasites of fish and invertebrates, chiefly annelids.
5. Spore cases are absent.
6. The spores are few in cysts and they are small.

Examples: *Ichthyosporidium and Haplosporidium.*

Subphylum III: Chidophora
1. All the animals are parasitic.
2. Spore function occurs throughout life.
3. Spores have several cells having one or more polar filaments which are coiled threads and can be shot out.
4. Adult trophozoites have many nuclei.
5. Zygote gives rise to one or more trophozoites without sporogony.

Class 1: Myxosporidea
1. Spores are of multicellular origin i.e. they develop from several nuclei and enclosed in two or three valves. Polar capsule present with 1, 2 or 4 filaments.
2. They are parasites in fishes.
3. Trophozoites are amoeboid and not intracellular.

Examples: *Myxidium, Triactinomyxon.*

Class 2: Microsporidea
1. Spores are small, with univalved membrane.
2. Polar capsule present or absent with 1 or 2 filaments.
3. They are cytozoic (intracellular) parasites in arthropods and vertebrates.

Example: *Nosema.*

Subphylum IV: Ciliophora

Subphylum Ciliophora
1. They are complex protozoa with a definite form and size.
2. Body is naked, bounded externally by a firm pellicle.
3. They possess simple cilia or compound ciliary structure as locomotor or food acquiring organelles at sometime in the life cycle.
4. They also show infraciliary system composed of basal granules below the cell surface and interconnected by longitudinal fibrils.
5. They have two nuclei, a vegetative macronucleus and a reproductive micronucleus.
6. Defined mouth (cytostome) and gullet (cytopharynx) are present except in parasitic forms. Anal aperture (cytopyge) is temporary.
7. Contractile vacuole one or more even in marine and parasitic types.
8. Asexual reproduction by binary fission.
9. Sexual reproduction by conjugation with the fusion of nuclei, autogamy and cytogamy also occur.
10. There are never any free gametes.
11. They show mixotrophic or heterotrophic nutrition.

Examples: *Paramoecium, Didinium, Vorticella, Nyctotherus, Balantidium coli.*

Class Ciliata

1. Cilia are present during the whole or a part of life cycle.
2. Mouth or cytostome and cytopharynx are often present.
3. Nutrition is holozoic.
4. Reproduction asexually by binary fission or budding and sexually by conjugation and autogamy.
5. They are mostly free living in freshwater, marine environments but parasites, colonial and sedmentary forms also occur.
6. Two types of nuclei, one vegetative (macronucleus) and the other reproductive (micronucleus).
7. They show infraciliary system, composed of basal granules below the cell surface and interconnected by longitudinal fibrils.
8. No formation of free gametes in sexual reproduction.
9. Some forms sessile, stalked ciliates are with the distal and bearing few to many tentacles.

Examples: *Paramoecium, Didinium, Vorticella, Nycotherus, Balantidium coli, Stentor, Ephelota.*

Some representatives of Protozoa

1. *Euglena*

It is a common and free living freshwater flagellate found in freshwater ponds, ditches and pools. Its body is elongated, spindle shaped with whiplike flagella. Flagellum is organ of locomotion but also useful in food capture or serve as sensory organelle. The body form is maintained due to thin covering membrane called pellicle. It is chlorophyll bearing protozoan. The animal possess cytostome or cell mouth at the anterior end. Cytostome leads into cytopharynx or gullet. It joints a large spherical vesicle called reservoir. Large contractile vacuole lies near it which is osmoregulatory in function. Just near posterior end, large nucleus is present. Paramylon granules are present in the endoplasm. Chromatophore or chloroplasts are radiating bodies present for photosynthensis. Animal shows holophytic or saprophytic or both modes of nutrition. Euglena reproduces asexually by longitudinal binary fission but sexual reproduction does not occur.

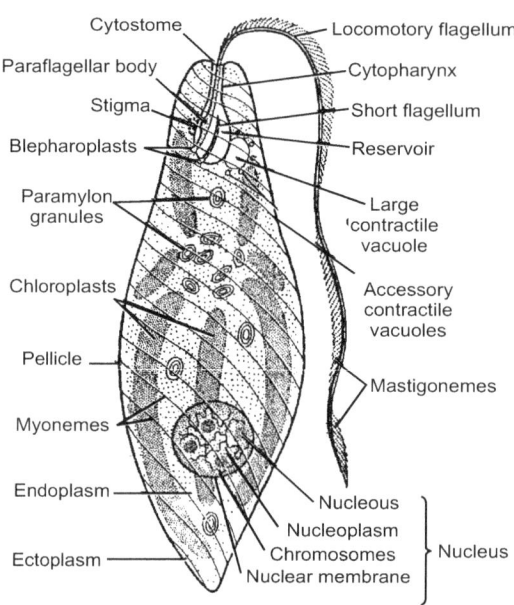

Fig. 1.5: *Euglena viridis*

2. Volvox

It is a colonial flagellate found in freshwaters. The colony has a genatinous matrix forming a round hollow ball filled with a fluid. The colony consists of thousands of zooids (somatic cells) arranged in a single peripheral layer. The cells are connected by protoplasmic threads. Each zooid shows two flagella, two or more contractile vacuoles, cuplike chloroplast, a single nucleus, a red stigma but no gullet. Nutrition is holophytic. Animal shows locomotion by combined action of flagella.

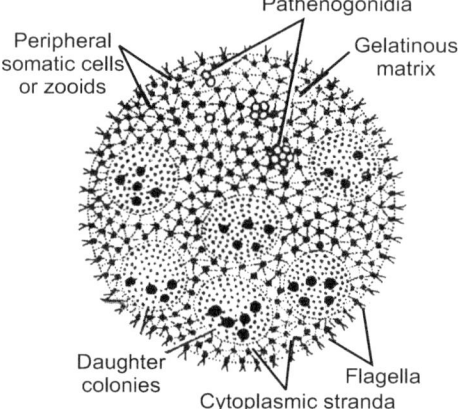

Fig. 1.6: *Volvox globator*. **Vegetative colony**

Size of the colony increases by binary fission. In the colony, the zooids called parthenogonidia repeatedly divide to form daughter colonies which are released from parent colony, biflagellate microgametes are formed by specialized cells called antheridia. *Archegonia* gives rise to non-flagellate macrogametes. By the fusion of both gametes zygote is formed that forms new colony after dormancy.

3. ***Trypanosoma***

It is heterotrophic and common parasite in blood, lymph and tissues of vertebrates. A part of life cycle is passed within alimentary canal of some blood sucking invertebrates hosts, such as insect, mites, ticks or leeches.

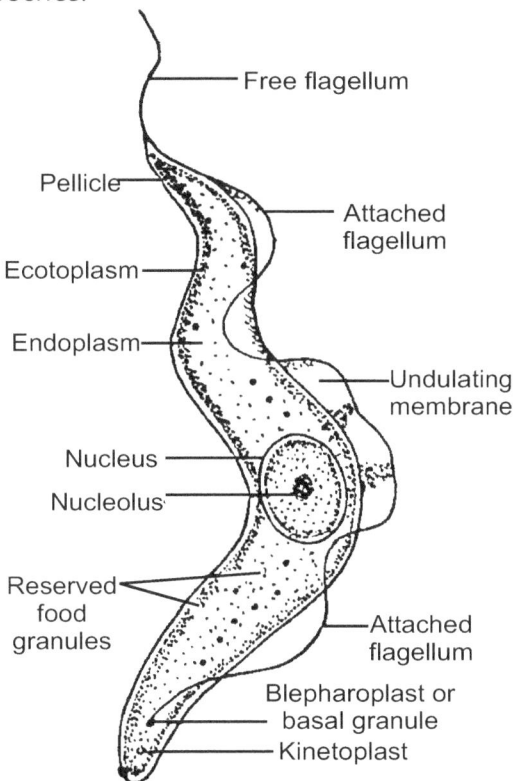

Fig. 1.7: *Trypanosoma gambiense*.
Structure under ordinary microscope

This protozoa parasite causes the most dreaded disease of Ganbia or African sleeping sickness. It is found in the blood, body fluids and spinal fluid of man. It is transmitted by insect host the tse-

tse fly. It lives in the blood of antelope, monkeys, pigs, buffaloes, dogs and other wild and domesticated animals. It is long, slender and spindle shaped but pointed at the both ends. Body is covered by thin, elastic and protective pellicle. It is uniflagellar animal bears a single, strong locomotory flagellum. It also shows membranous fold called undulating membrane useful for movement in the blood or body fluid. In the centre of the body nucleus is present. Cytoplasmic granules are present in the endoplasm. The animal reproduce by asexual method called binary fission.

4. *Noctiluca*

It is marine and pelagic protozoan, occurring near the shore. It is large globular animal with highly vacuolated cytoplasm. It has two flagella, one called tentacle and another which is a delicate flagellum. At ventral pole in a depression longitudinal oral groove representing sulcus. This groove has an oval mouth leading into the gullet. Nutrition is holozoic i.e. animal like. Reproduction takes place asexually by binary fission as well as by syngamy. Zoospores are formed by fusion of two organisms. When agitated, it glows with bluish or greenish light. The photogenic granules luciferin are responsible for luminescence. This reaction occurs in presence of enzyme luciferase and emits light.

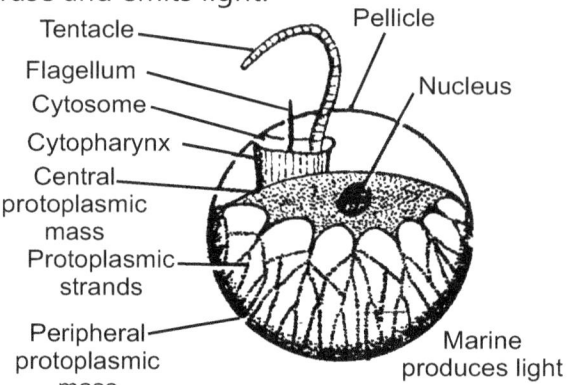

Fig. 1.8: *Noctiluca*

5. *Ceratium*

These are fresh water as well as marine organisms. Body is covered by cellulose plate which gives triangular shape to the animal. One anterior and two posterio-lateral processes giving it a triangular shape. The transverse groove is called as annulus and longitudinal groove is called sulcus. Cytoplasm is differentiated into ectoplasm and endoplasm. Cytoplasm contains starch granules, nucleus, chromoplast and contractile vacuoles. Nutrition is mainly hylophytic. Reproduction is by oblique binary fission.

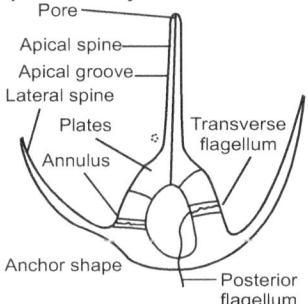

Fig. 1.9: *Ceratium*

6. *Giardia*

It is parasitic protozoan found in small intestine and colon of man, rats, mice, dogs, cats and frogs. Body is oval in shape with broad anterior end and narrow posterior end. The animal has two cesicular nuclei and four pairs of long flagella. The basal granules of foremost flagella are interconnected and also connected with pair of nuclei. Axostyle forms the median longitudinal axis of the body. On the ventral surface sucking disc is present. Animal exhibits caudal flagella towards narrow posterior end. Reproduction takes place by longitudinal binary fission. Thick walled cysts are formed and division occurs in the cyst forming four nuclei. This parasite prevents absorption of fats by the host in intestine which causes diarrhoea, fever, anaemia, allergy and acute enterocolitis.

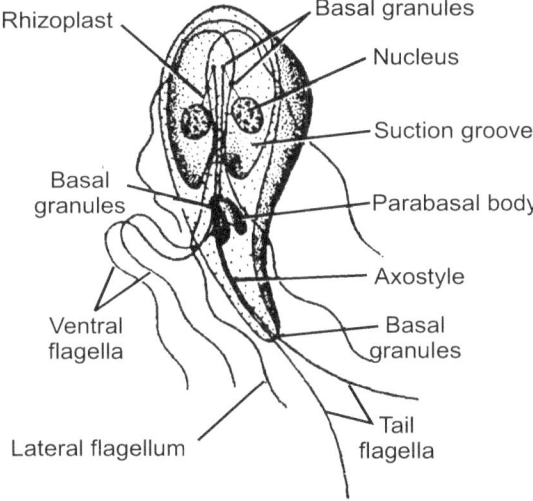

Fig. 1.10: *Giardia intestinalis*

7. Trichomonas

It is most common intestinal parasite of all vertebrates and also in termites and leeches. The body is pear shaped tapering posteriorly and provided with four flagella. Three are at the anterior end and one is directed backwards and joined with undulating membrane. Cytostome is present at the anterior end useful for ingestion of food. Blapharoplast is minute located at the anterior end. Cube shape parabasal body is extending posteriorly from the blapharoplast.

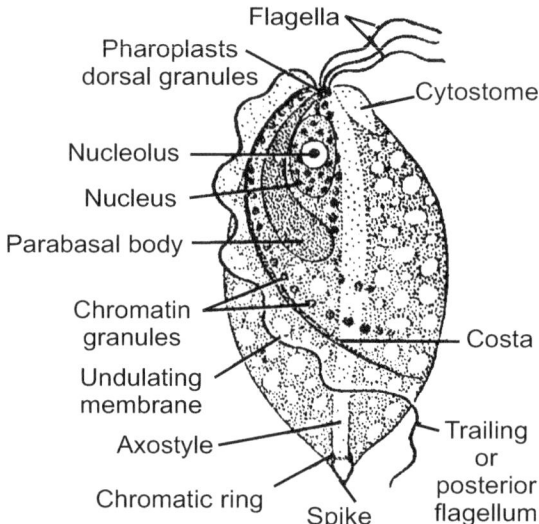

Fig. 1.11: *Trichomonas buccalis*

A contractile fibre called costa runs along the line of attachment of undulating membrane. The axostyle runs backwards and projects from posterior end as spike. The spike is useful as a anchoring organ while feeding. At the anterior end the large nucleus is situated in the endoplasm. Nutrition is sporozoic but some species ingest bacteria, yeast and other solid food. Reproduction takes place by longitudinal binary fission. In man, species of this parasite found in different body regions like mouth, colon and vagina. It causes inflammation of vaginal mucosa in females. *Trichomoniasis* is caused by this parasite.

8. Opalina

It is an endoparasite or endocommensal in the large intestine of frogs and toads. The body is flattened, leaf-like and oval in outline and covered by thin pellicle. Many rows of cilia are present. The mouth, cytopyge, food vacuoles and contractile vacuoles are absent. Nutrition is by pinocytosis. There are several small, spherical and similar sized nuclei present in the endoplasm. The nuclei are evenly distributed. The animal reproduces by longitudinal and transverse binary fission. It also shows reproduction by plasmotomy in which the cell division is repeated again and again without division of nuclei. Thus, many daughter cells are produced each having 3 to 6 nuclei. The daughter cells encysted and pass out in the faecal matter of the host. When tadpole swallows the cysts they hatch in the rectum as gametocytes. These gametocytes undergo longitudinal fissions and form uninucleate gametes. The small gametes are called microgametes and large gametes are macrogametes. After conjugation of gamete, there is formation of zygotes. This zygote undergoes encystment forming zygocyst. With rapid nuclear division and growth, each zygote reaches the normal multinucleate adult stage.

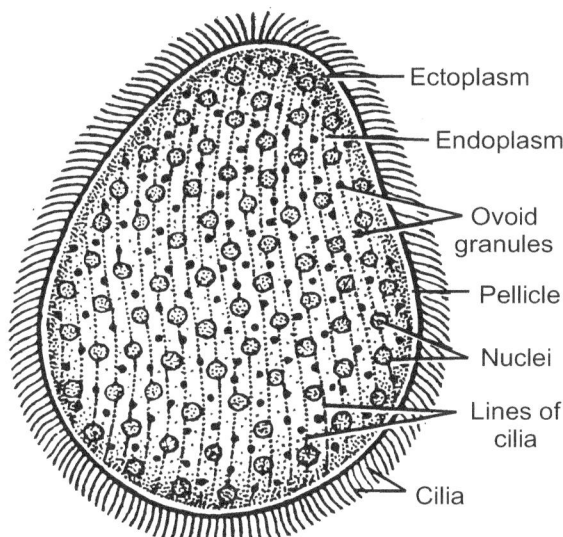

Fig. 1.12: *Opalina*

9. Amoeba

It is freshwater, unicellular, microscopic organism which can be seen only with the help of microscope. Its shape is more or less irregular, colourless, translucent. Amoeba continuously changes its shape. The finger-like blunt processes are called pseudopodia. These are locomotory organs. Body is a mass of naked protoplasm and it is not covered by pellicle or cell wall. However, relatively tough, elastic and semipermeable membrane or plasmalemma covers the body. Cytoplasm is differentiated into outer ectoplasm and inner endoplasm. Single, biconvex, disc like nucleus is present in the endoplasm. There are many food vacuoles and single contractile vacuole in the endoplasm. Contractile vacuole performs the function of osmoregulation. Amoeba reproduce by asexual method by binary fission and multiple fission.

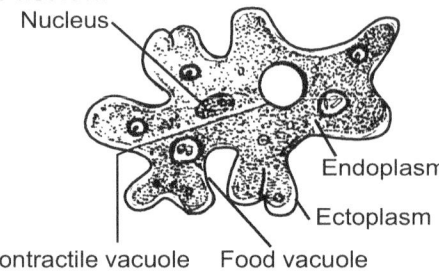

Fig. 1.13: *Amoeba*

10. *Arcella*

It is freshwater amoeba which secretes a pseudochitinous shell of brown or yellow colour. The cell is single chambered made up of siliceous prisms embedded in a chitinoid substance called tectin. On the ventral side the shell has an opening called pylome from which 3-4 pseudopodia project. The cytoplasm possess two or more nuclei and ring of granules called chromidia. There are several contractile vacuoles, food vacuoles and gas vacuoles in the cytoplasm. The animal reproduce by division of two nuclei into four. Two nuclei with some cytoplasm secretes new shell. Then this double shelled animal divides into two daughter cells with shell which forms two animals.

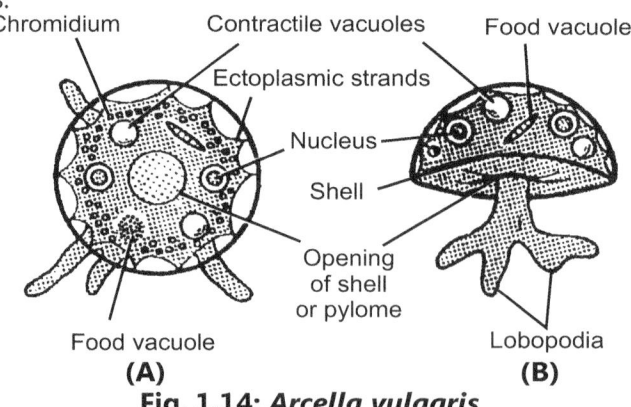

Fig. 1.14: *Arcella vulgaris*
A. Dorsal view, B. Side view

11. Polystomella

It is a large amoeba called chaos. The body shape changes constantly and it is asymmetrical. The animal shows single, large, blunt pseudopodium, the organ of locomotion. There are many nuclei, food vacuoles, rod like bacteria, sand particles and glycogen granules. The cytoplasm bears many fluid-filled vacuoles but they are not contractile in nature. This animal is found in the mud of pond rich in vegetable matter. It gets food by ingestion of mud.

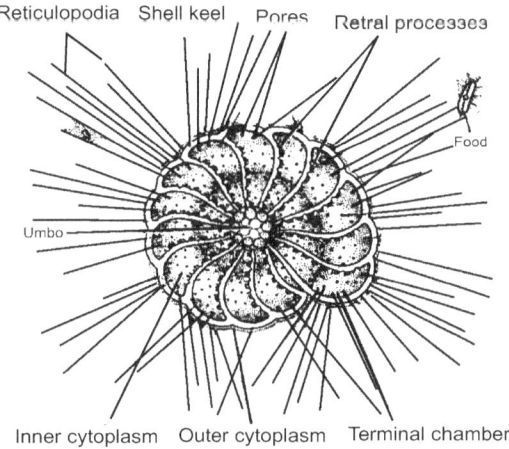

Fig. 1.15: *Polystomella*

12. Monocystis

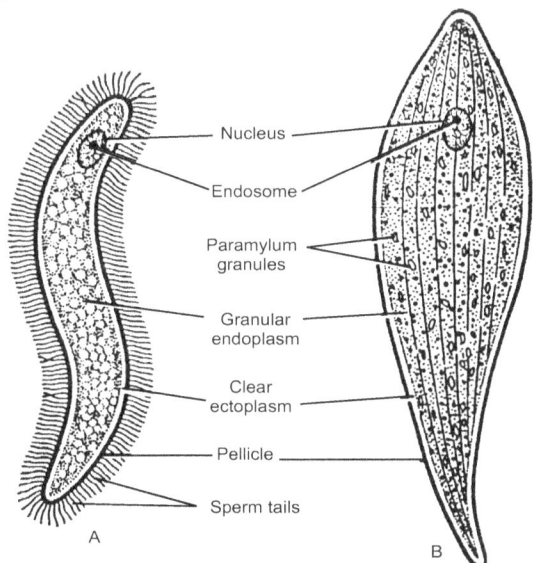

Fig. 1.16: *Monocystis*

Monocystis is an intra-cellular parasite of earthworms. Its life cycle is completed in one host only. It is microscopic, wormlike and unicellular. The adult *monocystis* is called trophozoite. It is elongated, spindle shaped, flattened and wormlike creature. Body is covered by thick smooth and permeable pellicle. Cytoplasm is well differentiated into ectoplasm and endoplasm. Endoplasm contains a large vesicular nucleus. Its nutrition is sporozoic. There are no locomotory organs but it shows wriggling and gliding movements. Infection in earthworm occurs when it ingests a sporocysts containing 8 sporozoites which are the infective stages. Reproduction takes place by spore formation. There is no sexual multiplication by schizogamy.

13. *Plasmodium*

Plasmodium is an intracellular blood inhabiting sporozoan parasite causing malaria. It completes its life cycle in man or other vertebrates and in the alimentary canal and salivary glands of mosquitoes. Sexual cycle is completed in the female *Anopheles* mosquito and asexual cycle is completed in man. The mature adult of *Plasmodium* is called trophozoite, which is amoeboid in shape, uninucleated having vacuolated and granular cytoplasm. It possess plasma membrane covering and cytoplasm contains organelles like mitochondria, golgi apparatus, haemozoin, vacuole, nucleus and endoplasmic reticulum. The mode of nutrition is sporozoic. There are no organs of locomotion. It shows anaerobic respiration. Reproduction occurs both by sexual and asexual method.

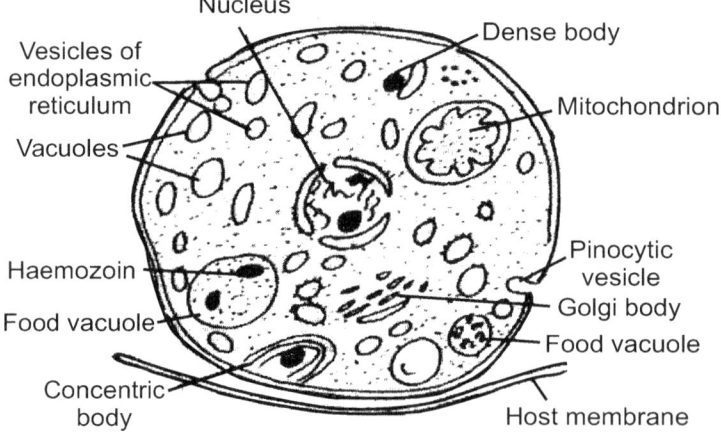

Fig. 1.17: *Plasmodium*

14. *Sarcocystis*

It is a vertebrate parasite found in sheep, pig, rabbit, rat, cattle, horses and also in reptiles and birds. Sometimes, it is found in man also. The parasite is in the form of long spindle shaped multinucleated cyst which is found embedded in the striped muscle fibres of the host. The spindle-shaped masses of parasites form long, slender, cylindrical bodies with pointed ends. They are called as Miescher's or Rainey's tubes. In each tube large number of sickle-shaped spores are formed and they are called Rainey's cells. There is no detailed information on the transmission of this parasite. It causes the disease in the host known as sacrcosporidiosis. The parasite produces toxic substance called sarcocystin in rabbits.

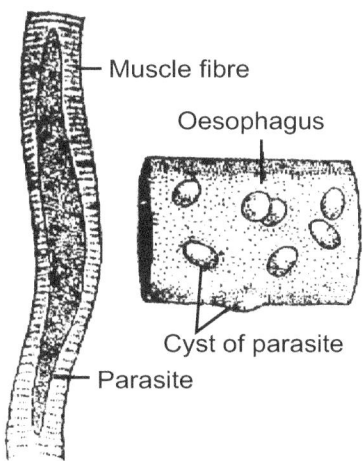

Fig. 1.18: *Sarcocystis*

15. Collozoum

It is colonial protozoan with subspherial body. Protoplasm is differentiated into intracapsular and extracapsular protoplasm by performated membrane. The extracapsular protoplasm is vacuolated and common to the whole colony having sexual central capsules embedded in it. Each central capsule is nothing but a zooid of the colony and it has single nucleus. Extracapsular protoplasm does not divide whereas central capsule undergoes repeated divisions. Contractile vacuole and skeleton is absent. Reproduction by merogony. Marine animals are found in deep sea.

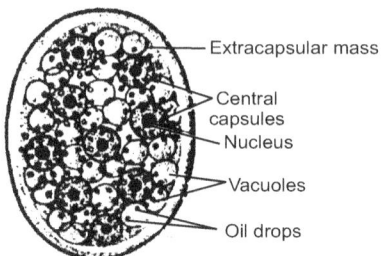

Fig. 1.19: *Collozoum*

16. *Babesia*

It is sporozoan parasite found in the blood of host sheep, cattle, goats, horses, dogs and other mammals. It is transmitted in the body of host by the bite of ticks. The sporozoites are transferred into the body of host when the tick feeds on it. The *Babesia* causes the formidable Texas fever or Red water fever in cattle in Australia and America. The female cattle tick serves as the intermediate host. There are different species of Babesia attacking on different animals.

Fig. 1.20: *Babesia*

17. *Nosema*

This parasite animal causes fatal disease 'pebrine' in silkworms. The parasite is found in eggs, larvae, pupae and imagoes of the host. In France, there was severe epidemic in sericulture and **Pasteur** discovered minute spore of the parasite in the eggs of silkworms. Next generation was infected due to hereditary transmission. To control the disease infected eggs were eliminated. Another species *Nosema apis* causes nosema disease in the honey bees.

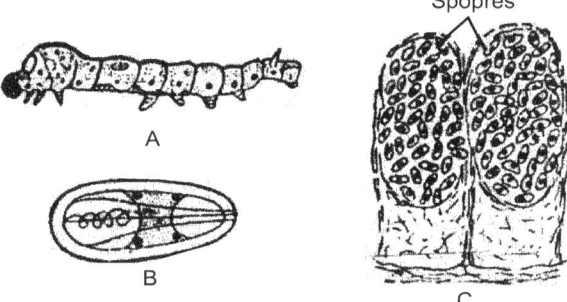

Fig. 1.21: *Nosema* A - An infected silkworm caterpillar, B - A spore enlarged, C - Two epithelial cells of bee's stomach filled with spores

18. *Didinum*

It is a freshwater ciliate found in ponds and ditches. The body of the animal is barrel shaped and encircled by two hoops of cilia. One circle is closed to the base of proboscis at the anterior end and other on the posterior end. The anterior end of the body is prolonged into tubular proboscis made up of parallel trichocysts. Cytostome or mouth is situated at the tip of the proboscis. The horse shoe shaped nucleus is situated in centre of protoplasm. The contractile vacuole and cytopyge are located at the posterior end. Nutrition is holozoic. Animal reproduce by transverse binary fission and conjugation.

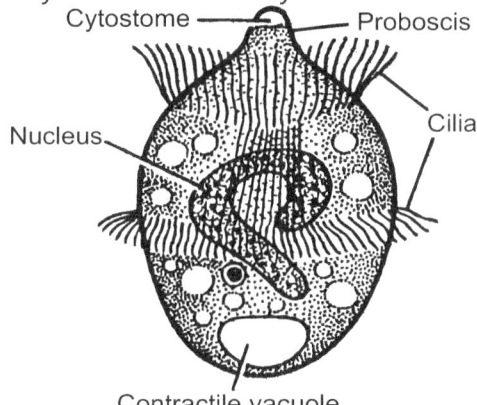

Fig. 1.22: *Didinium*

19. *Balantidium*

It is an endoparasitic ciliate found in the large intestine of man, pigs and monkeys. Some species are endoparasites of frogs, fish, cockroach and horse. The body is egg shaped pointed at anterior end and rounded posteriorly. The body has longitudinal rows of cilia. Peristome is located at the anterior end with longer cilia. Cytopharynx is next to the mouth or peristome. In the endoplasm large bilobed macro nucleus and small micronucleus located. There are two contractile vacuoles, larger one is at the posterior end. The food vacuoles are many containing blood cells of the host. The animal reproduce by transverse binary fission and occasionally by conjugation. In human beings *Balantidium coli* is responsible for ulcers and haemorrhage in the colon and coecum, which causes chronic dysentry.

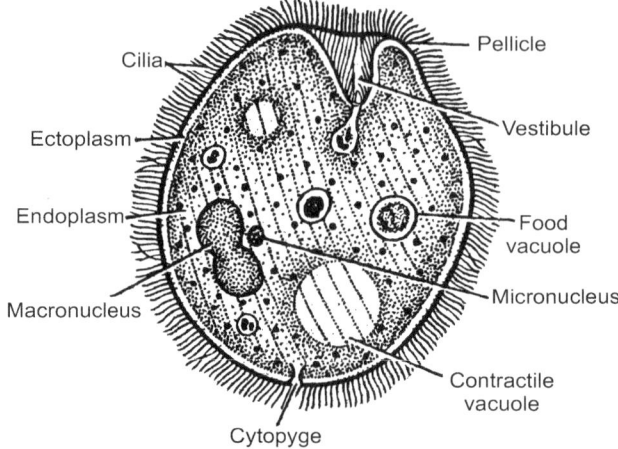

Fig. 1.23: *Balantidium coli*

20. *Nyctotherus*

It is also a parasitic ciliate in the rectum of frogs and intestine of the cockroaches. Its body is kidney shaped with horizontal rows of cilia. It has large peristome which leads into curved cytopharynx having large cilia. The macronucleus is kidney shaped and micronucleus is small embedded in endoplasm. Near posterior end there is single contractile vacuole and smaller one is at the anterior end. There is also permanent cytopyge at the posterior end. Animal shows conjugation for exchange of nuclear material and after separation it undergoes binary fission. The transmission of the parasites occur by ingestion of the encysted daughter cells passing through faeces.

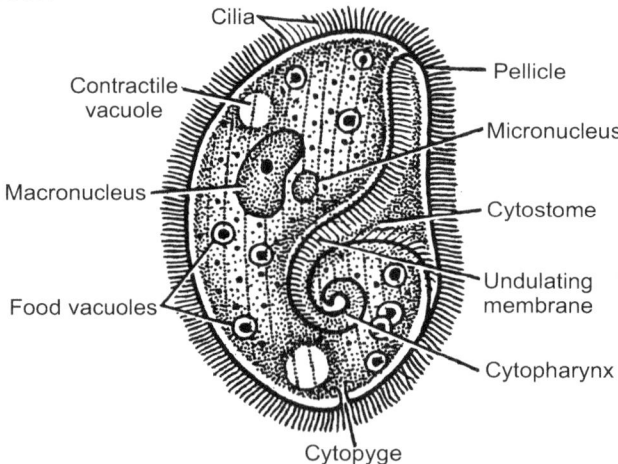

Fig. 1.24: *Nyctotherus*

21. Vorticella

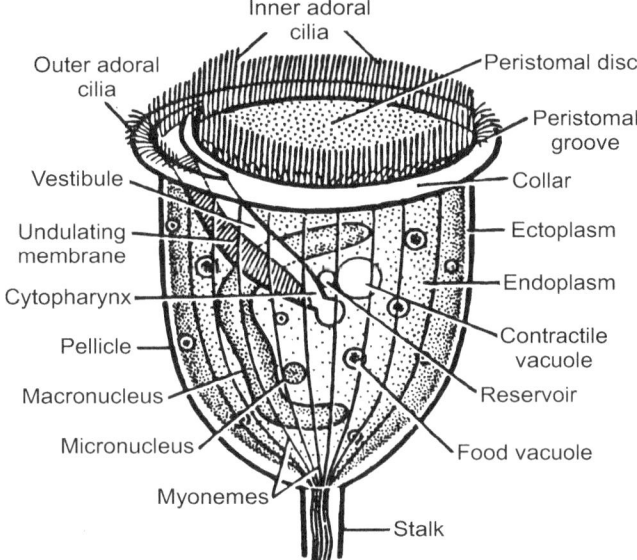

Fig. 1.25: *Vorticella*

It is a microscopic stalked form with an inverted bell-shaped body. It is found in freshwater ponds, lakes, rivers and streams with aquatic vegetation and rich in decaying organic matter. The animal feeds on bacteria. The rim of bell is called lip or peristomal collar. Inside there is peristome or oral groove, which surrounds the oral disc useful for closing and opening of the bellow. Border of cilia is present. There is vestibule, cytopharynx and undulating membrane beneath cytostome or mouth. The entire body of animal is covered by pellicle. Cytoplasm is differentiated into outer ectoplasm and inner endoplasm. Contractile and food vacuoles are also present in the body of the animal. Nutrition is holozoic. *Vorticella* normally reproduces asexually by longitudinal binary fission but it can reproduce sexually by conjugation. During unfavourable conditions, animal undergoes encystment.

Summary

- Protozoans are first microscopic, unicellular organisms.
- Body consists of protoplasm and one or many nuclei.
- They are solitary as well as colonial forms.

- Pseudopodia, flagella or cilia are the locomotory organs.
- Nutrition holozoic, holophytic or parasitic.
- All protozoa reproduce by asexual or sexual reproduction.
- Life cycle exhibits alteration of generation.
- Protozoa is divided into five important classes and they are Mastigophora, Opalinata, Sarcodina, Sporozoa and Ciliata.
- *Euglena, Trypanosoma, Opalina, Amoeba, Arcella, Monocystis, Paramoecium* are the examples of Protozoa.

Review Questions

1. Give an account of general characters of Protozoa and classify upto class level with suitable examples.
2. Give general characters of the following classes with suitable examples.
   (i) Mastigophora   (ii) Opalinata   (iii) Ciliata
   (iv) Sporozoa   (v) Sarcodina.

University Question

1. Write Short Note on Sarcodina.

***

1.5 Porifera

Introduction

The phylum Porifera means 'pore bearers' (Latin, porous-pore; ferre-to bear) and refers to the porous structure of the body having large number of openings on the surface.

General Characters

(1) They are aquatic, mostly marine and few freshwater, solitary or colonial, fixed to rocks, shells or other objects.
(2) The body is multicellular, cells are present in loose aggregation without forming tissues.
(3) They are diploblastic i.e. possess two layers of cells, outer dermal and inner choanocytic. In between these two cells gelatinous mesoglea is present which contains numerous free amoeboid cells of several kinds.

(4) The body shape is variable. Some are vase-like or cylindrical, globular symmetrical or asymmetrical.

(5) Body surface is perforated by numerous pores or ostia through which water enters the body. Canal system is present. Towards the free end large exhalent opening or osculum is present. Inside the body large cavity called spongocoel is present.

(6) All sponges possess internal skeleton made up of calcium carbonate or silicic acid called spicules and organic fibres of protein called spongin.

(7) No digestive cavity, nutrition is holozoic and digestion is intracellular.

(8) Respiration and excretion occurs by simple diffusion.

(9) Nervous system and sensory cells are absent.

(10) They show great power of regeneration.

(11) Reproduction is asexual as well as sexual.

(12) Fertilization is internal and cleavage is holoblastic.

(13) Life cycle includes free swimming larva for dispersal.

The phylum Porifera is divided into three classes: Calcarea, Hexactinellida and Demospongiae.

Class-Calcarea

(1) They are commonly called calcarious sponges.

(2) Size is small being a few to 15 cm in height.

(3) Body is cylindrical or vase-shaped, radially symmetrical occuring solitary or colonial.

(4) Skeleton consists of monaxon, triradiate and tetraradiate spicules of calcium carbonate.

(5) Canal system may be of asycon, sycon or simple leucon type.

(6) Choanocytes are large.

(7) Asexual reproduction by budding. The free swimming larva is called amphiblastula.

Examples: *Clathrina, Leucosolenia, Scypha, Grantia.*

Class-Hexactinellida

(1) They are popularly known as glass sponges.

(2) Size is moderate ranging from 10-30 cm in height.

(3) Body is radially symmetrical, cylindrical, vase like or funnel shaped.

(4) The skeleton consists of 6-rayed or hexactine spicules. The larger spicules are megascleres and smaller microscleres made up of silicic acid.
(5) Canal system is of eurypylous leucon type.
(6) Choanocytes are small and limited.

Examples: *Euplectella, Hyalonema*.

Class-Demospongiae
(1) They are numerous and highly organised sponges.
(2) They are found in shallow and deep sea as well as in freshwater.
(3) Body compact, often massive and brightly coloured.
(4) Skeleton consists of monaxon or tetraxon (8-rayed) spicules of silicic acid or of spongin fibres or of both.
(5) Canal system is of leucon type eurypylous, aphodal or diphodal.
(6) Asexual reproduction occurs by gemmules.
(7) Larva is called stereogastrula.

Porifera includes the sponges which are most primitive of multicellular animals. They are all aquatic mostly marine except one family spongillidae which lives in freshwater. **Spongilla** is the best known freshwater sponge.

Approximately, 10,000 species of sponges are known at present which show great animal diversity. The phylum porifera is divided into three classes namely Calcaria, Hexactinellida and Demospongiae.

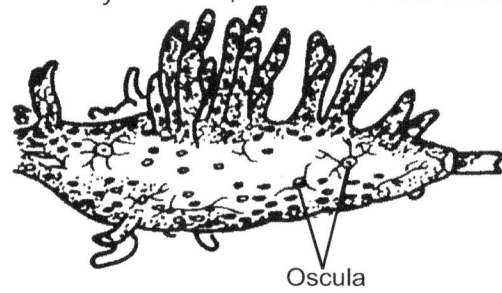

Fig. 1.26: *Spongilla*

The classification is chiefly based on the types of skeleton found in them.

General Organisation: The sponges show varied general organisation. Their shape and size also varies. The sponges are cylindrical like **Lencosolenia**, vase-shaped like **Scypha** and **Grantia,** tree-like e.g. **Microciona** finger-like (e.g. **Haliclona**), leaf-like (e.g. **Phyllospongia**), cushon shaped like **Euspongia,** rope like **Hyalonema,** bowl shaped like **Pheronema** etc.

Some sponges are solitory (e.g. **Scypha**), while others are colonial (e.g. **Lencosolenia**).

They are attached to rocks, shells of molluscs and corals. **Scypha** is shallow water sponge found upto a depth of 50 fathoms (1 fathom = 6 feet). Some sponges are boring sponges-like **Cliona.**

The sponges show different body colourations. They are mostly white or grey but yellow, brown, purple, orange, red and green coloured species are also reported. The green colour of the sponge is usually due to presence of symbiotic algae **Zoochlorella** in them. The size varies from few mm to massive having 1 or 2 meters diameter.

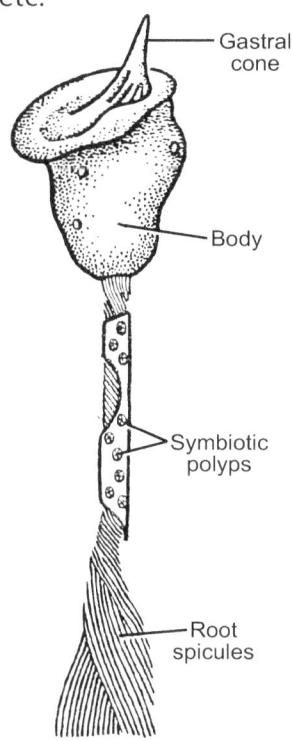

Fig. 1.27: *Hyalonema*

Canal System: The body of the sponge is perforated by ostia or pores. All the sponges show various types of canal system. All the cavities of the body traversed by the currents of water, which nourish the sponge from the time it enters by pores until it passes out by the osculum are collectively called canal system. There are usually three types of canal system met within sponges. They are Asconoid type, Syconoid type and Lenconoid type of water canal system. **Olynthus and Leucosolenia** show the Asconoid simplest type of canal system. The more advanced type of canal system is called Syconoid type. The calcarious sponges especially members of gems **Sycon** show this type of canal system. Still more advanced type of canal system called Lenconoid type is found in **Leucilla, Geodia** and **Stelleata.** The Rhagon type of canal system is exhibited by **Spongilla.**

Skeleton in Sponges:

All the sponges are classified on the basis of skeleton pressure within them. In sponges two types skeleton is present which is secreted by themselves. They are spicules and spongin or in the combination of both.

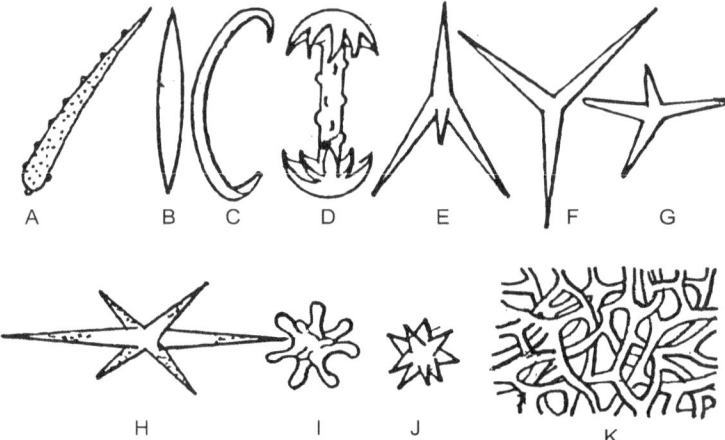

Fig. 1.28: Spicules and spongin A – Monactinal monaxon; B – Diactinal monaxon; C – Curved monaxon; D – Monaxon with hooked ends; E – Tetraxon; F – Triradiate; G – Calthrops; H – Hexactinal triaxon; I, J – Polyaxon; K – Spongin fibres

There are different types of spicules found in sponges. Megascleres are larger which support the body of sponge. They are classified into monaxon, tetraxons, triaxons, polyaxons and spheres. Polyaxons, spheres, desma are the different types. Spires and asters are microscleres.

Leucosolenia, Clathrina show calcarious monaxon or tetraxon spicules. In **Euplectella** spicules are hexasters i.e. star-like in shape. **Hyalonema, Pheronema** show amphidiscs spicules.

Fig. 1.29: *Chalina*

Spongin is an organic substance like silk. It also forms skeleton in the body of sponge. **Chalina, Spongilla, Euspongia** and **Hippspongia** show the presence of spongin fibres in the body. Spongin fibres with siliceous spicules are present in class Demospongiae.

Reproduction in sponges: The sponges show asexual and sexual reproduction. Regeneration, formation of reduction bodies budding, exogeneous budding, endogenous budding are the methods of which budding are the methods of asexual reproduction in sponges. **Spongilla** shows reproduction which by gemmule formation. Sponges also exhibit sexual reproduction. They have no sex organs but ameobocytes form sex cells in the mesenchyme. First, eggs are produced and later the sperms hence sponge is protogynous in which cross fertilization takes place.

Grantia, Scypha, Clathrina, Leucosolenia and many other species of sponges shows sexual reproduction.

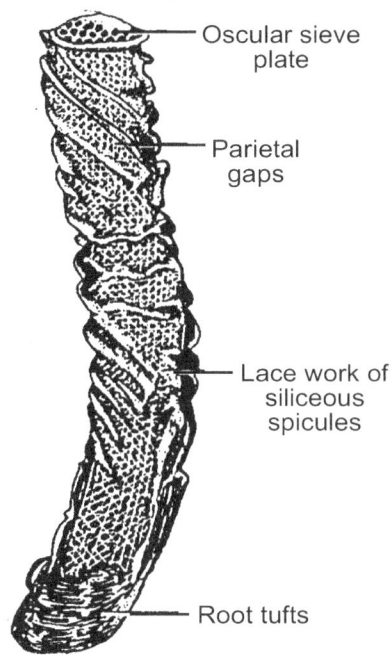

Fig. 1.30: *Euplectella aspergillum*

Many sponges like **Euplectella** (Venus flower basket or glass sponge) are found attached to the bottom of sea. **Euspongia** is common bath sponge. The cleaned spongin skeleton of **Euspongia** is used as commercial bath sponge. **E. officinalis** is found in Mediterranean, West Indies and Australia upto a depth of 180 metres.

Spongilla is fresh water sponge found in ponds, lakes and slow streams, growing on submerged sticks and plants. The colony is green due to presence of symbiotic algae **Zoochlorellae.** The sponge show rhagon type of canal system. Skeleton consists of siliceous spicules and spongin fibres. Asexual reproduction is by gemmule and sexual reproduction by way of unusual free swimming larva which is characteristic of **Spongilla.**

Thus, the large number of sponge species show diversity. Sponges are economically important. Some sponges are beneficial to mankind and other animals as a food, as commensals, as a material for bathing, polishing, washing cars, walls, furniture and scrubbing floor etc. **Euplectella** has a great commercial value and used as decorative pieces.

There are also harmful sponges. They cause death of some sessile animals by growing over them and cutting off their food and oxygen supply. The boring sponges like **Cliona** attach themselves to the shells of oysters, clams and barnacles etc. It bores into the shells of these animals and completely destroy them. The boring sponges also cause great harm to oyster.

Sponge fishing and its industry is of great economic value. Millions of sponges are sold every year making sponge fishing a source of income.

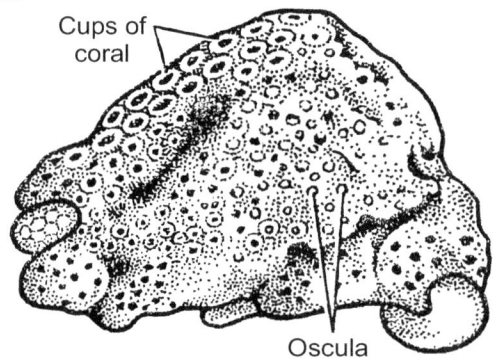

Fig. 1.31 (a): *Cliona*

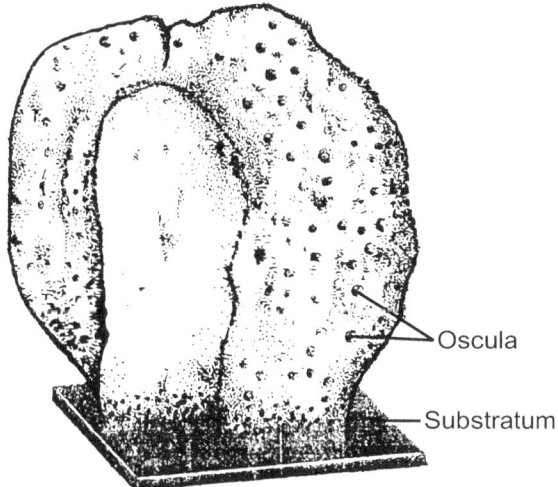

Fig. 1.31 (b): *Euspongia*

Summary

- Phylum porifera consists of the animals with number of pores on the body. They are called sponges.
- The sponges are marine or freshwater, solitary or colonial and fixed on rocks.
- They are diploblastic animals.
- They possess internal skeleton made up of $CaCO_3$ or silicic acid called spicules.
- Reproduction is asexual as well as sexual.
- Fertilization is internal.
- Porifera is divided into three classes namely, calcaria, hexactinellida and demospongae.

Review Questions

1. Give an account of general organisation of phylum porifera.
2. Mention distinguishing characters of phylum porifera. Give an outline of classification of porifera with characters and examples of each class.
3. Give distinctive characters of different classes in phylum porifera.

University Questions

1. Give an account of general characters of phylum porifera.
2. Give an account of classification of phylum porifera upto classes with suitable examples.
3. Give distinguishing characters of class calcaria, hexactinellida and demospongae with suitable examples.
4. Define:
   (i) Spongocoel (ii) Osculum
   (iii) Diploblastic animal (iv) Spongin
   (v) Water canal system
5. Define Spicules in Porifera.
6. Write short note on Specific Characters of Class Hydrozoa.

***

1.6 Classification of Coelenterata

Introduction

The name Coelenterata is derived from two Greek words koilos - meaning hollow and enteron meaning intestine. Thus, coelenterata literally means hollow intestine. But hollow bodied or 'hollow inside' gives better idea of coelenterates as they lack true intestine.

General Characters:

(1) The animals are aquatic, mostly marine, but few are freshwater.
(2) They may be either solitary or colonial and sedentary or free swimming.
(3) The animals are radially symmetrical.
(4) They are diploblastic i.e. body wall composed of two layers, an external epidermis or ectoderm and an inner gastrodermis or endoderm. The jelly like mesoglea is present in between these two layers which is structureless.
(5) Coelom is absent.
(6) Short, slender extensile tentacles encircle the mouth, useful for food capturing.
(7) On body and tentacles nematocysts or stinging cells are present. They serve for adhesion, offence and defense and food capture.

(8) They have two different structural types called polyps and medusa. Many species show polymorphism.
(9) Respiratory, circulatory and excretory systems are wanting.
(10) Nervous system is primitive consisting of a diffuse network of nerve cells.
(11) Sensory organs are simple or complicated. Eyespots or statocysts are present.
(12) Reproduction is both asexual by budding or sexual by ova and sperms.
(13) Development is indirect. There is oral, ciliated larva called planula during development.
(14) The life history shows the phenomenon of alternation of generations or metagenesis. In this phenomenon, sexual free swimming medusoid generation alternates with an asexual, sessile, usually colonial, polypoid generation.

The phylum Coelenterata includes the following three classes:
(1) Hydrozoa (2) Scyphozoa (3) Anthozoa.

Class-Hydrozoa:
Distinctive Characters of Hydrozoa:
(1) Most of the animals are marine and colonial (*Obelia*), a few solitary and freshwater (*Hydra*), sessile or free.
(2) Many animals show alternation of generation.
(3) Body shows radial symmetry, it may be tetramerous or polymerous.
(4) Bodywall is diploblastic, made up of outer ectoderm and inner endoderm and these layers are separated by a non-cellular, gelatinous mesoglea.
(5) Perisac is cuticular or horny layer secreted by exoderm and it gives rigidity and support. In some cases, it is calcarious forming stony structure called coral.
(6) Medusa is small and with true muscular and non-vascular velum.
(7) Gastrovascular cavity is simple but not divided by vertical mesenteries or partitions.
(8) Nematocysts are present on ectoderm or tentacles.
(9) Gonads are ectodermal in origin and discharge externally.
(10) The embryo is ciliated planula.

Examples: *Hydra, Obelia, Millepora, Physalia, Porpita, Velella*.

Class-Scyphozoa:
Distinctive Characters of Scyphozoa:
(1) Animals are exclusively marine and solitary.
(2) Polyp phase is absent or reduced. The scyphistoma is small, solitary stage which produce medusae by process of terminal budding or transverse fission called strobilation.
(3) Bell or umbrella shaped medusa phase is dominant which may be free swimming or attached by an aboral stalk.
(4) Animals exhibit tetramerous symmetry.
(5) Velum is reduced or absent.
(6) Margin of the bell is lobed containing sense organs. The sense organs are called tentaculocyst or rhophalia and they contain endodermal statolith.
(7) Tentacles are hollow, endodermal and gastric.
(8) The gastrovascular cavity is without stomodaeum. Its central part, the stomach is produced into four gastric pouches which has nematocyst bearing filaments.
(9) Mesoglea is thick and contains cells.
(10) Medusae are dioecious with four endodermal brightly coloured gonads. The gametes are released in gastric pouches and they pass out through the mouth.
(11) They are commonly called jelly fishes.

Examples: *Aurelia (Jelly-fish), Rhizostoma, Eriphylla, Pelagia.*

Class : Anthozoa (Actinozoa):
Distinctive Characters of Anthozoa:
(1) The animals are solitary or colonial, exclusively marine, and fixed to the substratum.
(2) Only polyp form is present and medusa form is absent, hence there is no alternation of generations.
(3) The symmetry is biradial with hexamerous, octamerous or polymerous arrangement of parts.
(4) Oral end shows flat oral disc with 6 to several hundred hollow tentacles around the mouth.
(5) Mesoglea contains cells and fibres in a gelatinous matrix.
(6) Exoskeleton of calcium carbonate is secreted by ectoderm forming massive corals.

(7) Gastro-vascular cavity is divided by 6 or more vertical partitions or septa called mesenteries which bear nematocysts.

(8) Nervous system is simple net-like.

(9) Most of the animals are unisexual. Gonads are endodermal.

(10) Fertilization is external. Egg develops into ciliated planula larva.

(11) Asexual reproduction occurs by budding.

Examples: *Tubipora, Alcyonium, Coralliiurn, Gorgonia, Fungia.*

Coelenterates are radially symmetrical, diploblastic animals with only epidermis and gastrodermis, between these two layers a jelly-like mesogloea is present, which is structure less material containing wandering amoebocytes. There are variety of cells in epidermis and gastrodermis and they show division of labour. These animals are equipped with tentacles and nematocysts for food capturing and defense. They show exo and endoskeleton. There is an oval ciliated **planula larva** during development.

Phylum coelenterata includes some 9000 living species which show great animal diversity. Almost all coelenterata are exclusively marine except few species are fresh water.

Fresh water forms: The class hydrozoa includes fresh water species of ***Hydra.*** Hydra represents good example of coelenterates to illustrate the fundamental characteristics of Metazoa. Different species of ***Hydra*** found in different parts of the world. ***H. vulgaris***, a orange red coloured animal found in America and Europe. ***H. fusca*** is brown hydra found in India, North America and Europe. The green hydra ***H. viridis*** is found in America and Europe. It gets green colour due to symbiotic green algae **Zoochlorellae** in endodermal cells. ***H. gangetica*** is found in ponds and water reservoirs along the river Ganges. ***Hydra*** usually remains attached to submerged vegetation or solid object in water. It has ability to extend or contract its body. ***Hydra*** is carnivorous animal, feeds on insects, larvae and small crustaceans. ***Hydra*** exhibits solitary habit i.e. it lives singly and reproduces sexually as well as asexually.

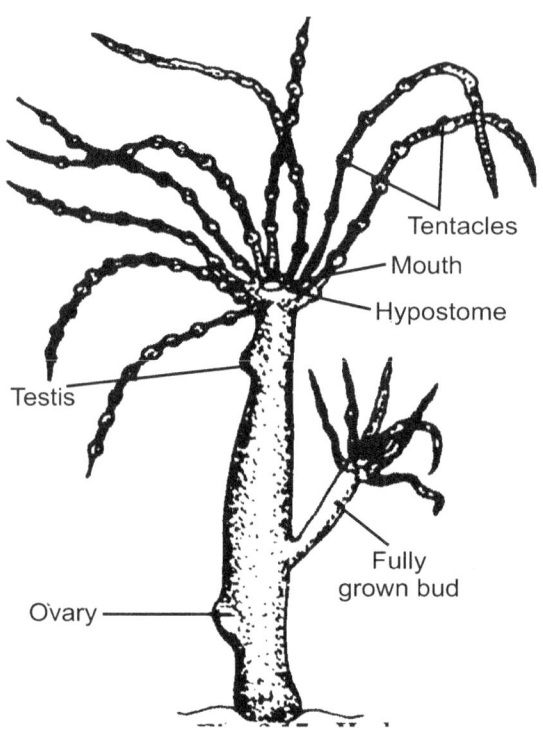

Fig. 1.32: *Hydra*

Hydra has tubular body with basal disc and hypostome which bears mouth. The mouth is enriched by a circle of 6 – 10 tentacles. They are long thread-like structures armed with nematocysts. By budding hydra forms another individuals. Gonads are present on the body where testes occur near oral end while ovaries are towards proximal end. Regeneration power is also exhibited by ***Hydra.***

Marine Coelenterates: There are large number of hydrozoa which are marine and exhibit colonial life. They also exhibit polymorphism i.e. there are two main types of zooids, the polyps and medusa. Polyps are sessile and asexual zooid, while medusa is free swimming and sexual zooid. Many hydrozoa exhibit **alternation of generation** or **metagenesis** in which asexual polypoid, sessile generation alternates with sexual medusoid, free swimming generations.

Obelia or sea fur hydrozoans are colonial forms. The individuals are called zooids and there are more than one zooids hence phenomenon of polymorphism is exhibited by these animals. The zooids perform different functions for colony. Polyps or hydrant are nutritive zooids, gonangia or blastostyles are budding zooids and medusae are sexual zooids. Thus, **Obelia** is trimorphic colony. **Bougainvillea** is dimorphic colony with only polyps and medusae.

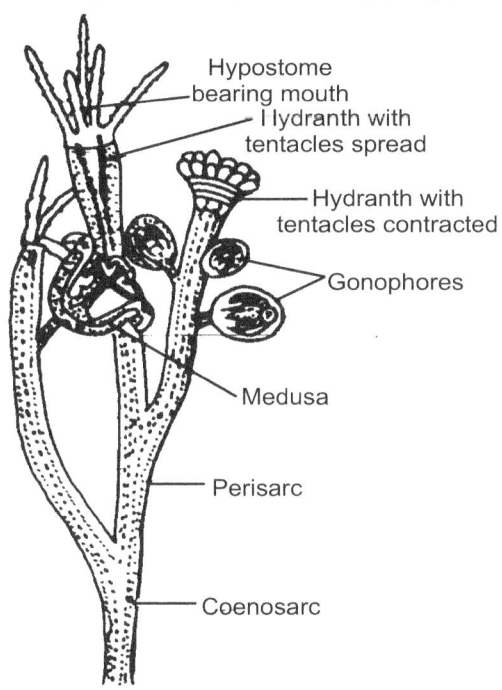

Fig. 1.33: *Bougainvillea*

Hydractinia is colonial hydrozoan which commonly grow on gastropodal shells occupied by hermit-crabs. This animal shows polymorphic colony containing five functional forms of polyps. They are gastrozooids (nutritive), dactylozooids (defensive), tentaculozooids (sensory), skeletozooids and gonozooids (reproductive).

Tubularia occurs either solitary or in colonies. The hydrants are large, brilliantly coloured and flower like. The colony is dioecious. The gonophores or medusae remain attached to the hypostome in clusters and are never set free. This animal represents structure of the ancestral coelenterate. ***Piennaria, Sertularia, Plumularia, Campanularia*** are the colonial hyrozoans showing structural modification.

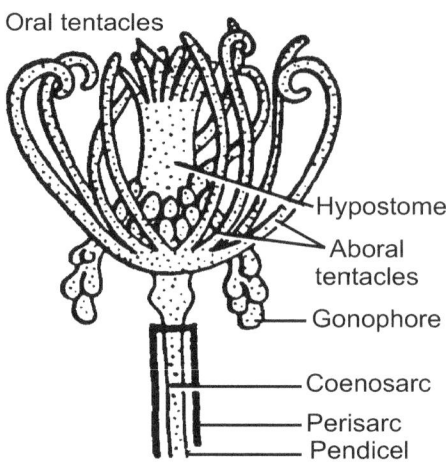

Fig. 1.34: *Tubularia*

Millepora*, *Stylaster are hydroid corals mostly associated with coral reefs in tropical segs. Colony consists of much branched anastomosing hydrorhiza forming broad basal mass encrusted on rocks.

The perisac forms massive solid calcarious exoskeleton (Corallium). Surface bears numerous pores of two kinds larger gastropores and smaller dactylopores. In living condition two kinds of polyps protrude from these pores into water. They are gastrozooids (nutritive) and dactylozoids (defensive).

In Physophoran siphonophores, there is a pneumatophore or float at the apex of the colony above the water level. This is filled with a gas, secreted by gas secreting tissue, enclosed within an oval disc.

In **Physalia** underneath the disc bears groups of cormidia, each including a gastrozooid, a small and large dactylozooid, both with long tentacles, and a branched gonozooid with both male and female gonophores.

In case of **Velella** and **Porpita**, the colony seems to be highly organised. There is a single central gastrozooid with a mouth. Around it are concentric rows of gonozooids surrounded by a few rows of dactylozooids. The whole colony looks like a single individual animal.

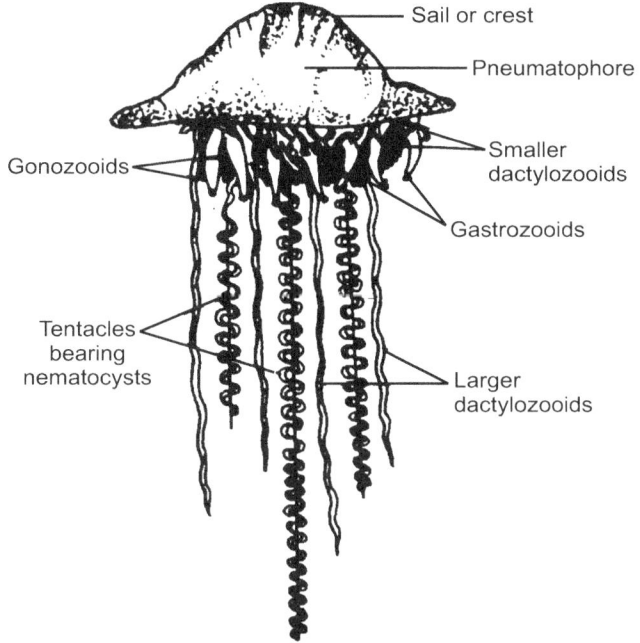

Fig. 1.35: Physalia

Halistemma is polymorphic colony consisting of a long, slender, floating stem to which polymorphic zooids are attached along its length. The upper stem has small pneumatophore which is like an invaginated cup it is gas filled. Below the pneumatophore are several closely set nectocalyces or swimming bells. Below this dactylozooids, gastrozooid, batteries of nematocysts and tentacles are present.

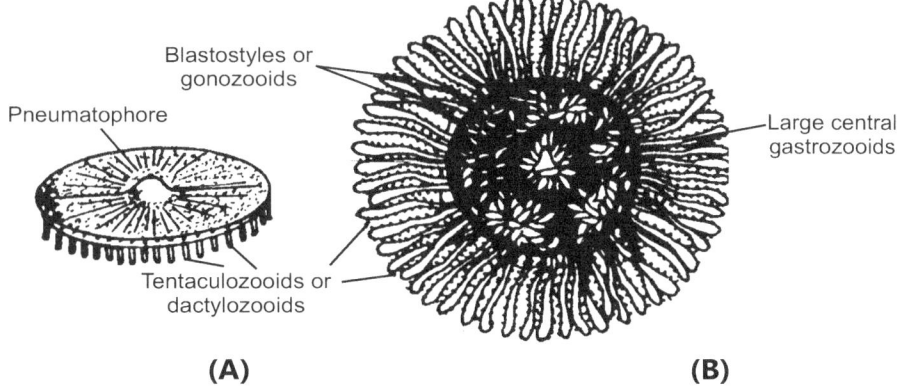

(A) (B)

Fig. 1.36: *Porpita* A – Colony in dorsal view; B – Colony in ventral view

The class Scyphozoa includes large jelly fish or true medusae. They are large, bell or umbrella shaped and free swimming or attached by aboral stalk. **Lucernaria** is a sessile, with trumpet shaped body provided with aboral stalk by which it is attached to sea weeds. The margin of the umbrella is divided into eight short and hollow adradial lobes. Each lobe bears a group of short knobbed hollow tentacles at its end.

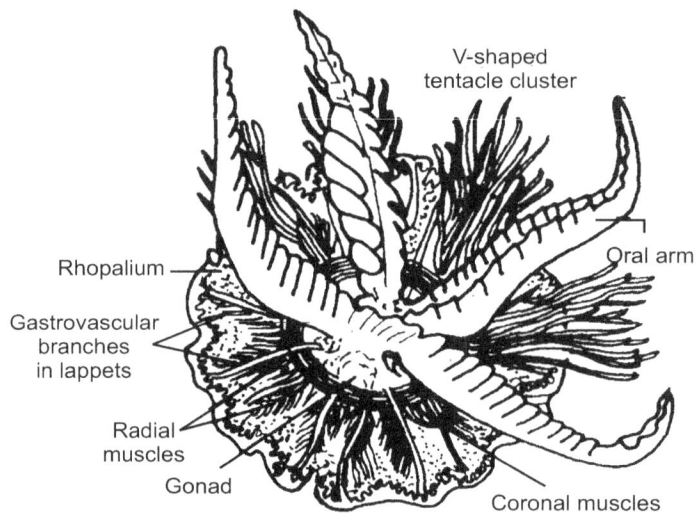

Fig. 1.37: *Cyanea*

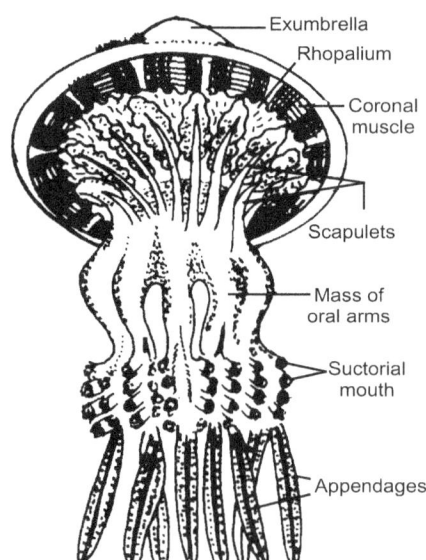

Fig. 1.38: *Rhizostoma*

Cyanea is a common jelly fish found in coastal waters. The disc or umbrella is bowl or saucer like with its margin scalloped into eight lappets. The larger species ***C. arctica*** upto 2 meters in diameter. It has very long and large frilly oral arms.

Rhizostoma is a large jelly fish found in shallow waters of Indo-Pacific region. It has saucer shaped umbrella with eight to sixteen tentaculocysts in different species. In young Rhizostoma there is central mouth but in adult it is closed by overgrowth and folding of 4 orals arms and it is replaced by thousands of pore like suctorial mouths which lie along the close grooves of oral arms. This polystomatous (many mouthed) condition is unique in animals.

Aurelia is a commonest jelly fish or moon jelly occurs in coastal waters of tropical and temperate oceans of world close to the surface of water. It lives singly or in a large groups found floating or swimming freely. It is carnivorous and reproduces both by asexual and sexual methods. Just below the umbrella 4 long arms are present which cover the mouth. Margin of the umbrella has tentacles. A system of five branched or unbranched radiating canals present on the surface of umbrella. Alternation of generation is seen in life cycle of ***Aurelia.***

Class **Anthozoa** includes flower like solitary or colonial polypoid forms. They show cylindrical body with hexamerous, octamerous or polymerous, biradial or radiobilateral symmetry. They form external or internal skeleton which is formed from calcium carbonate which often form massive corals.

The octocorallian order Alcyonacea which includes the well known genus *Alcyonium* (dead man's finger) is represented by soft corals. The coral is a colony of polyps with endoskeleton of separate calcarius spicules embedded in massive mesoglea or coenenchyme. The endoskeleton is common to whole colony. The order stolonifera includes a colonial coral called ***Tubipora*** or 'organ pipe coral'. In it the skeleton made up of calcarious spicules, is stained red with iron salts. Consists of vertical tubes connected by lateral platforms. The vertical tubes are also partitioned by smaller cross plates. These tubes contain polyps.

The order *coenothecalia* consists of single genus **Heliopora** which is commonly known as blue coral. In its colony of polyps, the secreted calcarious spicules form a massive **skeleton** or **corallium**. The larger cavities on the surface of the skeleton contain the polyps.

The order Gorgonacea includes the 'sea fans' or 'horny corals' in which the colony branches are made up of horny proteinaceous material intermixed with calcarious spicules arranged around the polyps.

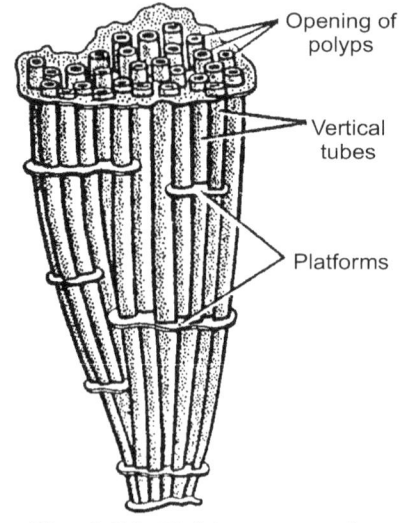

Fig. 1.39: *Tubipora musica*

Pennatula, Renilla are the members of order Pennatulacea. The colony is elongated and divided into proximal stalk or peduncle and distal rachis. **Pennatula** is called sea pen. It forms a quill-like bilaterally symmetrical colony. The rachis bears lateral branches containing nutritive polyps anthocodia and on the back of rachis siphonozooids are located.

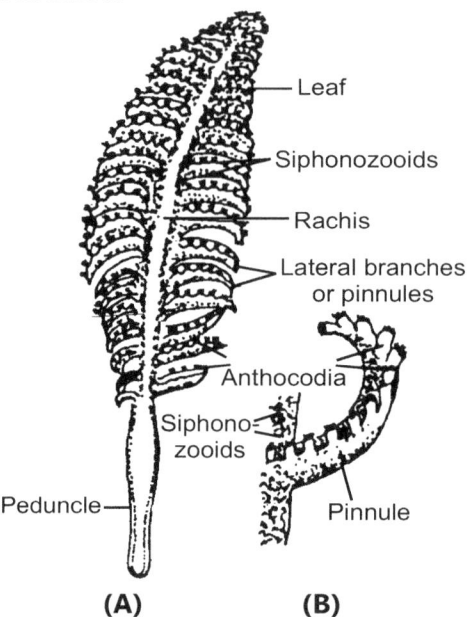

Fig. 1.40: *Pennatula*: A – Entire colony and B – Portion magnified

Pennatula sulcata has bright red colour and it grows upto 3 meters long and found in warm coast of Atlantic and Pacific oceans. **Renilla** is called sea pansy. It is also fan like and colony consists of a short peduncle which is embedded in the mud and circular kidney shaped (*reniform*) leaf like rachis. The colony is dimorphic containing two types of zooids called autozooids and siphonozooids. **Renilla** is colonial form occurs in shallow waters of coasts of North and South Carolina and West Indies.

The order **Actiniaria** of Hexacorallia includes sea anemones. **Metridium, Adamsia** are cylindrical animals with oral disc, column and pedal disc. Tentacles and mesentries are numerous and often arranged in the multiples of six. These animals show lack of skeleton. They are solitary, sessile animals found attached to the rocks where many individuals are fixed close together. Tentacles are present around the mouth which are armed with nematocysts. The tentacles are useful for food capturing. Anemones form remarkable symbiotic relationship with other animals, particularly with hermit crabs. Generally, **Adamsia** or **Sagaritia** are fixed to the shell of a gastropod snail inhabited by particular species of hermit crabs. **Metridium** is commonest sea anemones found at the depth of 90 fathoms.

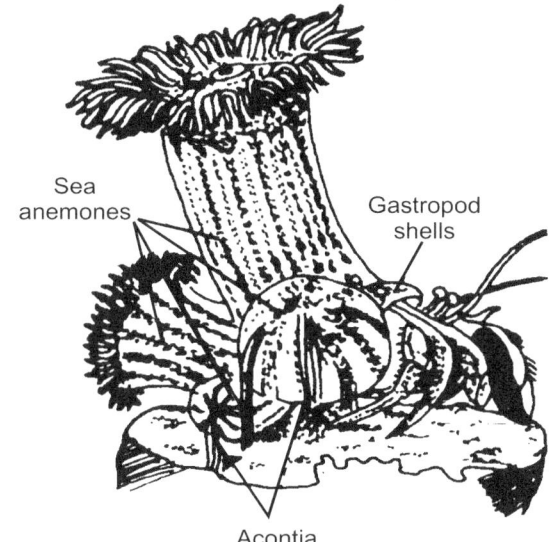

Fig. 1.41: *Adamsia*

Hexacorallian Corals

The members of the order Madreporaria constitute the stony corals or true corals. While some of them are solitary. Most are in colonies assuming a great variety of forms. These are main in building coral reefs. The coral organism is a small anthozoan polyp which secretes skeletal rudiment or protheca. It is secreted by ectoderm, first as a basal plate.

Fungia, Flabellum, Caryophylla etc. are the solitary corals or cup corals. The corallite is disc like, cup like mushroom shaped in form.

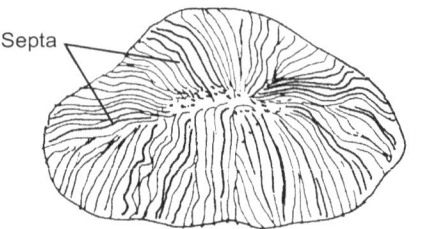 

Fig. 1.42: *Fungia*   **Fig. 1.43: *Astraea***

Majority of the stony corals are colonial with plate like, spherical cup like or vase-shaped skeleton (corallium) ***Oculina, Acropora, Favia, Madrepora, Meandrina*** are the typical examples of colonial corals. The single sexually produced polyp is responsible for the production of colony. It takes place by asexual methods of reproduction. The polyps live at the surface of the calcarious skeleton. By various methods of asexual budding different colonies are produced. Some of the colonies are branched. In stag horn coral, ***Acropora***, there is always a primary polyp at the top of the colony with lateral branches on either side. In some corals, like ***Oculina***, the polyps remain widely separated, each occupying a separate thecae. In others, like **Favia**, **Astraea** the thecae are so close together as to have common walls. ***Meandrina***, a brain coral the polyps and thecae become confluent occupying valley separated by ridges, on the surface of corallium.

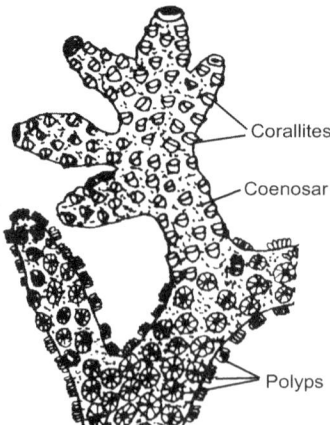

Fig. 1.44: *Madrepora*

Summary

- Coelenterates are hollow animals. They are aquatic mostly marine and few are fresh water.
- They are colonial or solitary and sedentary or free swimming.
- These animals are radially symmetrical.
- Diploblastic and coelom are absent.
- Mouth encircled with tentacles.
- Stinging cells or nematocysts are present.
- Polyps and medusae are the two different forms.
- Reproduction by asexual and sexual method.
- Alternation of generation or metagenesis is present.
- This phylum includes three classes namely, hydrozoa, scyphozoa and anthozoa.

Review Questions

1. Mention distinguishing characters of phylum coelenterata. Give an outline of classification of coelenterata with characters and examples of each class.
2. Give distinctive characters of different classes in phylum coelenterata.
3. Define:
   (i) Polyp
   (ii) Radial symmetry
   (iii) Alternation of generation
   (iv) Gastrozoids
   (v) Fringing reef.

University Questions

1. General characters of class calcaria.
2. Define:
   (i) Radial symmetry
   (ii) Alternation of generation
   (iii) Gastrozoids
   (iv) Fringing reef
   (v) Coral reef

***

1.7 Platyhelminthes

Platyhelminthes are called flatworms (Greek words Platy = flat and helmins = worms) because they possess flattened bodies. Their bodies are compressed dorsoventrally and show bilateral symmetry. They are triploblastic acoelomate animals. Some forms are free-living and many are parasitic. The parasitic flatworms possess suckers and hooks, spines for attachment. In parasitic forms, the body is covered with a thick and resistant cuticle but free-living tubellarians are clothed with cellular or syncytial epidermis. The digestive system is absent in tapeworms. But in other consists of mouth, pharynx and modified intenstine. Respiratory and circulatory systems are absent. Excretory system is well developed with flame cells. The nervous system is of primitive type consists of network and ganglia at the anterior end which serves as a brain. The flatworms show highly developed reproductive organs and most of the animals are hermaphrodite and rarely with separate sex. Cross-fertilization and self-fertilization both are common. Asexual reproduction is common among freshwater forms. Development is direct i.e. without larval stages or indirect with larval stages. Life cycle is completed in one or three intermediate hosts. Parthenogenesis and polyembryony is common among trematodes and cestodes.

Phylum Platyhelminthes is divided into three classes, namely *Turbellaria*, *Trematoda* and *Cestoda*. Turbellaria includes flatworms which are ciliated and free-living. Trematoda are non-ciliated parasitic flatworms or flukes. Cestoda are all endoparasitic flatworms commonly called tapeworms.

Turbellaria is derived from latin word *turbella* means a *stirring*. The animal produce turbulance in water by body cilia. These animals are broad, flat and leaf like in shape. They lead a free living life in fresh or salt water, in moist soil, some members are commensal or parasite. These animals are abundantly provided with adhesive organs. They possess incomplete adhesive organs. They possess incomplete alimentary canal i.e. the single opening, the mouth. These animals reproduce by sexual, asexual and regeneration methods.

General characters
- Helminthes constitute a large assemblage of worms of comparatively simple and varied organisation.
- Helminthes is derived from the Greek word *helmins* means worms.

- The term worms is not correct because it is used for elongated invertebrates without appendages and with bilateral symmetry.
- The term helminthes is restricted to a few phyla of invertebrate animals all of which are superficially worm-like but they differ markedly in their morphology, life history and bionomics.
- The two phyla Platyhelminthes or flatworms and Aschelminthes or roundworms are included under helminthes.
- The term Platyhelminthes means flatworms (Greek. Platys = flat + helmins = worms). The bodies of these worms are compressed dorsoventrally and show bilateral symmetry.
- They are lowest triploblastic acoelomate, metazoa. These animals are more advanced than coelenterata because their tissues are organized into organs.
- The mesoderm forms a type of connective tissue called parenchyma which fills the body spaces between the ectoderm and endoderm, so that there is no coelom, hence they are called acoelomate animals.
- Circulatory and respiratory systems are absent. Some forms also lack digestive system. Flame cells are the excretory organs which open outside the body.
- The reproductive organs are highly developed and the animals are hermaphrodite.
- Nervous system is in the form of network and it has ganglia at the anterior end which serves as a brain.
- This phylum includes free-living (Planeria) as well as parasitic animals (liver fluke and tape worms).
- The free living forms show ciliated body wall whereas parasitic forms show the presence of suckers, hooks, cuticle and hermaphrodite condition essential for parasitic mode of life.

Classification – Turbellaria, Trematoda and Cestoda

The name platyhelminthes is derived from two Greek words Platys-flat or broad; and helminthes – worms. Thus, platyhelminthes means flatworms as the animals have a flattened body.

General Characters

(1) They have soft, elongated, bilaterally symmetrical, usually dorsoventrally flattened body. The body is devoid of metameric segmentation.

(2) The flatworms are triploblastic i.e. three definite layers of cells ectoderm, endoderm and mesoderm are present.

(3) Anterior end of the body forms definite head.

(4) The body wall consists of single layered epidermis or tough cuticle made up of scleroprotein and musculature.

(5) Cuticle is modified into hooks, spines, thorns, spicules, teeth etc.

(6) They are acoelomate animals i.e. no body cavity or coelom.

(7) Respiratory, circulatory systems are absent.

(8) Digestive system if present, is incomplete.

(9) The excretory system includes characteristic flame-cells called protonephridia.

(10) Nervous system is primitive and ladder like and comprises the brain and two main longitudinal nerve-cords connected at intervals by transverse commissures.

(11) Sense organs are more in free-living and reduced in parasitic forms.

(12) Some are free-living while some live as endoparasites.

(13) Flatworms are bisexual or hermaphrodite with special copulatory organs, penis and vagina for mating purposes.

(14) Fertilization is internal.

(15) Development may be direct or with one or more larval stages.

(16) Life cycle requires one or more hosts.

(17) Asexual reproduction is also common in some forms. Parthenogenesis, endogenous or exogenous budding is common.

The phylum Platyhelminthes is divided into three classes Turbellaria, Trematoda and Cestoda.

Class-Turbellaria
Distinctive Characters

(1) They are free living habitant of fresh water or salt water, some live in soil and some are commensal or parasitic.

(2) Body is dorsoventrally flattened, bilaterally symmetrical and unsegmented.
(3) Anterior end of the body is differentiated into head.
(4) Body is covered by single layered epidermis which is cellular or syncytial. It may be partly or wholly ciliated and contains crystalline, rod-like, curved rhabdoides.
(5) Adhesive organs namely glandulo-epidermal adhesive organs and glandulo muscular adhesive organs are present.
(6) Mouth is usually ventral, pharynx is protrusible. Intestine is present which shows great variation.
(7) Protonephridia are excretory organs.
(8) Tango and chemoreceptors are present.
(9) Mostly hermaphrodite with few exceptions. Cross fertilization is common.
(10) Reproduction by sexual and asexual methods and by regeneration.

Examples: *Dugesia (Planeria), Conoluta, Microstomum, Bipalium.*

Class-Trematoda

Distinctive Characters

(1) The adult individuals are ecto or endoparasites and commonly called flukes.
(2) Body may be leaf like or elongated or oval.
(3) The animals lack epidermis, rhabdites and surface cilia but body is covered by thick cuticle.
(4) Suckers are adhesive organs.
(5) Mouth is anterior, digestive system shows pharynx, oesophagus, large bifid intestine.
(6) Protonephridia are excretory organs.
(7) Nervous system consists of pair of cerebral ganglia and longitudinal cords.
(8) They are hermaphrodite with few exceptions.
(9) Adults lack sense organs.
(10) Cross-fertilization is common.
(11) Life cycle may be simple or complicated with one or more intermediate hosts and larval stages.

Examples: *Fasciola hepatica (Liver fluke), Schistosoma, Polystomum, Diplozoon.*

Class-Cestoda
Distinctive Characters
(1) They are commonly called as tapeworms.
(2) They are endoparasites.
(3) They lack epidermis, rhabdites and external cilia.
(4) Body is divided into segments called proglottids.
(5) Body of the animal is divided into three parts : scolex, neck and strobila.
(6) Head or scolex is provided with suckers and hooks useful for attachment.
(7) There are three types of proglottids - immature, mature and gravid. The last, i.e. gravid proglottids are shed by the process apolysis.
(8) Mouth and alimentary canal are absent.
(9) Sense organs are also absent.
(10) Organs of excretory system called protonephridia, also perform the function of osmoregulation.
(11) Mostly hermaphrodite, each proglottid contains one or two complete sets of male and female reproductive systems.
(12) They show self-fertilization.
(13) Life cycle is complicated involving one or more intermediate hosts.

Examples: *Taenia solium (Tapeworm), Diphylidium (Dog Tapeworm), Amphilina*

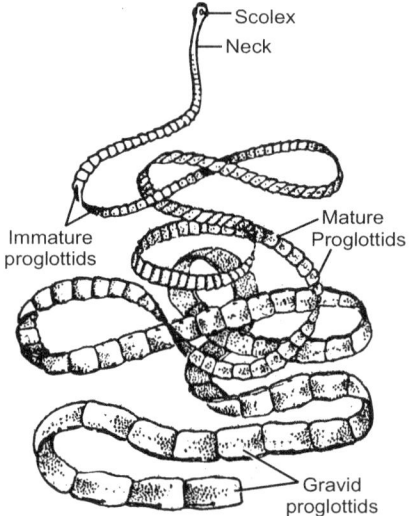

Fig. 1.45: *Taenia solium* (Tapeworm)

Dugesia or *Euplanaria* is a common free-living fresh water flatworm. There are several species of *Dugesia* found in India which occur in the mud at the bottom of the fresh water ponds, lakes and springs. It is gregarious (lives in groups) animal found on the underside of leaves, logs, deloris, stones or rocks submerged in cool, clear and running water of streams and lakes. Their movement is visible by naked eye. Their colour is similar to the surrounding plants and stones on which they cling. These animals prefer to live in damp surrounding because their bodies are not protected.

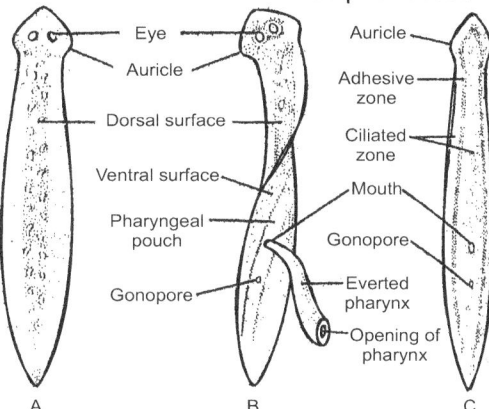

Fig. 1.46: *Dugesia*. External features
A – Dorsal surface; B – Body twisted to show a part of ventral surface; C – Ventral surface

Dugesia is dark brownish or blackish in colour with anterior moving end. The flat body shows upper dorsal lower ventral surface. Body shows triangular head with pair of eyes. Head shows lateral projections called auricles. The head is separated from body by neck like constriction. The mouth is present on the ventral side behind the middle of the body which leads into a pharyngeal sheath containing a cylindrical pharynx. The ventral side exhibits an adhesive zone at the margin which secretes adhesive substance from the glands. The animal clamps itself to the substratum by the adhesive zone. The mucus trail is left by the animal when moving, which is secreted by mucus glands opening on the ventral surface. Just behind the mouth aperture genital aperture or gonopore is present in sexually mature forms on the ventral surface.

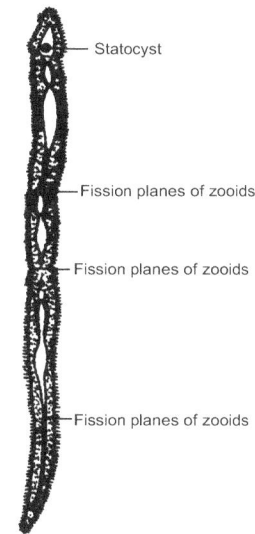

Fig. 1.47: *Catenula*

Dugesia moves by two ways i.e. gliding and crawling. It is carnivorous animal feeding on living small worms, crustaceans, snails and pieces of dead animals. Digestion is both extracellular and intracellular. The reproduction is by both sexual and asexual methods. It has great power of regeneration.

Catenula is a fresh water turbellaria. It has single protonephiridium. There is no sexual reproduction but asexual reproduction is by fission with chains of zooids. *Microstomium* is a microscopic fresh water form.

There are also marine free-living turbellaria, *Convoluta* is exclusively marine form living under stones among algae. It is a small worm with sides of the body curved ventrally. The anterior end has a cluster of frontal glands, a pair of eyes and a statocyst. The body has pigmented lens.

Mouth is situated ventrally near the anterior end. Intestine and excretory system is absent. It is hermaphrodite but protandry is common. *Convoluta* exhibits symbiotic phenomena by having algal cells in symbiotic association in its body.

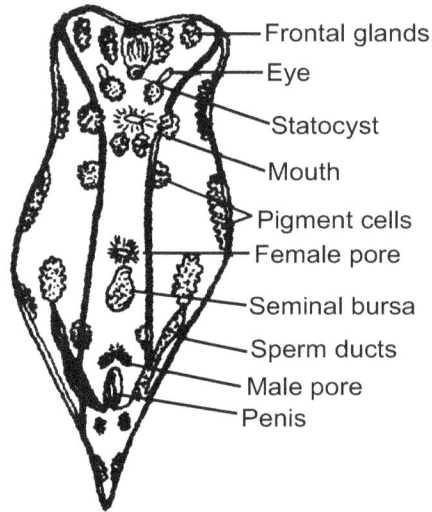

Fig. 1.48: *Convoluta*

Bipalium is a long terrestrial turbellarian living in the humid soil floor of tropical forests. It has expanded lunate head and cylindrical long body. Numerous eyes are present on the margin of the head and sides of body. It reproduces by asexual methods and propogates by fragmentation.

Though most of the turbellarians are free-living but *Temnocephala* is found as an ectocommensal on cray-fishes, prawns and other crustaceans. This animal has 12 finger-like tentacles at anterior end and an adhesive disc at the posterior end. It feeds upon diatoms, rotifers and other small animals.

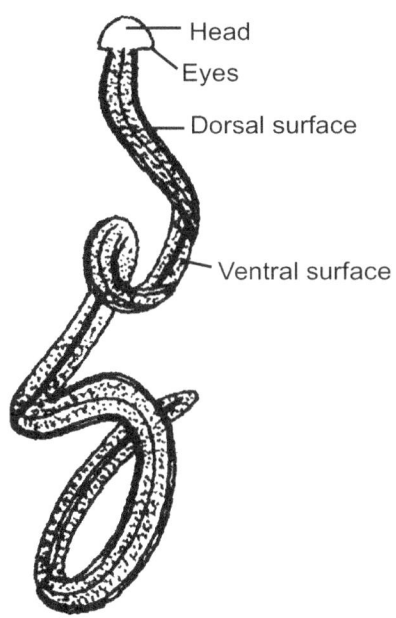

Fig. 1.49: *Bipalium*

The class *Trematoda* includes the animals which are mostly ectoparasitic or endoparasitic forms and they are commonly called flukes. There are no free-living forms. These animals are usually leaf-like and possess dorsoventrally flattened body. This is suitable for parasitic mode of life. There are no cilia on the body but covered with cuticle. The animals are equipped with well developed suckers. Digestive system is incomplete consisting of mouth, pharynx and two forked or branched intestine and anus is absent.

All trematodes are hermaphrodite with single ovary and two or many testes - Life cycle of these individuals is simple or complicated which includes intermediate hosts. These animals are armed with suckers for firm attachment. Trematodes occurs as an ecto and endo parasites in mussels, fishes, turtles, frogs and man.

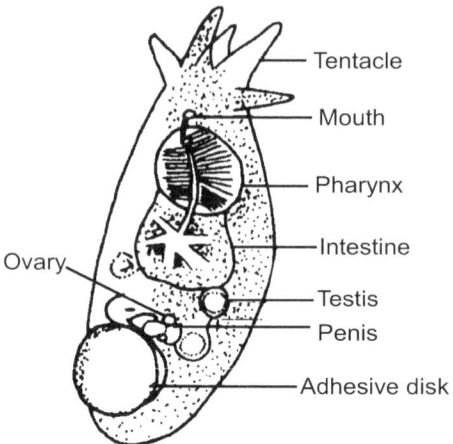

Fig. 1.50: *Temnocephala*

Gyrodactylus is an ectoparasite animal on the gills and skin of freshwater fishes. It has no anterior sucker but adhesive organs and adhesive glands are present at the anterior end. Its body is minute and elongated and eyes are absent. At the posterior end opisthaptor is disc shaped and bears one pair of anchors and eight pairs of marginal hooks or hooklets. It is viviparous. A remarkable feature is that a second embryo is produced within the first one, a third within the second and a fourth within the third. The first embryo, on completing its development passes out, still enclosing the other embryos and attaches directly to a host fish.

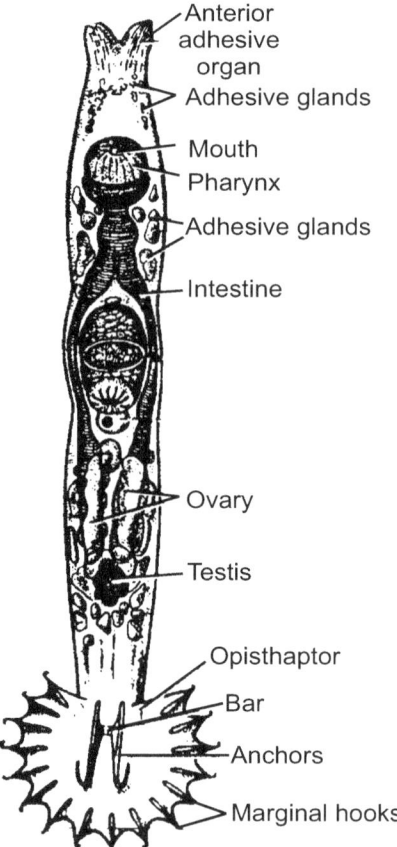

Fig. 1.51: *Gyrodactylus*

Aspidogaster trematodes is an endoparasite in the pericardial and renal cavities of fresh water mussel and in the gut of fishes and turtles. Its body is elongated and dorsoventrally flattened with anterior narrow end with subterminal mouth. A large sucker is present on the ventral side. Its life cycle is simple without alternation of host.

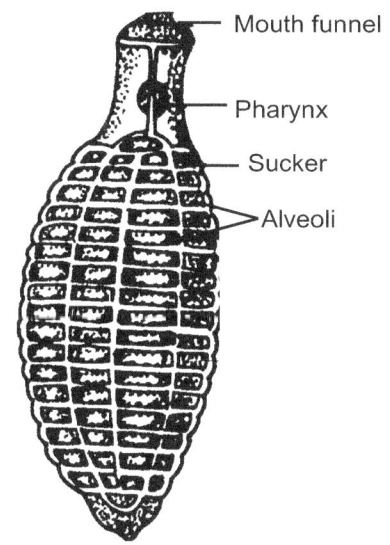

Fig. 1.52: *Aspidogaster*

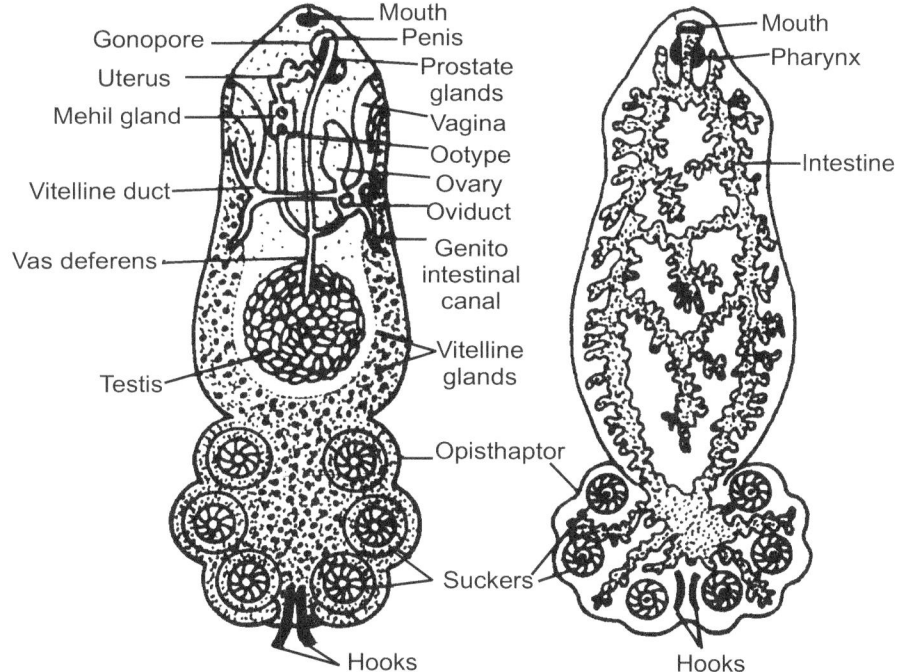

Fig. 1.53: *Polystomium*

Polystomium is an endoparasite in the urinary bladder of frogs and turtles. Its body is leaf like and dorsoventrally flattened. Its unique feature is presence of disc shaped opisthaptor with six-cup like suckers and 2 to 4 large chitinous hooks. Its mouth is also surrounded by an oval sucker. It produces egg in urinary bladder of frog and discharged into the water along with the urine of the host. After 4-5 weeks hatching takes place and larva attaches to the gills of tadpole and later develop into adult in the alimentary canal of metamorphosed tadpole.

Diplozoon is an ectoparasite found attached to the gills of freshwater fishes; feeding on their blood. Two individuals are always found attached permanently together in the form of X. *Opisthorchis* bears eight suckers arranged into rows of four each.

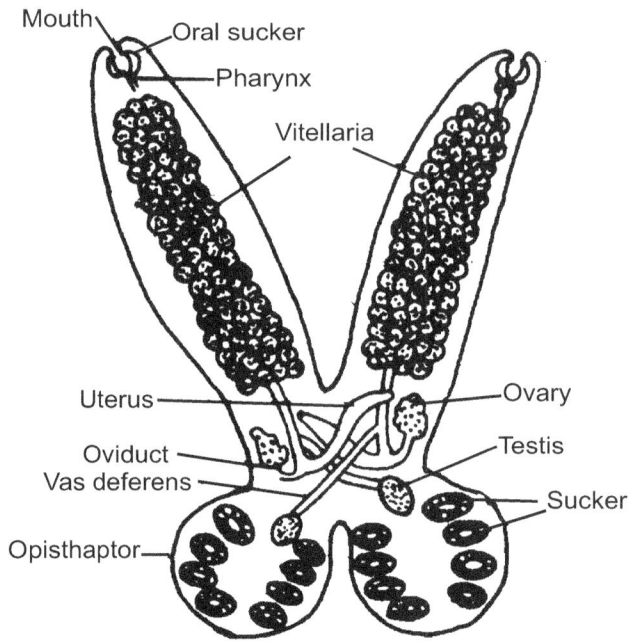

Fig. 1.54: *Diplozoon*

Fasciola hepatica is world wide in distribution and inhabit the digestive tract or accessory tubes and cavities. It occurs primarily in the sheep, but also occurs in other hosts like goat, horse, dog, ass, ox, deer, antelope, rabbit, elephant, monkey, etc. Humans are occassional host. It is digenetic fluke i.e. life history is completed in two hosts a primary host and a secondary host or intermediate host. Adult fluke occurs in the liver and bile passages of sheep. A single host may harbour as many as about 200 of these flukes in its liver which may create abnormal function of the organ. The disease caused is called liver rot. The part of the life cycle is completed in the body of intermediate host, a fresh-water snail *Limnea truncatula*. Miracidium, sporocyst, cercaria, are the larval stages in the life cycle of the fluke. Being an endo-parasite, it produces enormous number of eggs. Due to large number of eggs chances of survival of animal are more. Multiplication takes place by paedogenesis during larval stages.

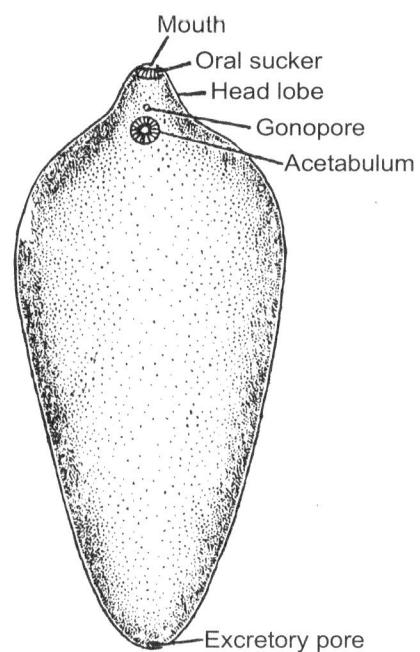

**Fig. 1.55: *Fasciola hepatica*.
Adult in ventral view**

Liverfluke has oral sucker and mouth at anterior end and acetabulum or ventral sucker just below the gonopore.

Opisthorchis is called Chinese liver fluke which inhabits in the bile ducts of man in China, Japan and India. It is generally found in fish eating mammals. The size ranges from 10 to 20 mm.

When raw or insufficiently cooked fish is eaten, young flukes emerge from the cysts in human small intestine from where they reach the bile ducts within few hours.

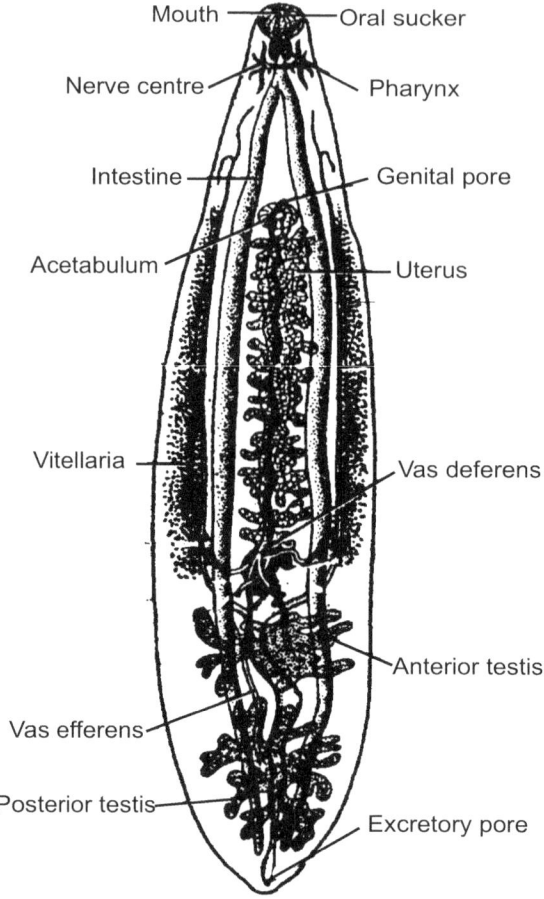

Fig. 1.56: *Opisthorchis sinensis*

Schistosoma is another dioecious digenetic trematode which is parasitic in the human hepatic portal or pelvis veins. Some species of this trematode are parasitic in veins of birds and mammals. The pecularity of this animal is both sexes are separate but male and female live together in pairs. The male is larger and thicker which carries longer and slender female in the gynaecophoric canal formed by folding of ventral body wall.

Body surface of male is rough and spiny with oral sucker and acetabulum. After fertilization female leaves the male to lay the eggs one at a time in the smaller blood vessels. The capsules lacerate the capillaries and reach the urinary bladder and are vioded with urine. Through urine the capsules are released in water where they hatch into miracidium larvae which enter a fresh-water snail and reach its liver. Sporocysts are formed from miracidium. Many generations are formed. Then they give rise to cercaria larvae which are with forked tail. There is no radia stage. The cercaria come out of the snail and swim freely in water. They penetrate human skin during bathing or washing or they may be swallowed by drinking infected water. Cercaria may enter the blood vessels, then pass to the heart, lungs and liver where they grow. They reach hepatic portal or pelvic veins where they become sexually mature.

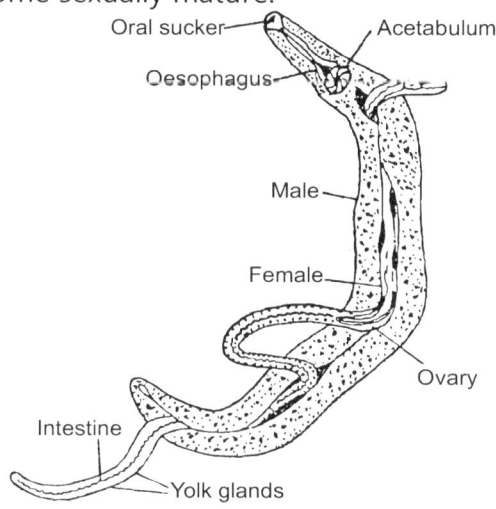

Fig. 1.57: *Schistosoma* (male and female)

There are three species of *Schistosoma* parasitic in human beings. They are *S. haematobium*, *S. mansoni* and *S. japonicum*. This parasite causes bladder injuries, bladder stones, skin diseases, haematuria which is disorder of kidneys with discharge of blood. In Egypt 60% of the population has sanitary control of water and use of compounds of antimony are the effective measures for control of the disease.

The class Cestoda includes endoparasites of vertebrate intestine and are commonly called tapeworms.

(1) These parasites are flat, elongated and ribbon-like with length from 1 mm to 10 metres.
(2) Body is usually divided into a scolex or head, neck and few to many proglottids.
(3) Scolex is provided with hooks or suckers or both.
(4) The tapeworms lack mouth and digestive system.
(5) Excretory system consists of protonephridia with flame cells.
(6) Nervous system consists of ganglionated nerve ring in scolex and two pairs of lateral nerve cords in proglottids.
(7) Each proglottid contains one or two sets of male and female reproductive organs. Thus, they are hermaphrodite.

(8) Fertilization is internal and self.
(9) Life cycle is complicated with hooked embyro, and is passed in more than one host.

There are about 3400 species in Cestoda. Following description gives an account of bio-diversity of some selected representatives of Cestoda.

The tapeworms are found in the intestine of fishes, frogs, reptiles, and birds and mammals.

Amphilina is an endoparasite found in the coelom of fish Acipenser. Its body is flat and leaf like, with no scolex. It has anterior protrusible proboscis. The intermediate host is crustacean *Gammarus* on which fish feeds. *Tetrahynchus* is found in the intestine of elasmobranch fishes. Its body is long and divisible into scolex and proglottids and broader at the posterior end. Scolex is elongated and divisible into a long proximal part containing the proboscis apparatus and distal part bearing the bothria. Scolex bears four bothria (suckers) each with a eversible proboscides armed with spines. Probscides or rostella are enclosed in muscular sheaths which end below in muscular bulbs.

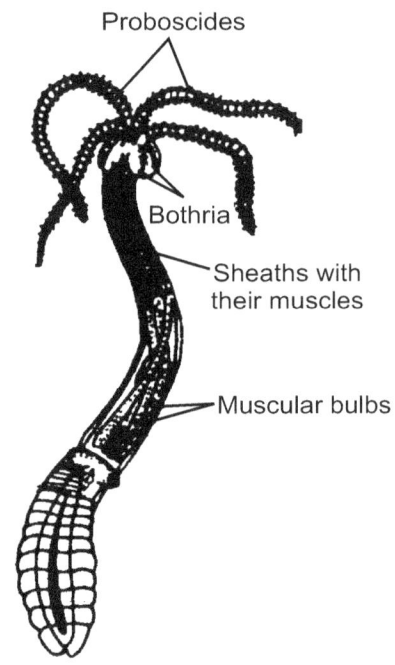

Fig. 1.58: Tetrahynchus

Diphyllobothrium is the broad fish tapeworm found in the intestine of man. It is largest and most injurious parasite to man with 18 to 20 metres in length. Body is differentiated into scolex, neck and proglottids. The number of proglottides is 3000 to 4000. Scolex is fusiform bears two slit-like bothria (suckers) followed by long slender neck. Life cycle involves two intermediate hosts, one is *cyclops* and other a fish.

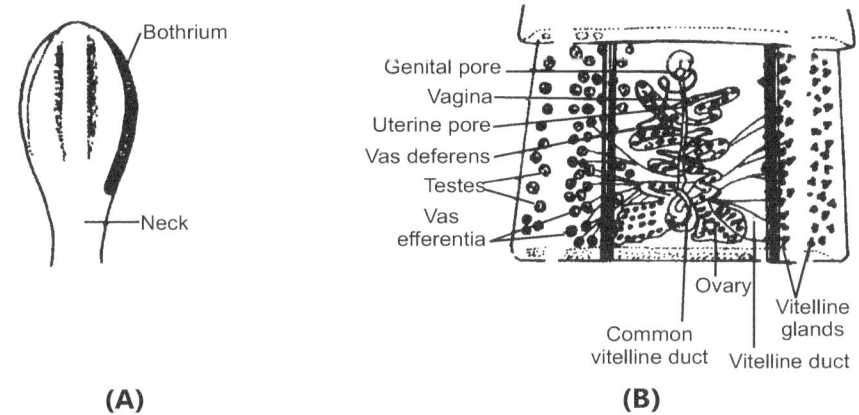

Fig. 1.59: *Diphyllobothrium*. A – Scolex; B – A mature proglottid

Taenia saginata is commonly called beef tapeworm which is endoparasite in the intestine of man. It is cosmopolitan in distribution. Body is dorsoventrally flattened and much larger than *T. solium*, reaches a length of 5 to 6 metres. The scolex bears four large suckers for adhesion. Rostellar hooks are absent. Intermediate hosts are cattle, usually cow and buffalo. Infection occurs by ingestion of improperly cooked beef.

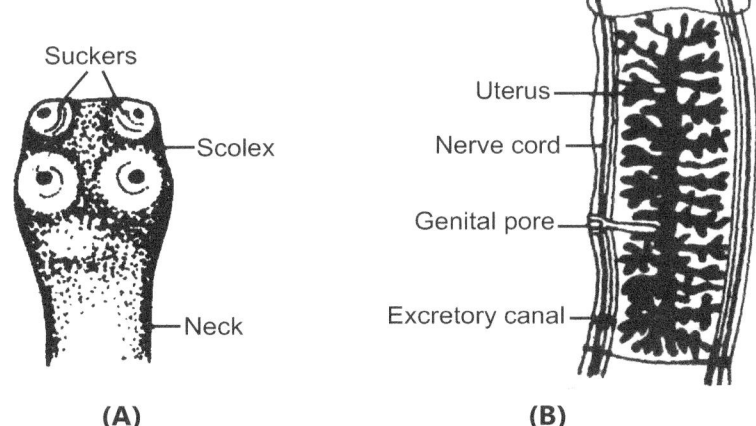

Fig. 1.60: *Taenia saginata*. A – Scolex; B – A mature proglottid

Echinococcus granulosus is a minute tapeworm found in the intestine of dogs, cats and wolves. The scolex possess with four suckers and a protrusible rostellum with two rows of hooks. There is neck and 3 to 4 proglottids, one immature, one or two mature with complete hermaphrodite reproductive organs and one large gravid proglottid. Intermediate host is man or herbivorous animals like rabbits, sheep and cattle, kangaroos.

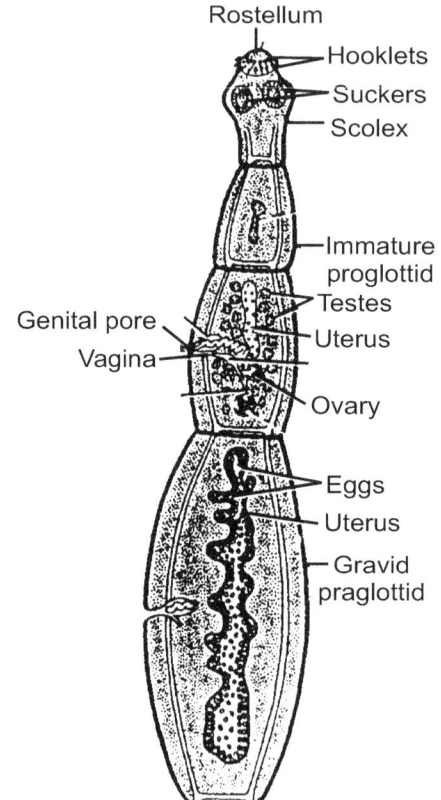

Fig. 1.61: *Echinococcus granulose*

Hymenolepis nana is called *dwarf tapeworm* found in the intestine of the man. Its length is 7 to 100 mm. The rostellum is well developed and retractile with single circlets of 20-30 hooks. Neck is long and slender. Life cycle is simple without any intermediate host. It causes abdominal pain and diarrhoea.

Raillietma is the tapeworm found in birds like pigeon, fowl, duck, crow, sparrow, etc. The scolex has four closely spaced suckers with spines. The cushion-shaped rostellum contains 20 to 110 small hammer shaped hooks in double rows. Neck is absent. About 500-700 proglottids are present having a single set of hermaphrodite reproductive organs. The parasite is digenetic. The primary host is a bird and intermediate hosts are houseflies and ants.

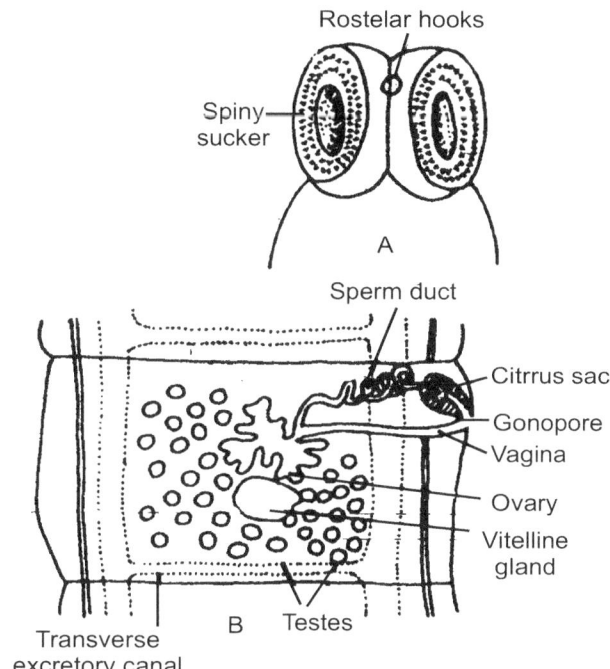

Fig. 1.62: *Raillietma*.
A - Scolex; B - Mature proglottid

Summary

- Platyhelminthes are flatworms.
- They are triploblastic.
- Animal possess definite head at anterior end.
- They are equipped with hooks, spines, thorns, spicules and teeth etc.
- Protonephridia or flame cells are the excretory organs.
- They are free living as well as endoparasites.
- They are bisexual or hermaphrodite.
- Life cycle is completed in one or two hosts.
- Platyhelminthes are divided into three classes namely Turbellaria, Trematoda and Cestoda.

Review Questions

1. Give an account of general characters of phylum Platyhelminthes.
2. Classify the phylum platyhelminthes upto class level and give the distinctive characters of different classes.
3. Give the distinctive characters of class Turbellaria, Trematoda and Cestoda.

1.8 Aschelminthes

Introduction

The Aschelminthes *(Greek askes = cavity; helmins = worm)* are pseudocoelomote, mostly vermiform fresh water and marine animals. Recently, Nematodes have been grouped in a class Nematoda in the phylum Aschelminthes.

They show the following characteristics:
1. Body of round worms is elongated, cylindrical, vermiform with tapering ends.
2. Body is unsegmented or superficially segmented covered with tough cuticle.
3. They are mostly minute to small size but some are of great length.
4. Caudal end of the body is generally straight in female but coiled in males and males are shorter than females.
5. Mouth is terminal surrounded by lips. In strongyloides the lips are modified into teeth known as leaf crown.
6. The sensory organs are amphids and papillae which are of great taxonomic value in ease of free-living forms.
7. Body is covered by rough resistant cuticle with bristles, spines, warts and papillae, etc.
8. Body cavity is pseudocoel.
9. Digestive tract is well developed generally made up of mouth, buccal cavity, pharynx or oesophagus, intestine and anus.
10. Nervous system consists of a nerve-ring encircling the oesophagus from it, nerves are given out anteriorily and posteriorly.

11. Protonephridia absent but excretory system is made up of canals.
12. Sexes are separate.
13. They are ovo-viviparous, oviparous or viviparous.
14. Life cycle is complicated with or without intermediate host.
15. The phylum includes free-living, epizoic and parasitic members.

- There are many nemotode worms which are marine, freshwater, and terrestrial and free-living forms which are included in subclass I.
- *Aphasmidea, Paracytholaimus, Anticoma, Tricoma,* etc. are the marine and free-living nematodes, whereas *Dorylaimus* is fresh water animal. Some species are terrestrial. *Mermis* and *Paramermis* are the free-living nematodes in adult condition but the larvae are parasitic in invertebrates.
- Majority of nematodes are parasitic in birds and mammals. The genus *Rhabditis* includes numerous free-living, semiparasitic forms. They are normally found in soil, organic matter or water and frequently in faeces of man and animals.
- *R. pellco* is occassionally found living in the human vagina, larvae escaping in the urine. *R. hominis* found in the stool of man and animals. They show H-shaped excretory system.
- The female is large with pointed tail whereas male has flattened copulatory bursa with two equal spicules. Life cycle is simple and direct.
- *Enterobius vermicularis (Oxyuris)* is commonly known as pinworm, which is more common in Europe and America.
- Pinworms are parasites in the human caecum, colon and apendix. Male has ventrally curved tail with a single spicule. Female has straigle tail which becomes long and pointed.
- Life cycle is simple and there is no intermediate host. Gravid females migrates to anus causing itching sensation. They crawl and deposit eggs on the perianal skin.
- Due to scratching, gravid females rupture and thus small eggs are liberated. The reinfection in children takes place by putting fingers in mouth. Eggs hatch in small intestine.

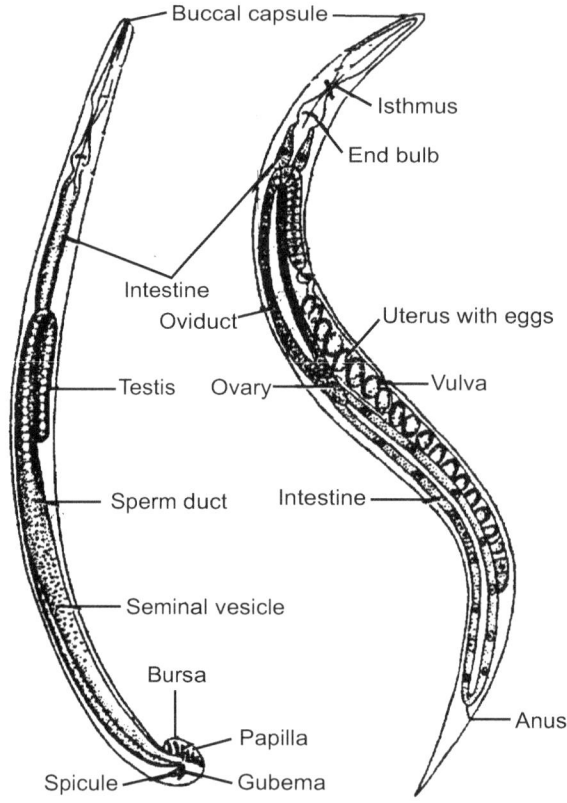

Fig. 1.63: *Rhabditis elegans*. (a) - Male; (b) - Female

- Juveniles descent slowly, moult 4 times and become adults. It causes disease enterobiosis. Symptoms are inflammation of caecal mucosa, abdominal pain, insomnia hysteria, restlessness, loss of apetite and sometimes apendicitis.
- *Loa loa* is commonly known as African eyeworm chiefly found in Africa. It is the parasitic in subcutaneous tissues of man.
- The male and female measure 20-35 mm and 20-27 mm in length respectively. The body is covered by numerous warts. The intermediate hosts are mango flies *Chrysops*.
- The larva moult and develop into infective stage in fly. These are transmitted in blood of man through proboscis.
- The adult worm moves and some times passes across the eyeball causing intense itching and swelling called calabar *swellings*. These are injurious and fatal when they penetrate brain and spinal cord.

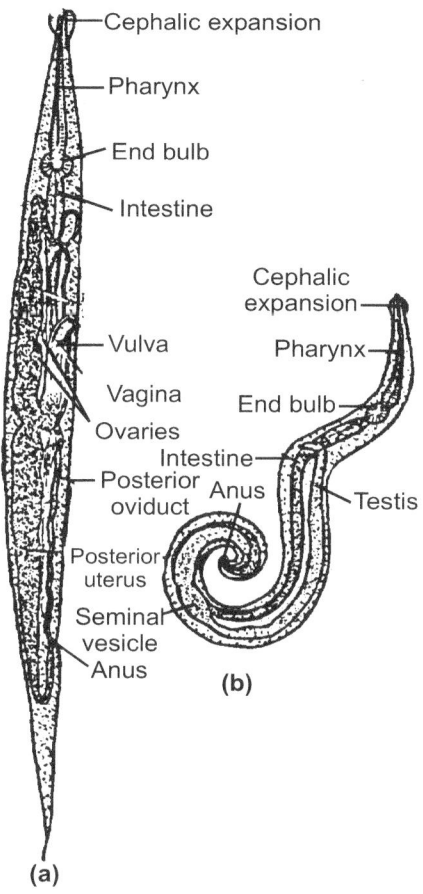

Fig. 1.64: *Vermicularis*. (a) – Female; (b) – Male

- *Dracunculus medinesis* is called guinea worm and found in tropical countries like India, Africa, East Indies.
- It lives in the deeper subcutaneous tissues of man. Anterior end is blunt and posterior end is pointed.
- Male measures 4 cm in length whereas female measures 70-120 cm. Females are viviparous.
- Mature female migrates to the superficial layers of the skin in those parts of the body which are likely to come in contact with cold water.
- Due to production of toxic substances. Under skin, blister is formed leading to an ulcer.
- It breaks when it comes in contact with water releasing larvae in water. They are swallowed by female cyclops which is an intermediate host.

- When cyclops are swallowed by new host with drinking water infection occurs. It causes guinea worm disease characterised by asthama, nausea, vomitting, diarrhoea etc.

Fig. 1.65: *Loa loa* in the cornea of man

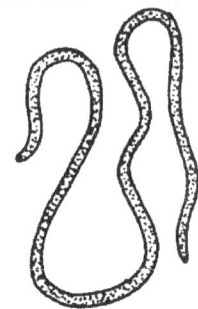

Fig. 1.66: *Dracunculus medinesis*

- *Trichinella spiralis* is commonly known as trichina worm. It is a small intestinal parasite of man in Europe and America.
- It is also parasitic in pigs and domestic animals and rodents. Man becomes infected by eating insufficiently cooked pork.
- Female is larger than male. The fertilized female bores through the intestine into a spiral lymph space and gives birth to juveniles.
- The juveniles travel through the lymph and blood vessels into every organ, but finally live in the form of cyst in voluntary muscles. If pork is eaten by man the embryos come out in intestine.

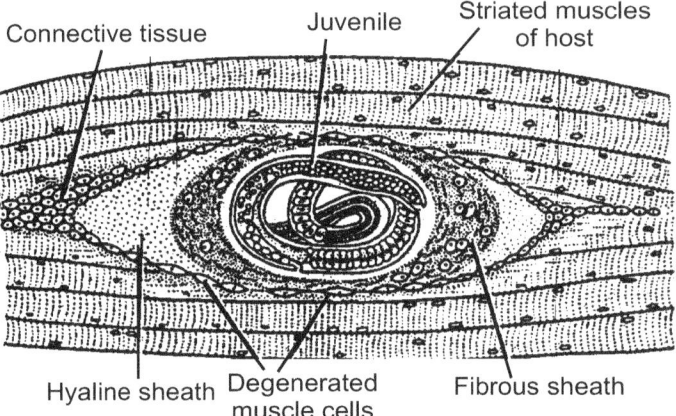

Fig. 1.67: *T. spiralis* ensheathed in host muscle

- *Trichuris* is commonly known as whipworrn. It is also a parasite of the intestine of man and other mammals. It feeds on blood and epithelial cells.

- Life cycle is simple with no intermediate host. Development of eggs take place in moist soil.
- Contaminated food and water is responsible for infection in man by swallowing eggs with juvenile.

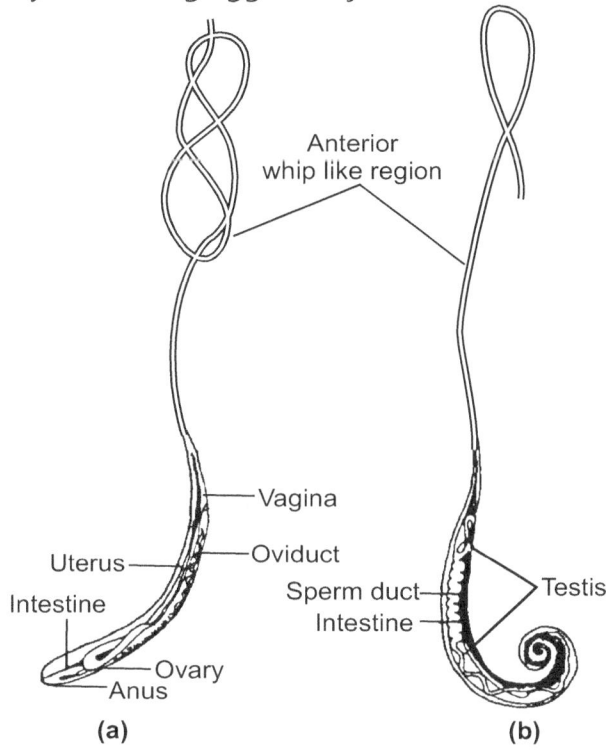

Fig. 1.68: *Trichuris ovis.* **(a) - Female, (b) - Male**

- *Ascaris lumbricoides* is the most common nematode parasite found in human intestine. They occur more commonly in human intestine. They occur more commonly in children.
- As many as 1000-1500 adult worms may be present in a single host. Female is larger than male and male has hook-like tail with penial setae. It requires only one host to complete its life cycle. It is pathogenic to man.
- When larvae migrate through the lungs, they cause lung inflammation and fatal pneumonia, vomitting, diarrhoea, apendicitis are also different disorders caused by them.
- *Ancylostoma duodenale* is called hook worm which infects humans. Other species are found in dogs, cats and bear.

- It causes diseases like elephantasis. Severe infection causes blockage of lymphatic vessels and causing lymphatic obstruction.
- So that lymph cannot get back to the circulatory system. Lymph gets accumulated in the organ and this condition is called lymphoedema.
- It causes elephantasis of feet, hands, scrotum, etc. producing a tumor like ugly look.
- *Wuchereria bancrofti* is dreadful endoparasite of man. Adults live in lymphatic vessels and lymph nodes.
- The larvae live in blood. Its life history is digenetic, as it involves a secondary host, the blood sucking insect mosquitoes of genus *Culex, Aedes* and or *Anapheles*.
- This parasite is largely confined to the tropical and subtropical countries of the world.

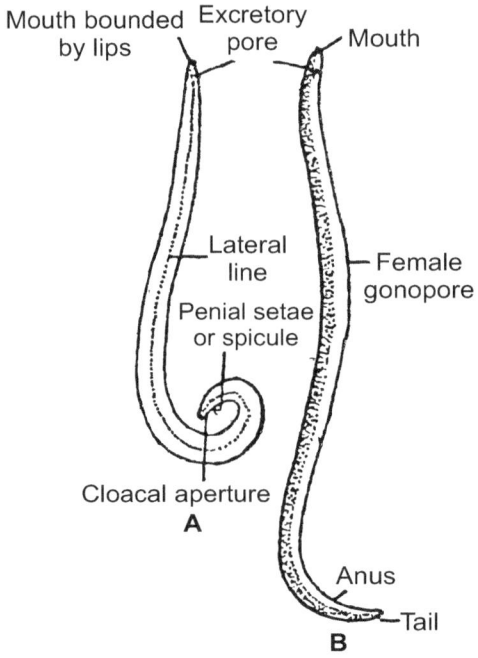

Fig. 1.69: *Ascaris lumbricoides*

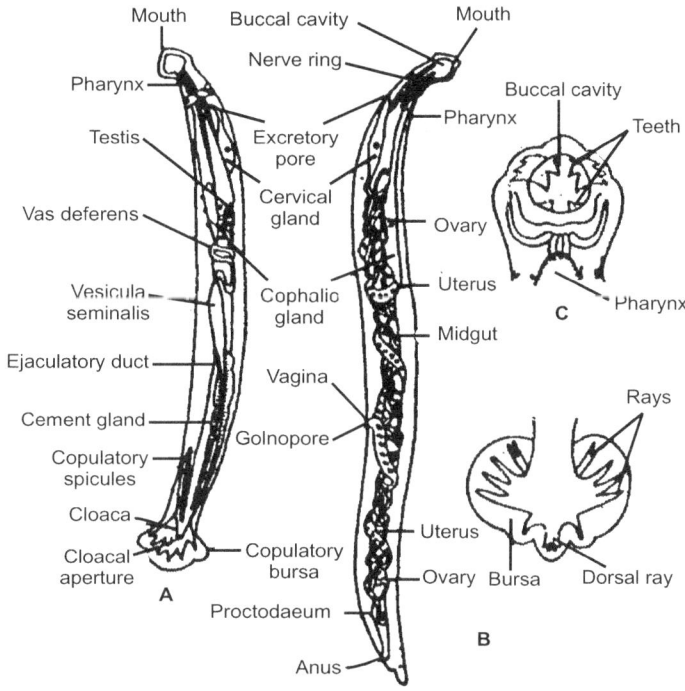

Fig. 1.70: *Ancylostoma duodenale*. A - Adult male; B - Adult female; C - Anterior end; D - Posterior end of male

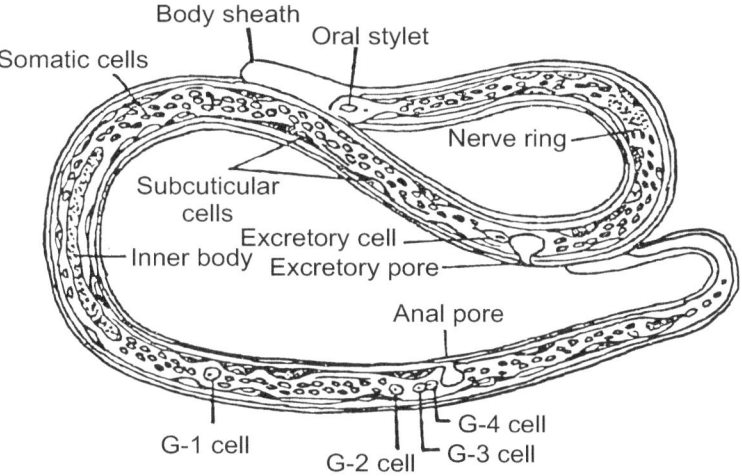

Fig. 1.71: *Wuchereria*. Microfilaria

Summary

- The Aschelminthes are pseudocoelomate, mostly vermiform freshwater and marine animals.
- Body elongated and cylindrical.
- Mouth is terminal.
- Amphids and papillae are the sensory organs.
- Well developed digestive tract.
- Sexes are separate.
- Complicated life cycle with or without intermediate host.
- This phylum consists of one class called nematoda.
- *Ascaris*, *Rhabditis*, *Trichinella*, *Dracunculus* are the examples of Nematoda.

Review Question

1. Give an account of general characters of Phylum Aschelminthes with suitable examples.

***

1.9 Annelida

Introduction

Lamark first used the name annelida for higher segmented worm means 'little ring' and refers to the ring like constrictions of the body. The name annelida has been derived either from Latin annelus (a ring), or French anneler (to arrange in rings) and the Greek eidos (form).

General Characters:

(1) Most of the annelids are aquatic, fresh water as well as marine, some are terrestrial which live in burrows or in tubes.

(2) Body is elongated, vermiform and bilaterally symmetrical.

(3) Body is metamerically segmented. Externally, segments are shown by transverse grooves and internally by muscular partitions called septa. The segments or metameres or somites are many and arranged one after the other in a single linear series.

(4) The outer most covering of the body is called cuticle secreted by underlying epidermal cells.
(5) The body wall is composed of circular and longitudinal muscles.
(6) Setae or chaetae are the locomotary organs.
(7) They are triploblastic animals.
(8) All annelids are true coelomate animals. The body cavity or coelomic cavity is lying between the two layers of mesoderm.
(9) Respiration is by general body surface or by special projections or gills of parapodia and head.
(10) Annelids shows well developed blood vascular system and it is of a closed type.
(11) Blood is red due to dissolved haemoglobin.
(12) Nephredia are the excretory organs which communicate the coelom with the exterior end.
(13) Nervous system consists of cerebral ganglion (brain), circumpharyngeal connectives and double ventral nerve cord with segmental ganglia.
(14) Sexes may be separate (Polychaeta) or united (hermaphrodite) e.g. Oligochaeta and Hirudinea.
(15) In indirect development, there is characteristic larva called trochophore larva.

The phylum Annelida has three main classes, such as,
(i) Polychaeta, (ii) Aelosomata, (iii) Clitellata

Class - Polychaeta:
Distinctive Characters of Polychaeta:
(1) Most of the animals are marine, few are fresh water and carnivorous.
(2) Body is elongated, cylindrical and segmented into similar somites.
(3) The animals show distinct head with sense organs such as eyes, tentacles, cirri, palps and mouth.
(4) Each body segment bears paired, flattened lateral outgrowths of body wall, called parapodia. They are locomotory and respiratory in function.
(5) Many bristles or setae extend from parapodia in bundles, hence animals are called polychaeta.

(6) The clitellum or cingulum is absent.
(7) Cirri or branchiae may be present on body segments.
(8) Sexes are generally separate (dioecious).
(9) Many show asexual reproduction like serial or lateral budding.
(10) Fertilization is external.
(11) Development shows metamorphosis with a typical free swimming trochophore larva.

Examples: *Nereis, Aphrodite, Chaetopterus, Terebella, Amphitrite.*

Class-Aelosomata:

(1) These are small to minute worms with many chaetae.
(2) They live in the interstitial zone of both freshwater and brackish water environment.
(3) They are hermaphrodites animals.
(4) Each animal possessing one ovary and two testis.
(5) There are about 25 species. They are little known to science and their classification is disputed with some authors considering them to be part of the Oligochaeta.

Class-Clitellata is divided into three subclasses like **Oligochaeta**, **Hirudinaria** and **Brachiobdella**.

Sub-class-Oligochaeta:

Distinctive Characters of Oligochaeta:

(1) Most of the animals are terrestrial, some are fresh water and marine.
(2) No distinct head, prostomium is small without sense organs and appendages.
(3) Rod like setae are present in the body wall of each segment for locomotion.
(4) Clitellum or cingulum is usually present.
(5) Some animals bear external gills for respiration. Integument or skin also shows respiration.
(6) They are bisexual or monoecious or hermaphrodite.
(7) Development is direct. No metamorphosis and larval stage. Development occurs inside cocoon secreted by clitellum.
(8) Some animals show asexual reproduction by transverse fission. All possess a great power of regeneration.

Examples: *Pheretima, Tubifex, Lumbricus, Branchiobdella.*

Sub-class-Hirudinea:
Distinctive Characters of Hirudinea:
(1) Some are terrestrial, some freshwater and a few marine.
(2) They are generally ectoparasitic and blood sucking.
(3) Body is dorso-ventrally flattened or cylindrical, segmented.
(4) Number of body segments is small but definite usually 33. Each segment again shows superficial divisions into 2 to 5 transverse rings or annuli.
(5) Anterior and posterior ends of body are provided with suckers called cephalic and anal suckers respectively. They are useful for locomotion and attachment.
(6) Head is not distinct and bears only eyes.
(7) Coelomic (body) cavity is greatly obliterated and filled by botryoidal tissue.
(8) Body is very muscular and has got great power of contraction and extension.
(9) Sexes are united.
(10) Nephridia are excretory organs.
(11) Fertilization is internal and development is direct and it occurs in cocoon secreted by clitellum.

Examples: *Hirudinaria (leech), Acanthobdella, Placobdella, Hirudo.*

Sub-class-Brachiobdella:
(1) They are small (about 1 cm long) aquatic whitish animals.
(2) These animals are either commensals or parasites on crayfish.
(3) They are mostly found in the northern hemisphere.
(4) Different species attach to their hosts at different places on the body. For example, *Branchiobdella parasitica* attaches to the underside of the abdomen while *B. astaci* attaches to its hosts gills. Some forms are considered as parasitic feeding on the tissue of host but some forms are considered as commensals.

- *Nereis* is typical polychaet worm living in burrows in sand or mud often with clams, hence it is called clamworm or sandworm. It is found on sandy shores between tide marks.
- It spends more time in burrow which is formed by its jaws. The burrow is generally U-shaped upto 60 cm deep and inside coated with mucus which cements the sand particles.

- The constant water current is mantained by the worm, in the burrow by dorsoventral undulations of its body. The worm is nocturnal and carnivorous. At night, it keeps its head protruded out of the burrow in search of prey.
- The worm is armed with chitinous teeth and jaws for capturing food. Occassionally, the worm leaves its burrow and creeps about beneath stones and rocks or among sea weeds.
- During breeding season the worm leaves its burrow permanently and swims actively in the surface layer of water. During this phase it is called heteronereis.

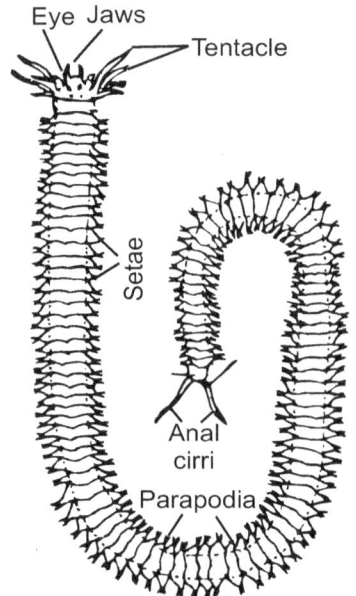

Fig. 1.72: *Nereis*. Dorsal View

- *Aphrodite* is another marine polychaet called 'sea mouse'. It is found crawling on the sea bed or burrowing in the mud or sand of the sea bottom.
- Its body is oval, broad and dorsoventrally flattened and consists of 30-35 segments.
- Dorsal body surface is covered by overlapping 15 pairs of scales or elytra.
- It has protective stiff spine like setae and lateral iridescent bristles. It's head is small and hidden beneath the dorsal felt.

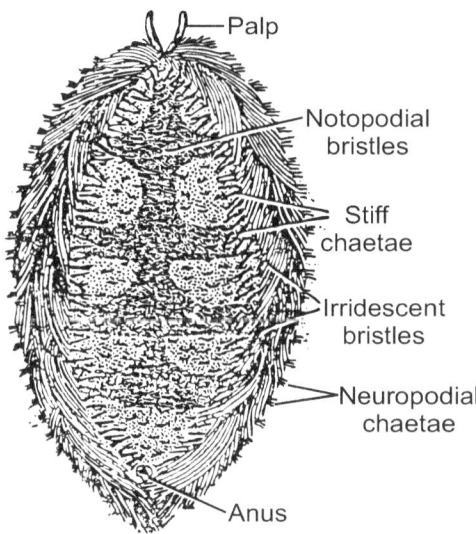

Fig. 1.73: Aphrodite

- *Eunice* also marine worm living in rock and coral crevices below low tide mark. The body is long with many segments. Its body shows two regions, anterior no sexual or atoke and posterior epitoke is sexual region.

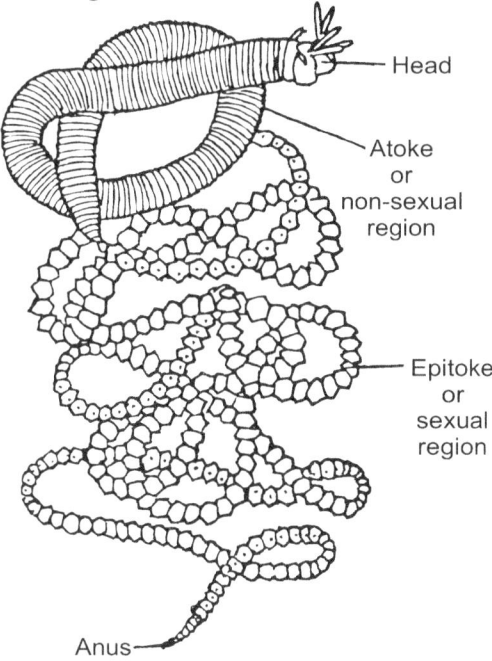

Fig. 1.74: Eunice

- In the early morning, the worms come out from burrows and male by spiral swimming movements breaking free their epitokal regions. The epitokes rupture at sunrise, which is immediately followed by fertilization.
- *Chaetopterus* is tubicolous, marine polychaet worm living in a parchment like, U-shaped tube formed by sand particles or mud in the intertidal zone.
- The body of the worm is divided into three regions. The anterior, middle and posterior regions.
- Middle region is without parapodia. The worm is filter feeder. It has remarkable power of regeneration. From single segment it can regenerate whole body.
- *Arenicola* is commonly called lugworm and lives in sea or estuaries having less water salinity. It shows presence of gills which act as the respiratory surfaces and water current is maintained through the burrow.
- The class Oligochaeta includes the worms which mostly terrestrial or fresh water forms. They show distinct external and internal segmentation.

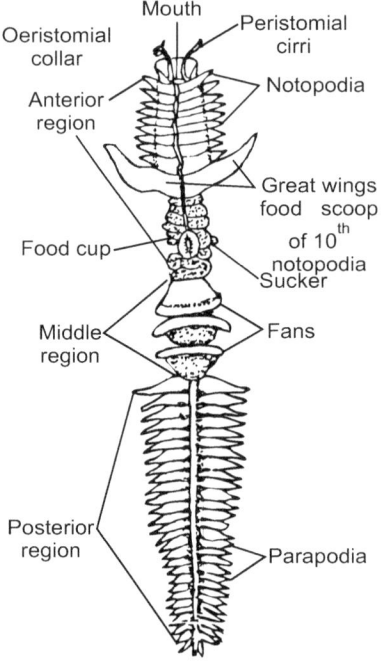

Fig. 1.75: *Chaetopterus*

- Parapodia are absent but setae are segmentally arranged which are useful for locomotions. Clitellum is usually present.
- Animals are herma-phrodite. The worms show direct development which occurs in cocoons secreted by clitellum.
- *Pheretima posthuma* is the terrestrial earthworm which lives in burrows made in moist soil. It is nocturnal animal found in the soil rich in decaying organic matter.
- The worm is generally found in upper layer of earth to a depth of about 30 to 45 cm. However, during summer it may go down upto 3 metres or more in search of moisture.
- The worms are hermaphrodite but prefer cross-fertilization and breeding occurs in rainy season.
- The earthworm makes its burrow partly by boring with its pointed anterior end and partly by sucking and swallowing the earth.
- It's food is soil containing organic matter. The residual soil discharged by its anus is called castings.

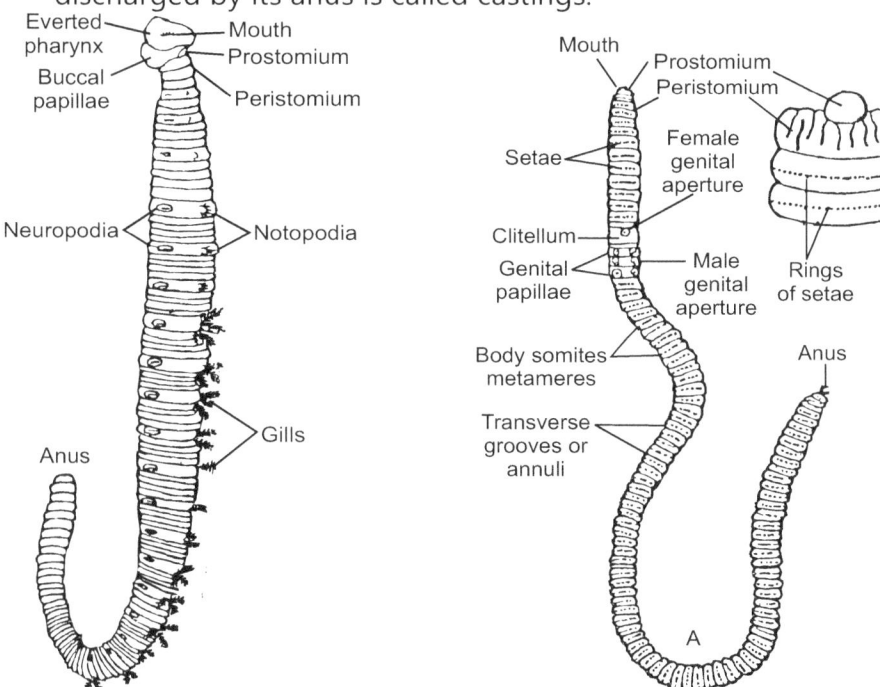

Fig. 1.76: *Arenicola*

**Fig. 1.77: *P. posthuma*. A – Entire worm in ventral view.
B – Anterior end in dorsal view**

- *Megascolex* is large earthworm found in South India. It has two species namely *M. maurittii* and *M. konkonesis*.
- The worm measures about 8 to 12 cm in length and bears 80 to 100 or more segments.
- *Lumbricus terrestris* is the earthworm found in Europe and America. The body shows about 250 segments.

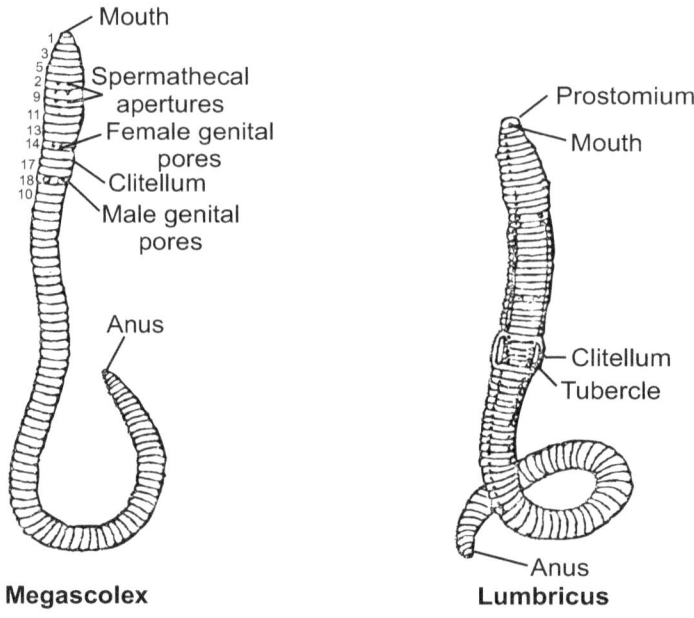

Fig. 1.78: *Megascolex* and *Lumbricus*

- *Tubifex* worms are fresh water oligochaets found at the bottom of deep lakes. It lives in tubes made of mud and mineral cemented together with mucus. It is 4 cm long, cylindrical, red coloured worm very much similar to earthworm.
- *Aelosoma* is a fresh water worm and lives in fresh water ponds or occurs attached to or in the liver of fresh water snails. Body is transparent, dorsoventrally flattened. External segmentation is not visible. Reproduction is by asexual method.

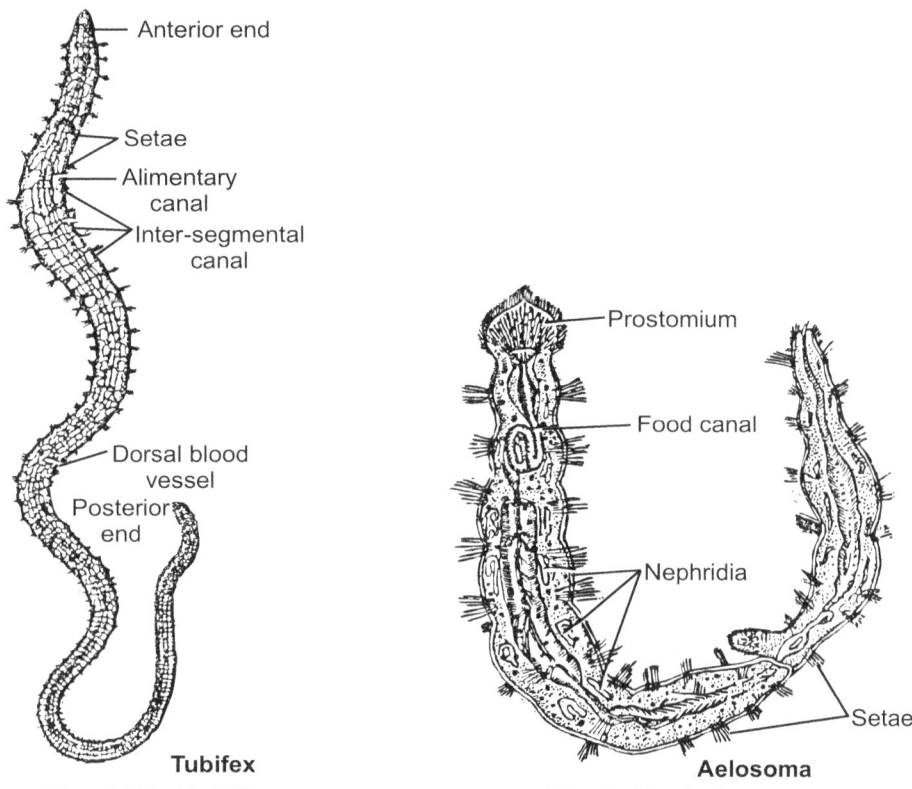

Fig. 1.79: *Tubifex*   **Fig. 1.80: *Aelosoma***

- Class Hirudinea includes mostly ectoparasitic and fresh water animals. There are also marine ectoparasites which feed on fishes and other animals. They have elongated and dorsoventrally flattened body.
- These animals show definite number of body segments. For the parastic mode of life the worms are equipped with anterior and posterior suckers which are situated ventrally.
- They are blood sucking, freshwater, terrestrial and marine animals. They are also carnivorous animals.
- *Glossiphonia* is a fresh water leech which feeds on snails and is carnivorous animal. *Pontobdella* is marine leech ectoparasitic on elasmobranch fishes. Its anterior sucker is saucer shaped whereas posterior sucker is cup shaped.
- It lays eggs in empty mollusca shells and guards them for over 100 days till they hatch. *Branchellion* is another ectoparasite marine leech found on the skates and rays.

- Anterior region forms long proboscis and anterior sucker is present, situated on its posterior region possess lateral leaf-like gills and large posterior sucker.

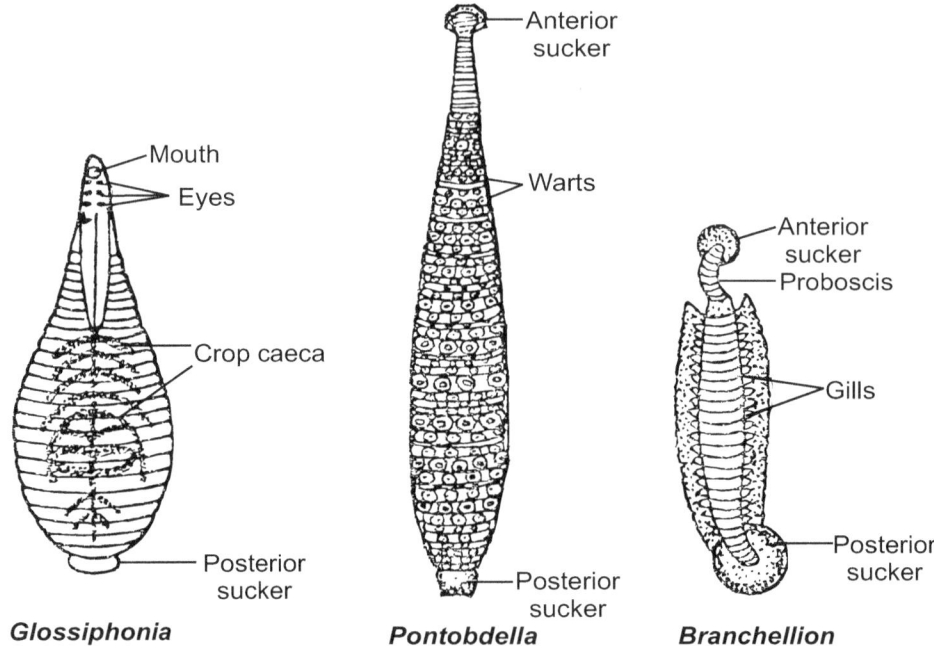

Glossiphonia　　**Pontobdella**　　**Branchellion**

Fig. 1.81　　**Fig. 1.82**　　**Fig. 1.83**

- *Hirudinaria granulosa* is the common Indian leech found in tanks, ponds, lakes, swamps and slow streams. It lives in shallow water and remains concealed under logs, stones and weeds.

- It is sanguivorous (blood sucking) animal sucks the blood of fishes and frogs, cattle or human beings.

- Leeches show diversity in their habit and habitat. They are fresh water, marine and terrestrial.

- Though some species are blood suckers yet many species are not ectoparasites but they are predatory carnivorous, feed on worms, snails and aquatic insect larvae.

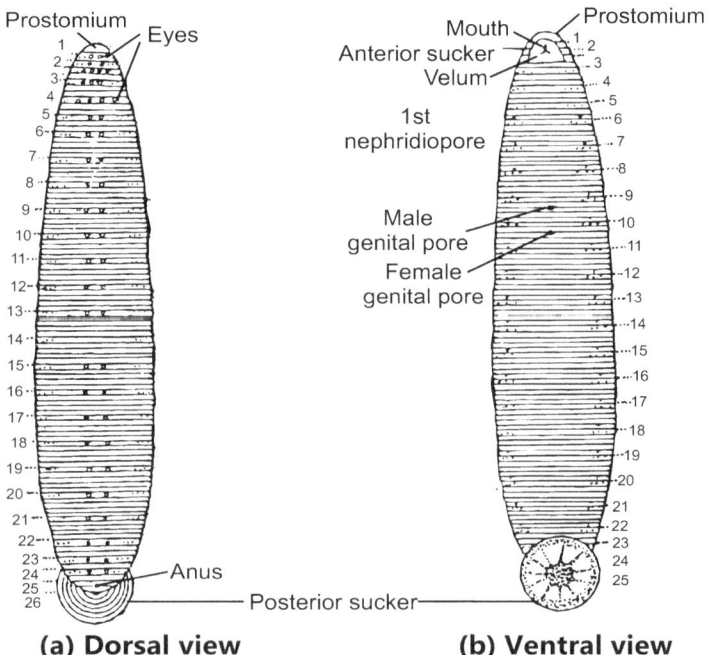

(a) Dorsal view (b) Ventral view
Fig. 1.84: *Hirudinaria*. External features

Summary
- Annelids are aquatic and terrestrial animals.
- Body is metamerically segmented.
- Setae or chaetae are the locomotary organs.
- They are triploblastic and true coelomate animals.
- Closed type of circulatory system.
- Nephridia are the excretory organs.
- Nervous system consists of brain, nerve cord and segmential ganglia.
- Sexes may be separate or united.
- The Phylum Annelida has three classes, such as Polychaeta, Oligochaeta and Hirudina.

Review Questions
1. Give the distinctive characters of Polychaeta.
2. Give the distinctive characters of Oligochaeta.
3. Give the distinctive characters of Hirudinea.

University Question
1. Give an account of general characters and outline of classification of Phylum Annelida with suitable examples.

(B) Protista - *Paramoecium*

1.10 Protista - *Paramoecium*
1.11 Systematic Position, Habit and Habitat
1.12 External Morphology and Structure of *Paramoecium*
1.13 Locomotion
1.14 Nutrition
1.15 Respiration
1.16 Excretion
1.17 Reproduction

1.10 Introduction

- The ciliates are more specialized protozoans distinguished by the presence of hair-like organelles, the cilia which serve for locomotion and food capturing.
- Another unique feature of these organisms is that they possess two kinds of nuclei.
- There are several species of *Paramoecium* like *P. aurelia*, *P. bursaria*, *P. multimicronucleatum*, *P. trichium* but the largest and most commonly studied species is *P. caudatum* and it is described in detail in this chapter.

1.11 Systematic Position, Habits and Habitat

1.11.1 Systematic Position

Kingdom	:	Protista
Phylum	:	Ciliophora
Class	:	Ciliata
Subclass	:	Euciliata
Order	:	Holotricha
Family	:	Paramecidae
Genus	:	*Paramoecium*
Species	:	*caudatum*

1.11.2 Habits and Habitat

- *Paramoecium* is a common free-living freshwater ciliate found in ponds, pools, ditches, streams, lakes, reservoirs and rivers.
- It is specially abundant in the stagnant ponds rich in decaying organic matter and in the sewage water. Since, free living, it is worldwide in distribution.
- It has very similar habit to that of *Amoeba* and *Euglena* hence, they may be generally found living together. The individuals frequently come in contact with floating object, thus, they form a white scum on the surface of water.

Culture:

- *Paramoecium* can be easily grown in the laboratory.
- The simplest way to culture the *Paramoecia* is to take submerged weed or decaying vegetation in a litre of pond water in a glass container, cover it and leave for 2-3 days.
- If present, swarms of *Paramoecia* will appear in a few days. For preparing culture, hay infusion method can be employed.
- Boil hay in water, decant infusion and add few grains of wheat and allow it to become turbid with bacteria. Inoculate few *Paramoecia* from the first container into this culture medium, where they multiply rapidly (Refer Fig. 1.85).

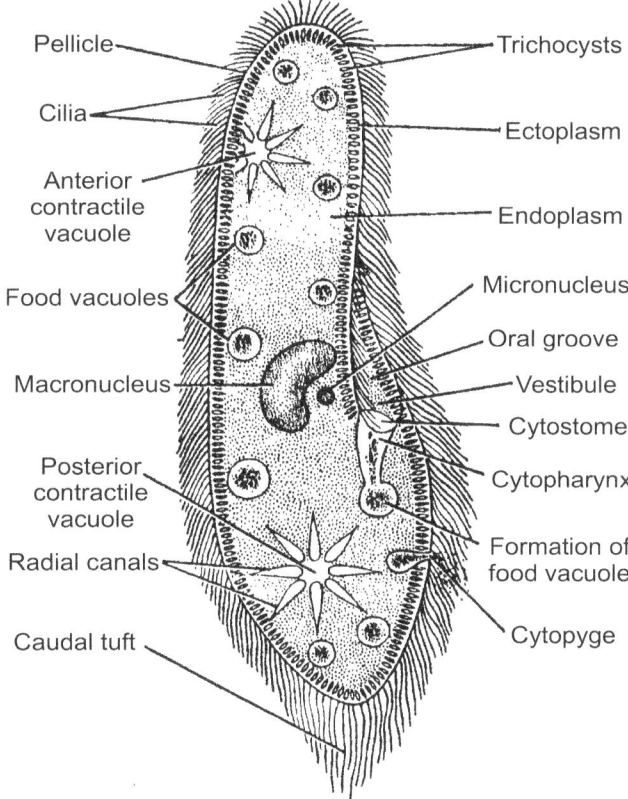

Fig. 1.85: *Paramoecium caudatum*

1.12 External Morphology and Structure of *Paramoecium*

1.12.1 External Morphology

Size: *Paramoecium caudatum* is minute microscopic organism just visible to the naked eyes as elongated, whitish bodies. It is the largest species, varies in length from 170 to 350 microns. Certain environmental factors also influence the size.

Shape: Its general appearance is like a sole of slipper, hence it is popularly known as slipper animalcule.

Joblot gave the name '*Chausson*' to caudatum which means 'Slipper Shaped Animalcule.' The name *Paramoecium* was given by **John Hill** in 1752 which also refers to the characteristic shape of the animal (Greek, *Parameses* means oblong).

The body appears roughly circular in transverse section and shows flattened *ventral surface* and upper convex *dorsal surface*. The anterior end of the body is slender and blunt while the posterior end is some what pointed or cone shaped. The body of the animal is somewhat wider slightly below the middle region. The rounded end is directed forwards during locomotion.

Pellicle : The shape of the body is definite and constant because the body is covered by a thin but firm and flexible, outer covering the *pellicle* which is secreted by its outer surface or underlying ectoplasm.

It is a colourless cuticular membrane. The pellicle has double membrane, the outer is continuous with the cilia and the inner with the ectoplasm.

The pellicle is not a smooth layer, under high magnification of microscope, it reveals large number of *hexagonal* or *rectangular depressions* on its surface.

Each hexagonal depression is perforated by a central aperture through which single cilium is projecting out. The anterior and posterior margins of hexagons possess the openings of *trichocysts*. Because of the complex structural organisation, some authors call the pellicle by the name cuticula or cuticle.

The pellicular pattern of the dorsal surface may differ from that of the ventral surface. The pellicle is soon regenerated if lost in an injury.

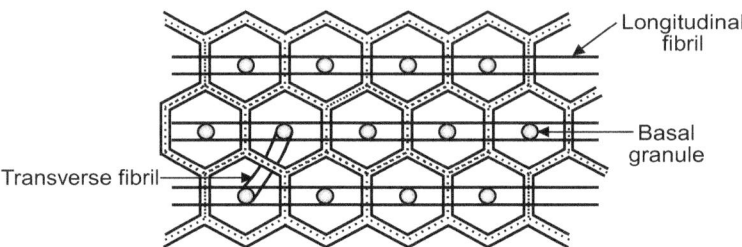

Fig. 1.86: *Paramoecium*: **Pellicular Structure Showing Basal Granules and Longitudinal Fibrils**

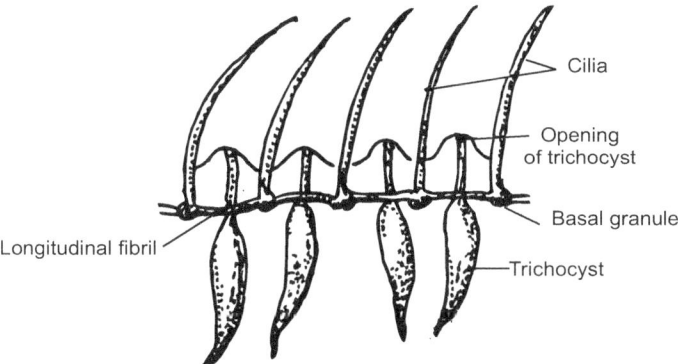

Fig. 1.87: *Paramoecium: Pellicular* **Structure (side view)**

1.12.2 Structure of *Paramoecium*

Cilia:

- The entire body of the *Paramoecium* is covered by short hair-like fine protoplasmic processes called *cilia*.
- They serve as organs of locomotion and food capture.
- These mobile organs are arranged in regular longitudinal rows called holotrichous arrangement.
- The length of the cilia is uniform throughout, but at the extreme posterior tip they become longer, forming the caudal tuft, hence, the specific name is *caudatum*.
- The ciliation of the oral region is more complicated.

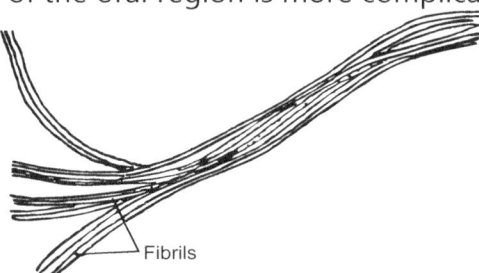

Fig. 1.88: *Paramoecium*: **A Cilium as seen Under Electron Microscope**

- The basic structure of cilia and flagella is the same. The outer free part of the cilium is surrounded by *plasma membrane* or *protoplasmic sheath* which is in continuation with outer cell membrane of the body surface.
- In the protoplasmic sheath, there are nine double longitudinal fibrils present in the peripheral ring. There are two central longitudinal fibrils which are thinner than the outer nine fibrils.
- Beneath the pellicle, each cilium is connected to a small, spherical *basal granule* or *kinetosome* embedded in the cytoplasm.

- The layer containing the basal granules, with their connections is also called as *alveolar layer*.
- The nine pairs of peripheral fibrils fuse together to form the wall of the kinetosome, thus kinetosome is a tube which is either opened or closed at its lower end. The two central fibrils stop at the levels of the pellicle in the most ciliates.

Ultrastructure of Cilium:

At the basal region, the cilium has the diameter of about 0.2 micron (or 2000 A°) but it increases about 10 micron above the cell surface. The cilia are covered by unit membrane of 90 A° thickness which remains continuous with plasma membrane. The bounded space of the cilium is filled by a watery substance called matrix, and they are typically 2 pairs of peripheral fibres and a pair of central fibres enclosed within a delicate inner membrane sheath. The diameter of peripheral fibres is 260 A° and the fibres are composed of two subfibrils, having diameters of 180 to 250 A°. The subfibrils are called subfibril A and subfibril B. The subfibril A is slightly larger than subfibril B. The subfibril A gives out two fork-like thick arms or projections from its one side, which show clockwise direction. The central fibrils are without subfibrils and their diameter is about 250 A°. The thickness of their wall is about 60 A°. Both the central fibrils are separated by a space of 350 A° and are enclosed by a common sheath. **Gibbnos** (1967) has reported that the sheath of the central fibrils and the peripheral subfibrils A are connected by radially arranged connections, called *spokes*.

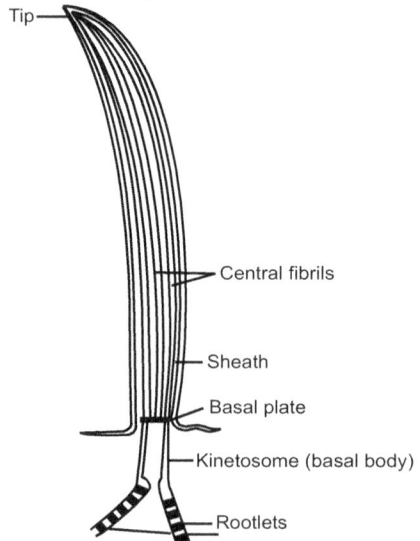

Fig. 1.89: *Paramoecium*: **V.S. of Cilium**

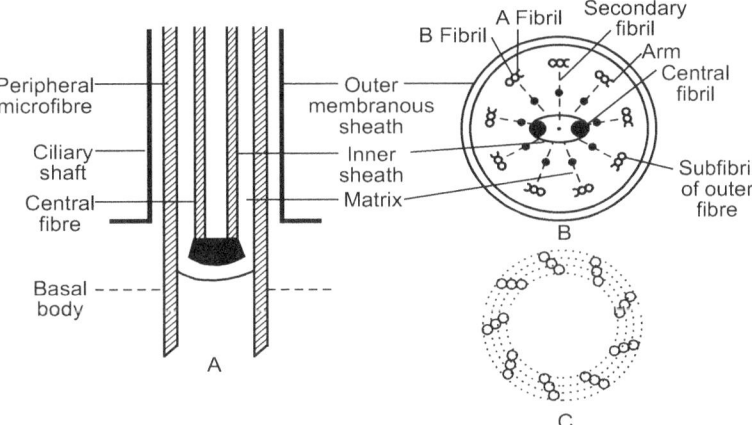

Fig. 1.90: *Paramoecium*: Structure of a Cilium and its Basal Body
A – L.S., B – T.S. of Cilium, C – T.S. of Basal Body

- The peripheral and central fibrils under high resolution of electron microscopy showed that they are also composed of 10-12 microfilaments of 40 A° thickness and each filament is beaded.
- Each bead remains arranged in the lattices of 40 by 50 A° in the plane of the wall of the tubule. These beads are considered as the basic subunits of the tubule structure.

Infraciliary System:

- The cilia on the body of *Paramoecium* are connected below pellicle with the fibrillar system, called infraciliary system.
- It consists of *basal granules* or *kinetosomes* and from each kinetosome, a fine fibril is given out, called *kinetodesmos*.
- Each cilium arises from the kinetosome, which appears as a solid granule when stained with haemotoxylin or impregnated with silver under light microscope.
- It is also formed by 9 pairs of peripheral fibrils of cilium and each peripheral pair is further augmented by third fibril forming triplet.
- All the nine triplets in the cross-section of basal granule appear in the form of twist.
- The basal granules are the self-reproducing units which give rise to new cilia.

- From each kinetosome, arises a single rootlet or fibril, the kinetodesmos which extends to the right and then forwards to run closely parallel to similar fibrils from other *kinetosomes* in the same row.
- This bundle of parallel fibrils is known as the *kinetodesma*. A longitudinal row of *kinetosomes* with their *kinetodesmata* (plural of kinetodesma) forms a longitudinal unit, called a *kinety*.

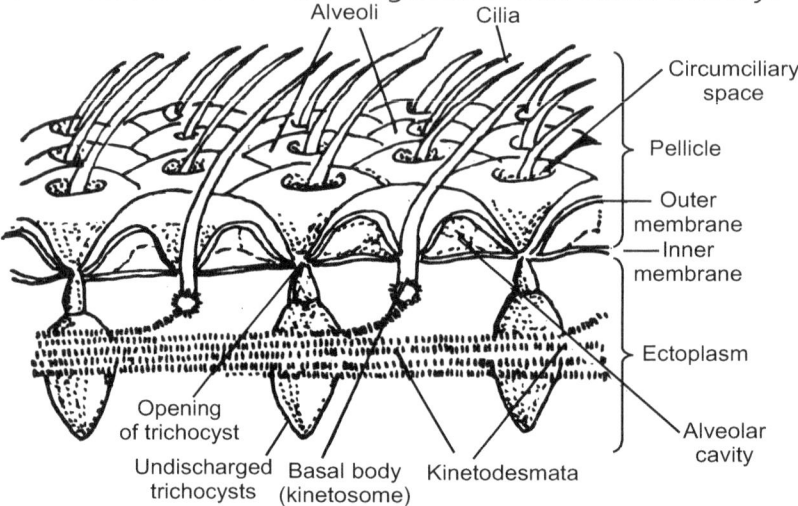

Fig. 1.91: *Paramoecium*: Pellicle and Associated Organelles (Diagrammatic three dimensional view)

- The individual kinetodesmos do not run more than 5 kinetosomes, hence, in each kinetodesma 5 fibrils are present.
- The basal granules are also connected with each other by longitudinal fibres resembling the beads on a string.
- The *longitudinal fibres* are joined by *transverse fibres* which pass from one basal granule to another in adjacent rows. These structures are visible by a special technique of *silver impregnation*.
- The infraciliary system is thought to co-ordinate the beating of cilia or movement of its row. Also it brings about formation of organelles in cell division.

Neuromotor System:
- Under the influence of certain stains, another system of fibres (other than kinetodesmata) is also present in the pellicle.

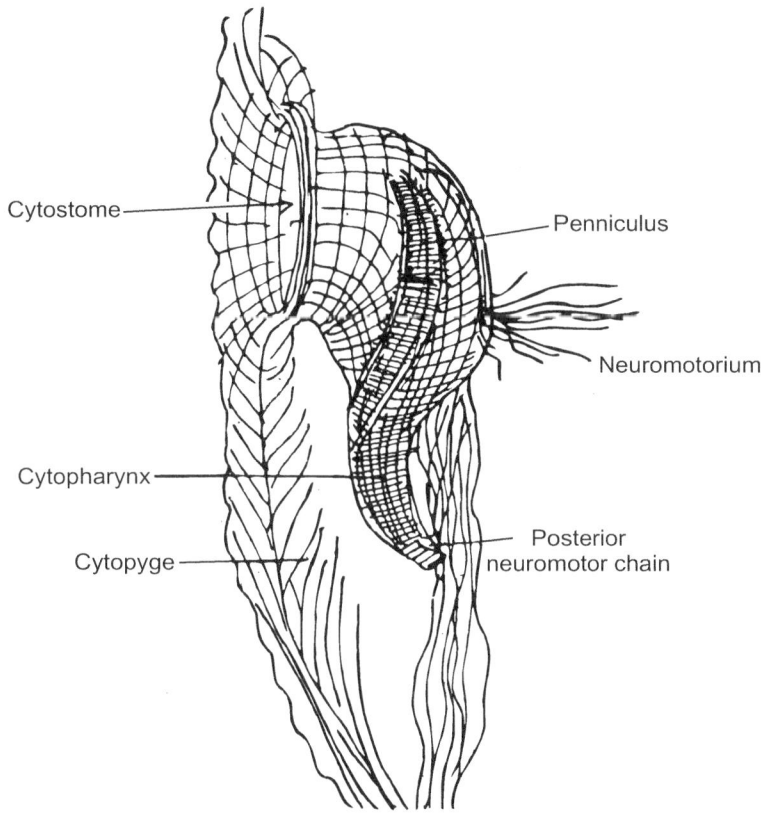

Fig. 1.92: *Paramoecium* Multimicronucleate Part of Neuromotor System (after Lund)

- This is called the fibrilar or *neuromotor* system. It is visible with the help of nuclear stains, especially *Heidenhains*.
- These fibrils directly connect together to the kinetosomes and internal fibrilar network with a darkly staining conspicuous, bilobed body, the motorium, lying near the cytopharynx and also probably with trichocysts.
- The motorium together with associated fibrilar network, forms a neuromotor apparatus or system.
- This system was described by **Rees** (1922) and **Lund** (1933). However, the true nature of the system is not properly understood and the electron microscopic studies do not show any evidence regarding the existence of neuromotor system in *Paramoecium*.

- The so-called neuromotor system as seen under light microscope is due to deposition of stains in alveoli.
- This system is now regarded as a part of the buccal infraciliature.
- Regarding the functions of the system, it co-ordinates the ciliary movements and also helps in contractibility, conductivity, elasticity and mechanical support.

Oral Groove and Cytopyge:
- The *oral groove* or *peristome* is a large, oblique, shallow depression, present on the ventral surface.
- It starts from the left side of anterior end of the body, where it is broad and runs obliquely backwards towards the right side upto the middle of the body.
- The oral groove leads into a short conical funnel-shaped depression, called *vestibule*.
- It leads through a large oval opening into a wide tubular passage, called *buccal cavity*.
- The buccal cavity which extends backwards and ends directly to the fixed, oval-shaped, opening called *cytostome* or *cell mouth*. The cytostome leads in a short narrow tube, cytopharynx which forms a food vacuole at its inner end.
- A minute permanent anal aperture, called *cytoproct* or *cytopyge* is situated near and behind on the right side of the body, through which undigested food particles are egested.

Ciliation of Oral Groove:
- As compared to the ciliation of body, the ciliation of oral groove is very complicated. Here they show a good deal of variation in size and arrangement.
- The cilia on the oral groove are as long as the body surface. In the vestibule, the cilia are relatively short and are arranged in a crescentic manner.
- At the junction of vestibule and buccal cavity, there is an undulating or endoral membrane. It is formed by fusion of row of specialized cilia and runs transversely along the right wall and partially encircles the opening of vestibule into buccal cavity.
- Besides, there are three membranelles in the buccal cavity, each consisting of three rows of cilia. These are *ventral penniculus, dorsal penniculus, and quadrulus*.

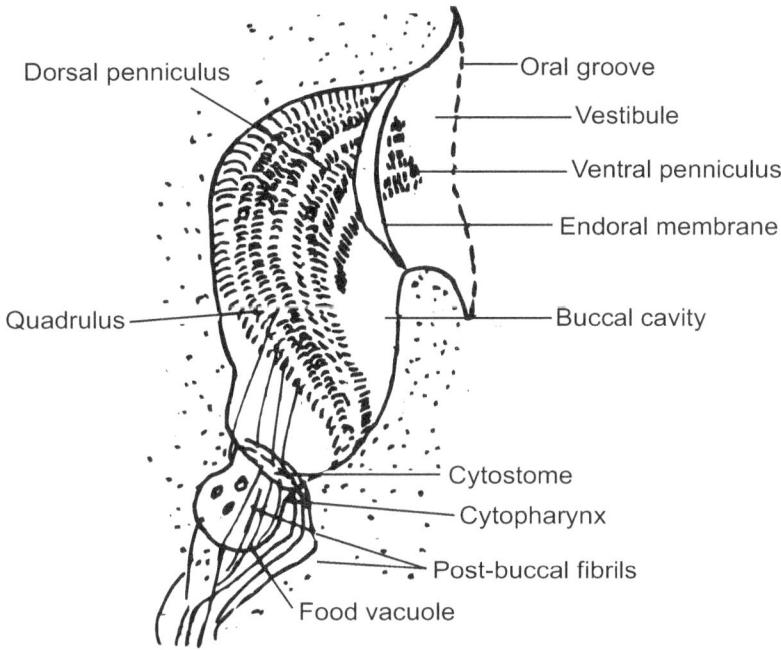

Fig. 1.93: *Paramoecium*: Oral Apparatus Showing Buccal Ciliature in Dorsal View

- The two peniculi run down the left wall of the buccal cavity. The ventral penniculus is short and ends at the cytostome, while dorsal penniculus longer, crosses over to the right wall at the cytostome and extends on the right wall of the cytopharynx.
- The penniculi beat longitudinally in opposite direction. The *quadrulus* is also made up of four rows of cilia but they are not fused at the ends.
- It extends along the dorsal wall (roof) of the buccal cavity, crosses over to the wall near the cytostome and ends close to the dorsal penniculus. End of the buccal cavity gives off very long dorsal cilia or post buccal fibrils cilia.
- Detail structure and ciliation of oral groove was studied by **Gelei** (1934) and **Lund** (1941). The penniculi and quadrulus control the passage of food. It is not properly understood, how cilia work, but probably their fibrils contract in rhythmic way which causes bending. According to **Gelei** (1925) the function of penniculi is to force the food elements into the body.

Trichocysts:
- The trichocysts are small fusiform or carrot-shaped organelles embedded in the ectoplasm at right angles to the body surface.

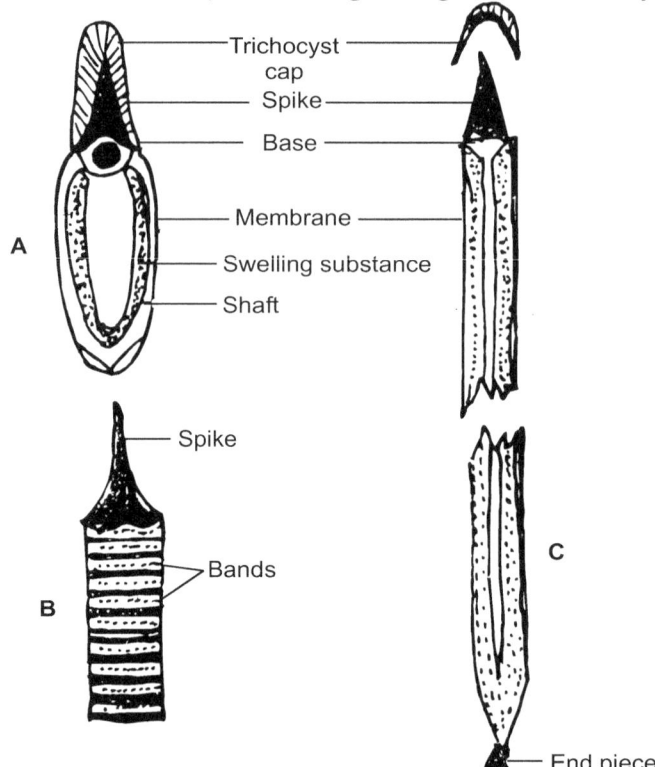

Fig. 1.94: *Paramoecium*: Trichocyst A–L.S. of Undischarge trichocyst, B–Tip of the trichocyst, C–Discharged trichocyst

- They are located in the centre of the anterior and posterior walls of the pellicular polygons alternating between the basis of cilia.
- In resting stage, each trichocyst measures 4 microns in length and extends 1-2 microns below the surface of pellicle attached by a very delicate fibre.
- A trichocyst is made up of a large, roughly oval sac-like shaft containing refractive, dense fluid with swelling substance.
- At the outer end, is a conical head or *spike* which rests on the basis. The spike is covered by a cap. On being stimulated, the trichocysts discharge to the exterior as a fine elongated needle like filament and may be 6-10 times the length of the resting cones.

- The different stimuli such as contact, electric shocks, chemicals and desiccation can evoke discharge. Due to stimulus the ectoplasm suddenly contracts.
- This separates the cap of the trichocyst to let the water enter the sac. By absorbing water the substance of the shaft greatly swells and suddenly shoots out as a elongated needle-like thread on the body surface.
- The thread shoots out through the pore in the pellicle, bringing the spike at its tip. The discharged trichocyst thus consists of two parts; a sharp pointed, dense spike and a long, thread-like shaft with alternating dark and light cross bands. The trichocysts are discharged very rapidly in only few milliseconds.
- The degree of discharge varies, some may discharge partly with a given stimulus, others fully, while still others may be discharged and set free from the body.
- Once discharged, the trichocysts cannot be withdrawn. They are broken off and replaced by new ones. New trichocysts develop from minute granules, the *trichocystosomas*, which are in turn formed from basal granules or kinetosomes.
- There is controversy regarding origin of the trichocysts. According to some workers, the basal granules give rise to trichocysts while others say that they originate in the endoplasm and later come to lie in the ectoplasm.

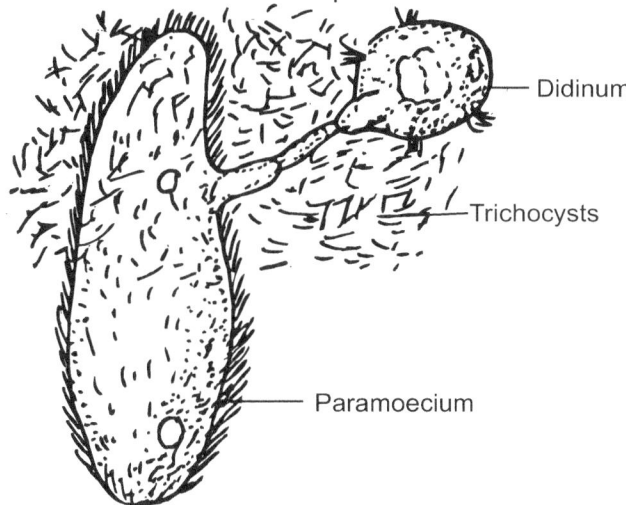

Fig. 1.95: *Paramoecium*: Throwing out Trichocysts when attached by a small *Didinum*

- The true nature and function of trichocysts are uncertain, but they are regarded by some authors as the organelles of defence and offence.
- The trichocysts discharge a gelatinous poisonous fluid, strong enough to paralyse small unicellular organisms. This fluid hardens into water forming sticky threads in which enemy may get trapped or form a sort of screen that gives some degree of safety to the organisms.
- It also seems to be uncertain because the trichocysts are ineffective against *Didinum*, the chief predator of *Paramoecium*. The trichocysts are also considered to be organelles for fixing the animal to a spot during feeding.
- The tips of the discharge trichocysts are sticky and *Paramoecium* uses them for attachment to an object where greater concentration of bacteria is there for feeding.

Cytoplasm:
- The cytoplasm is differentiated into two regions: an outer thin, clear, dense and relatively firm *ectoplasm* or *cortex* and the central, granular, more fluid and voluminous *endoplasm* or *medulla*.
- The ectoplasm is permanent part of the body, strikingly delimited from the endoplasm.
- It is further differentiated into a thin outer alveolar region and thick inner denser region.
- In the outer alveolar region, contains the basal granules, trichocysts and kinetodesma.
- It also contains fine contractile threads, the *myonemes* running in longitudinal direction.
- The myonemes enable the animal to bend and squeeze its body through narrow passages by their differential contraction.

Endoplasm:
- The endoplasm or medulla is soft, more or less fluid and contains many cytoplasmic organelles as well as other inclusions.
- The cytoplasmic inclusions are mitochondria, Golgi bodies, reserve food granules of starch, glycogen and fat. Other structures like nuclear apparatus, contractile vacuoles and food vacuoles are also found in the endoplasm.

Nuclear Apparatus:
   The nuclear apparatus is lying in the endoplasm approximately at the centre of the body. It consists of two nuclei, the larger *macronucleus* and the smaller *micronucleus*.
- **Macronucleus:** It is granular and roughly kidney-shaped or bean-shaped and without nuclear membrane. It is a compact structure containing fine threads and tightly packed discrete chromatin granules of variable sizes. It is also called *trophic* or *vegetative* nucleus as it controls the vegetative activities of the organism. It usually divides amitotically. The macronucleus is also responsible for the genetic control of the phenotype.
- **Micronucleus:** The micronucleus is smaller and spherical in shape with nuclear membrane. It lies in the depression of the macronucleus. It controls the reproductive activities of the organism, hence it is also called as *generative nucleus*. Fine chromatin granules and threads are uniformly distributed in the micronucleus. *Paramoecium* devoid of micronucleus survives but, fails to reproduce.
   According to **Moses** (1950), both the nuclei are identical in chemical composition.

Contractile Vacuoles:
- There are two large, liquid filled contractile vacuoles in *Paramoecium*, each situated near one end of the body close to the dorsal surface.
- The contractile vacuoles are located in the innermost part of the ectoplasm. Each contractile vacuole is surrounded by six to ten elongated, radiating canals called *feeding* or *tributary* canals.
- These canals run parallel to the surface but may extend far into the endoplasm. Each radiating, spindle-shaped canal can be differentiated into three parts-outer, middle and inner.
- The outer or blind terminal part is away from the contractile vacuole and are surrounded by fine *microtubules* or nephridial tubules.
- These tubules are visible only under electron microscope. These microtubules are present in the endoplasm and they collect the excretory fluid.
- The *ampulla* or the middle part of the radiating canal becomes swollen like a bulb, when filled with excretory fluid.
- The inner part or the *injector canal* empties into central vacuole, which in turn opens to the outside through a distinct *discharge*

canal, having a permanent aperture in the pellicle of the dorsal body surface.

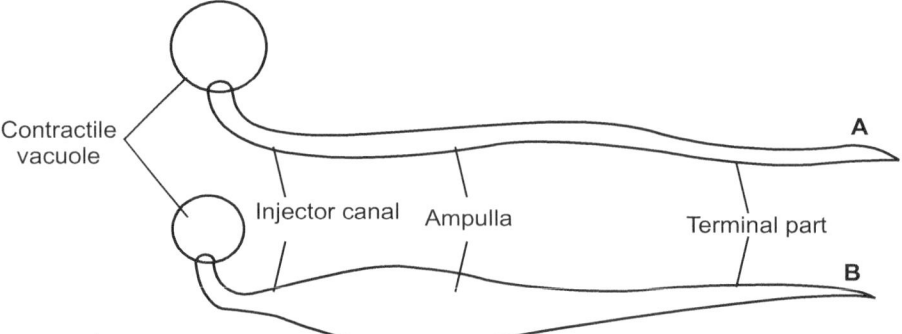

Fig. 1.96: *Paramoecium*: Radial canal A-Empty, B-Full

- The contractile vacuoles serve to excrete excess water taken up from the outside. Thus, they regulate the water contents of the body.
- The pulsating rate of the contractile vacuoles is different, the posterior is faster than the anterior.

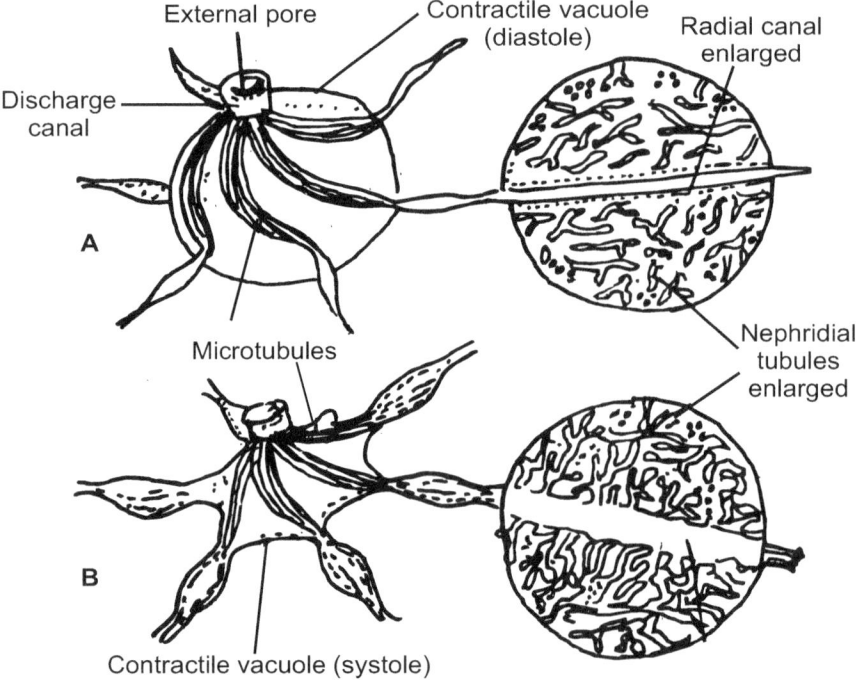

Fig. 1.97: *Paramoecium*: A Contractile Vacuole in Diastole (A) and systole (B) with radiating canal and nephridial tubules

Food Vacuoles:
- These are non-contractile, spherical bodies vary in number. There may be about 50 food vacuoles seen moving in the endoplasm.
- Depending on the nature of ingested food particles, the food vacuoles differ in shape and size.
- But mostly they are rounded in form, food vacuoles contain ingested food particles principally bacteria and small amount of fluid bounded by a thin definite membrane.
- **Volkonsky** (1934) proposed the name *gastrioles* for these vacuoles serve as temporary stomach as food is digested in them. They are seen moving with the streaming endoplasm and process is called *cyclosis*.

1.13 Locomotion

Paramoecium performs locomotion by two methods, viz, metaboly or body contortion and ciliary locomotion.

Metaboly or body contortion: *Paramoecium* can show the movement by contracting and twisting its body. Being elastic body, it can squeeze itself through a passage narrower than its body, after which the body assumes its normal shape. These movements are caused by the contractions of the myonemes present in the ectoplasm. The temporary change of body shape is called metaboly or body contortions.

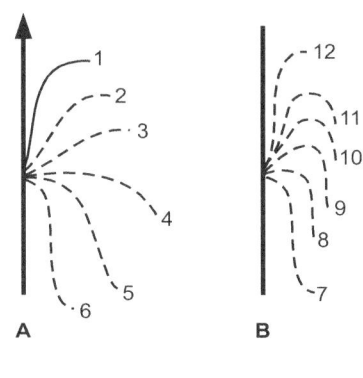

Fig. 1.98: *Paramoecium*: **Ciliary Movements (A) Effective stroke; (B) Recovery stroke; (C) Metachronous movement of a row of cilia**

Ciliary Locomotion:

- *Paramoecium* swims in water by rhythmic beating of cilia which is the main method of locomotion. The cilia can beat forwards or backwards direction.
- A ciliary beat consists of two phases: an effective stroke and a recovery stroke.
- During effective stroke, the cilium stiffens and bends almost as a straight rigid rod to become parallel to the body surface.
- During the recovery stroke, a cilium becomes lump and return to its original vertical position in a greatly flexed condition, thereby exposing less surface to the resistance of water.
- The effective stroke of a cilium is caused by the active contraction in one plane of its axial filament, and the recovery stroke, by the elasticity of the protoplasmic sheath.
- The resistance of water gives push to the body to the forward direction. Thus, when cilia beat backwards animal moves forward.
- All the cilia of the body do not beat simultaneously and independently but progressively in a remarkable co-ordination and metachronal *rhythm*.
- Cilia of the same transverse row beat simultaneously or synchronously and those of the same longitudinal row do not beat all at once but in a characteristic wave, beginning at the anterior end and progressing backwards.
- This co-ordinated movement is called metachronal rhythm. It is due to the infraciliary system and causes forward swimming.
- But the cilia do not beat straight backward. Instead they beat obliquely to the right, thereby causing the animal to roll over the left.
- As a result of this, the *Paramoecium*, while swimming forward rotates on its long axis in the manner of left hand spiral.

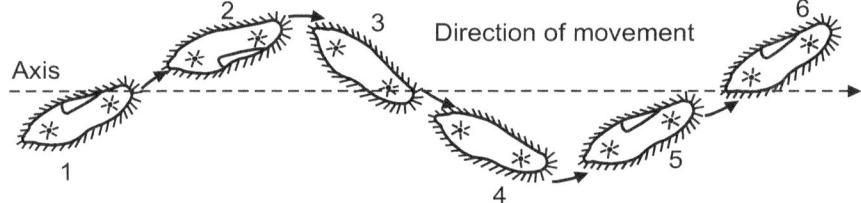

Fig. 1.99: Spiral path of *Paramoecium*

- The effective strokes of the cilia, lining the oral groove, are more powerful than those of the body cilia which causes anterior end of the body swerve (turn) to the left i.e. away from the oral side.

- The action of cilia of body and oral groove makes the animal to rotate on its long axis, swerving occurs alternately to all sides.
- In the beginning, the oral side is downwards and the body bends upward, a little later (due to rotation) the body, swings downwards.
- Finally, the oral side shifts to the left and the body swerving in one direction is compensated by an equal swerving in the opposite direction, the *Paramoecium* progresses along a spiral path round a straight axis.
- The spiral is anticlockwise when viewed from behind. The body rotates once for every spiral revolution so that the same surface of the body always faces the centre of the spiral.
- In the spiral locomotion of *Paramoecium*, involve three factors forward push, axial rotation and swerving of the anterior end to the aboral side.
- When cilia beat forward, the *Paramoecium,* can swim backward.
- The mechanism of ciliary movement in *Paramoecium* is little studied. The cilia are not moved by any co-ordinating system.
- **Seravin** (1967) showed that ATP plays an important role in the ciliary action. The cilium in *Paramoecium*, beats about 10-11 times per second and it swims at the rate of about 1 mm per second.

1.14 Nutrition

- In *Paramoecium*, nutrition is *holozoic*. Its food consists essentially certain species of bacteria (*Bacterium coli*), small Protozoa, unicellular plants (like algae, diatoms, yeasts, etc.) and small fragments of larger animals and vegetables.
- Therefore, *Paramoecium* is omnivorous organism.
- It does not wait for the food but hunts for it actively. It feeds only at rest or when swimming very slowly and does not feed when swimming fast.

Ingestion
- *Paramoecium* captures the food material with the help of cilia lining the oral groove. While feeding, the cilia of the oral groove beats more strongly than the body cilia.
- This draws a current of water in the form of *vortex* or feeding cone towards the oral groove near anterior end. This current

- sweep the food particles suspended in water into the buccal cavity through the vestibule.
- The cilia of the penniculi pushes the food particles into the cytopharynx through the mouth.
- According to **Mast** (1947), not all the food particles entering the vestibule and buccal cavity are actually ingested, some larger particles are rejected even before they enter the mouth.
- This work is done by cilia. The passage through which selected food particles are pushed towards mouth by ciliary action, is called the **selection path**, while the passage along which the unwanted particles are driven outside, is called the **rejection path**.

Formation of food vacuoles
- The accumulated food particles, at the posterior end of the cytopharynx, are directed by the long cilia into the rounded, ball-like mass in the endoplasm called *food vacuole*.
- The food vacuole develops at the distal end of the cytopharynx. It grows rapidly and then pinched off from the cytopharynx by a constriction of the surrounding endoplasm.
- Then again another food vacuole begins to form in its place. The vacuole quickly passes into the endoplasm.
- The mechanism by which the food vacuole is liberated is not properly understood. Probably the pharyngeal cilia helps in this process.
- For the formation of the food vacuole, time required 1 to 5 minutes however, it depends on the food supply and feeding rate.

Cyclosis: As soon as the food vacuole is separated from the cytopharynx, it circulates through the endoplasm along a definite path which is functionally similar to the alimentary canal. The food vacuoles are circulated by the streaming movement of the endoplasm which is called *cyclosis*. Several vacuoles may be seen thus circulating in a definite direction in the endoplasm of well fed *Paramoecium*. The tract begins from the end of the cytopharynx, then to the posterior side then to the dorsal surface, then towards the anterior end, then downwards to the anus or cytopyge.

Digestion: During cyclosis, digestion occurs by enzymes secreted by endoplasm into the food vacuoles and it is accompanied by changes in pH. The contents of the food vacuoles show first an acidic and then an alkaline reaction. The size of vacuoles also changes, first decreasing and then increasing, associated with changes in pH. The enzymes reported from *Paramoecium* include the *amylase* which converts starches into sugars, *proteinase* which break the proteins into the peptides during the acid phase of the food vacuole and *dipeptidase* that changes the peptides into amino-acids during the alkaline phase. Regarding the digestion of fat, there is controversy among the Zoologists. According to some scientists, the lipids found in the endoplasm are formed from the glycogen, while others hold that fats are digested by an enzyme called *lipase* during alkaline phase of digestion.

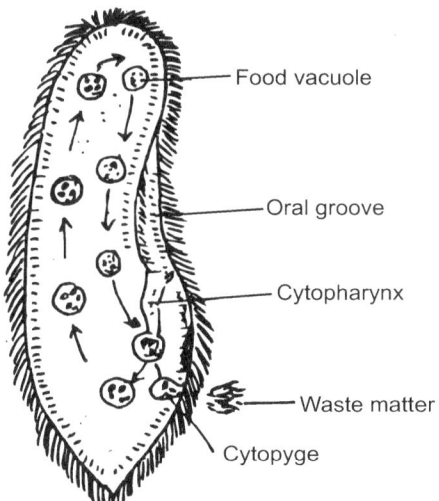

Fig. 1.100: *Paramoecium*: Showing Cyclosis and Course of Vacuoles in the Endoplasm

Absorption: The digested simple food materials pass through the thin membrane of the food vacuoles into surrounding endoplasm. This process is called the absorption of the food. As absorption progresses the food vacuoles decrease in size till only indigestible matter is left in them. The digested food gets thoroughly distributed to all the body parts during cyclosis.

Assimilation: The food absorbed into endoplasm is partly synthesized into protoplasm and partly converted into storage products, like glycogen and lipid droplets. Both these processes occur by enzymatic activity.

Egestion: The vacuole gradually becomes smaller, containing indigestible residue or faeces are eliminated through the cytopyge.

1.15 Respiration

- Body surface is the main respiratory organ in *Paramoecium*. The pellicle is semipermeable through which gaseous exchange takes place.
- The oxygen present in the water in dissolved condition diffuses into the body. In addition, some oxygen enters the body, dissolved in the water of the food vacuoles.
- The oxygen, taken inside the body is utilized in the oxidation of food materials, particularly carbohydrates.
- In this process, energy is released and carbon dioxide is produced. The energy is utilized by the animal for movement and growth.
- The carbon dioxide simply diffuses out into the surrounding water, because its concentration is higher in the body. Some dissolved carbon dioxide is eliminated in the water, pumped out by the contractile vacuoles.

1.16 Excretion

- The nitrogenous waste materials formed as a result of metabolic processes, are ammonia and urea in *Paramoecium*. They are also eliminated out by diffusion through the entire body surface.
- The crystals present in the cytoplasm are infact the excretory products, which first get dissolved and then eliminated with fluid of the contractile vacuoles.

Osmo-regulation:

- Like *Amoeba* and *Euglena*, *Paramoecium* has also to face the problem of eliminating excess of water from its body.
- Two contractile vacuoles regulate the water content of the body of *Paramoecium*.
- The surplus water from the cytoplasm collects first in the microtubules.
- These pass the water into feeding canal, which consequently swells up from more streaks.
- When feeding canals become fully filled with water, their injectors emit droplets of fluid which unite to form contractile vacuole.

- When the vacuole has grown to its maximum size, it contracts and throws its water to outside through the canal that connects it with a pore in the pellicle.
- The pore opens at the time of discharge, getting closed by the membrane soon after it.
- At the time of diastole, the radial canals disappear for a while and reappear as small streaks, soon after the systole or contractile vacuoles do not, at the same rate, but posterior vacuole works more quickly than the anterior one.
- It may be probably because of presence of buccal cavity, and pharynx provides more surface for endosmosis. In *Paramoecium*, the contractile vacuoles can eliminate a volume of water equivalent to its body volume in about half an hour.
- The rate of discharge depends upon several other factors. It varies with temperature, rise of temperature leads to an increase of frequency of discharge. The rate of discharge is also higher in an inactive animal than in one that is swimming about. It is higher in water containing less salts.

1.17 Reproduction

Paramoecium reproduces by asexual as well as sexual methods. Commonly it reproduces asexually by *transverse binary fission* under good conditions of food. The sexual reproduction occurs usually by conjugation but at times by the processes of nuclear reorganisations such as *endomixis*, *autogamy*, *cytogamy* and *hemimixis*.

1. Binary fission
- Binary fission is the commonest type of reproduction in *Paramoecium*, but the division is the horizontal or transverse i.e. right angle to the longitudinal axis of the body.
- This type of division is called *homothetogenic division* in which transverse plane is cutting across the kinetics. It takes place during favourable conditions.
- Before the beginning of fission *Paramoecium* stops feeding, develops two minute pores near the middle of its body for the future contractile vacuoles of daughter individuals and doubles its cilia.
- When the process starts, the animal becomes less active and assumes spindle-like form, its oral groove disappears. In

- binary fission, the micronucleus divides by mitosis into two daughter micronuclei and they move away from each other.
- During mitosis, the nuclear membrane remains intact. The chromosomes (36 to 150 in number) which appear in mitosis are very small, numerous and compactly arranged.
- The *macronucleus* divides amitotically by simply becoming elongated and constricted in the middle, forming two daughter nuclei. Meanwhile a transverse constriction forms a round in the middle of the body.
- A new cytopharynx and cytostome are formed for the future posterior daughter *Paramoecium* by budding from the original cytopharynx and cytostome which remain in the future anterior daughter *Paramoecium*.
- The furrow deepens until the cytoplasm is completely divided. The resulting two daughter *Paramoecia* are of equal size, each containing a set of cell organelles. Each daughter individual receives one contractile vacuole from the parent and develops one new contractile vacuole.
- Then each individual grows into adult. The anterior one is called *proter* and the posterior daughter called *opisthe*. They grow to full size before another division occurs. The time required for the process of binary fission is two hours and it may occur one to four times per day, yielding 2 to 16 individuals.
- About 600 generations are produced in a year. The rate of multiplication depends upon external conditions of food, temperature, age of the culture, population density, also on the internal factors of heredity and physiology.
- The individuals produced from a *clone* and the members of a clone are genetically alike.
- The binary fission cannot go on indefinitely. After several generations, the rate of fission gradually declines. The vigour of the descendants is diminished, the nuclei and protoplasm show symptoms of decay and eventually death seems inevitable.

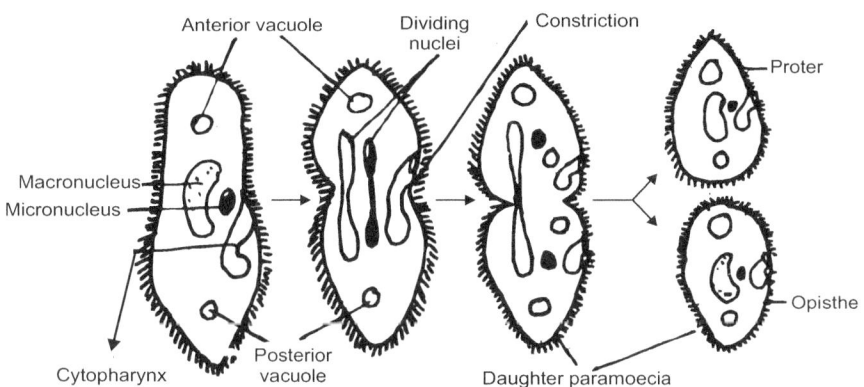

Fig. 1.101: *Paramoecium*: Binary fission

2. Conjugation

Usually, *Paramoecium* reproduces by binary fission but it is interrupted by *conjugation* which is referred as sexual reproduction.

Conjugation is simply a temporary union of two individuals of one and the same species for the purpose of exchanging a part of their micronuclear material. It corresponds to cross-fertilization of higher animals and it is necessary for the continued vitality of the species.

For the process of conjugation, following conditions are necessary:

(i) Conjugation occurs after about 300 asexual generations of binary fission or it alternates with binary fission at long intervals to rejuvenate the dying clone.

(ii) There should be change in physiological condition of the animal, such as smaller size, due to repeated binary fission. Then conjugation begins to prevent the death of old age *Paramoecia*.

(iii) Conjugation occurs in certain species of *Paramoecium* and each species of variety further contains generally two mating types. For example, *P. caudatum* has five sexually different varieties. Variety 1 has mating types I and II, the variety 2 has mating types III and IV and so on. Conjugation can occur only between the individuals of different mating types of the same variety.

Process of Conjugation: The detail account of process of conjugation was described by **Hertwig** and **Maupas** (1889) in *P. caudatum*.

1. In conjugation, two individuals from two different mating types come in contact and adhere to one another by their oral surfaces. Adhesion probably results from the secretion of a sticky substance by the cilia. Now the individuals which take part in conjugation are called *conjugants*. The pellicle and ectoplasm of both individuals from the attached surface disintegrate and a *protoplasmic bridge* is formed between them. They continue swimming but stop feeding.

2. The *macronucleus* which is vegetative in function does not take any part in conjugation. It begins to disintegrate and the fragments are absorbed by the cytoplasm. This process is very slow.

3. The micronucleus enlarges and undergoes two successive divisions, one of them being a reduction division. Thus, four haploid micronuclei and produced in each conjugant so that only one remains.

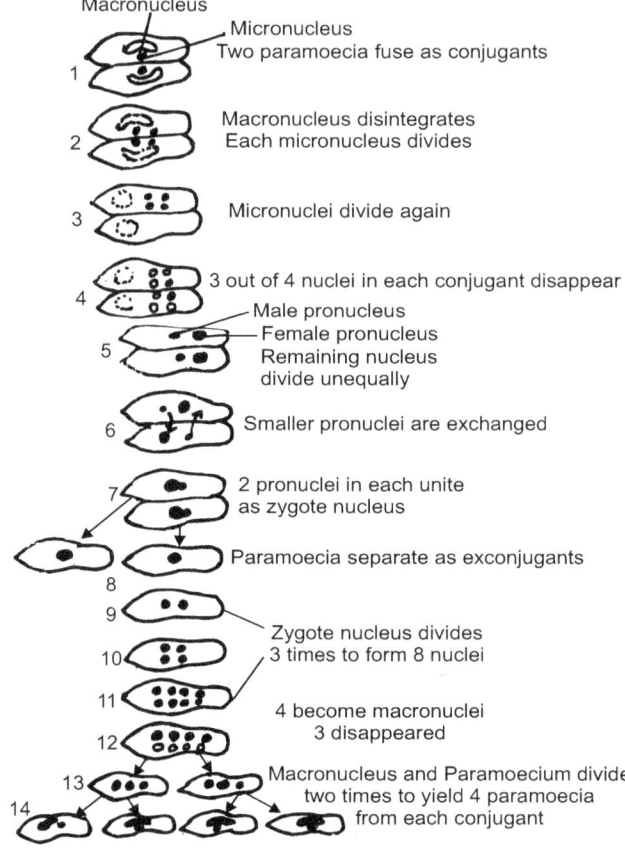

Fig. 1.102: Conjugation stages of *Paramoecium*

- The remaining micronucleus of each conjugant divides mitotically into two unequal *pronuclei* or *gametic nuclei* which are genetically identical. Of these, the smaller one is active, is called *male pronucleus*. It is also called migratory or wandering *pronucleus*.
- The larger one is passive and is called *stationary* or female *pronucleus*. The male pronucleus of each conjugant migrates through the cytoplasmic bridge into other and fuses with the female pronucleus therein forming a fusion nucleus called *synkaryon* or *zygote* nucleus in which diploid number of chromosomes is restored.
- The fusion of the nuclear material from two individuals is known as *amphimixis* and corresponds to the cross-fertilization of higher animals. The conjugants now separate and are called *exconjugants*.
- In each exconjugant, the zygote nucleus divides three times successively by mitosis, producing eight nuclei. Four of the eight nuclei enlarge and become *macronuclei* and other four become *micronuclei*.
- Three micronuclei disintegrate and disappear in the cytoplasm. Each exconjugant now has four macronuclei and one micronucleus. The micronucleus divides mitotically into two micronuclei. At the same time the exconjugant divides by transverse binary fission into two in such a way that each individual formed receives two *macronuclei* and one *micronucleus*.
- The micronucleus of each individual again divides with the division of each daughter *Paramoecium* forming two individuals each containing one macronucleus and one micronucleus. Thus, from each exconjugant four young *Paramecia* are formed at the end of conjugation.

Significance of Conjugation: In true sense, conjugation is not a sexual reproduction, because it is not concerned with increasing the number of individuals, but only with the union of nuclei. Its function is not reproduction but variation. Conjugation begins and ends with two individuals. Multiplication that follows conjugation, occurs by binary fission.

However, conjugation has two-fold significance, physiological and genetic for *Paramoecium*.

1. **Rejuvenation:** Physiological significance lies in rejuvenation i.e. restoration of vitality of *Paramoecium*. *Paramoecium* loses its vigour if binary fission is continued repeatedly for several generations, and animal shows depressed physiological state. Because of this condition individuals cease to multiply, reduce in size, degenerate in organisation and eventually die off. Thus, to avoid these things, conjugation is essential which rejuvenates and revives the lost vigour for asexual reproduction. However, **Woodruff** and **Jennings** do not support this view.

2. **Nuclear reorganisation:** In the process of conjugation, nuclear, material is reorganized and readjustment occurs between cytoplasm and nuclear apparatus. Probably the macronucleus loses its potentialities while performing vegetative functions. Conjugation brings about the replacement of meganucleus with material from synkaryon and the new macronucleus has renewed vigour and vitality to enhance the metabolic activities.

3. **Hereditary variation:** The genetic significance of the conjugation lies in the production of variations. During asexual reproduction by binary fission, the hereditary material of the progeny remains the same. But conjugation involves meiosis and fusion of pronuclei of different individuals and this results in the formation of new combinations of genes in the descendants. This hybridization brings an increase in the vigour and of the offspring which may be better suited than others to survive in new conditions of life.

Summary

- *Paramoecium* is free living freshwater ciliate with slipper like shape.
- Body shape is constant because body is covered with firm and flexible pellicle.
- The entire body is covered by cilia.
- Below the pellicles fibrillar infraciliary system is present.
- Trichocysts are useful for defense and offence.
- *Paramoecium* possess two nuclei namely, macronucleus and micronucleus.

- Contractile vacuoles regulate the water content of the body.
- Food vacuoles are useful for digestion of food.
- Nutrition in *Paramoecium* is holozoic.
- Reproduction is by asexual method called binary fission and conjugation by sexual method.

Review Questions

1. Explain the following:
   (i) Trichocysts in *Paramoecium*.
   (ii) Binary fission in *Paramoecium*.
   (iii) Describe structure and function of contractile vacuoles in *Paramoecium*.
   (iv) Explain conjugation stages of *Paramoecium* with diagram add note on its significance.
   (v) Give the general characters of protista.
2. Describe external morphology of *Paramoecium*.
3. Write short notes:
   (a) Cilia
   (b) Ultrastructure of cilium
   (c) Trichocysts
   (d) Ectoplasm
   (e) Osmo-regulation
   (f) Food vacuoles
   (g) Cytostome
   (h) Distinguishing character of opalinata

University Questions

1. What is nutrition? Describe the process of nutrition in *Paramoecium*.
2. Define:
   (a) Aquaculture
   (b) Holozoic nutrition
   (c) Cytostome
   (d) Rejuvenation
   (e) Pellicle
   (f) Conjugation
   (g) Food vacuole
   (h) Cyclosis
   (i) Osmoregulation

3. Write short notes on:
   (a) Conjugation in *Paramoecium*
   (b) Binary fission in *Paramoecium*
   (c) Ultrastructure of cilium
4. Explain trichocyst in *paramoecium*.

✳✳✳

Chapter 2...

Porifera and Coelenterata

(A) PROFIERA - SYCON (*SCYPHA*)

2.1 Systematic Position, Habit and Habitat
2.2 External Morphology
2.3 Histology of Bodywall - Cell Types
2.4 Skeleton
2.5 Canal System
2.6 Nutrition
2.7 Respiration
2.8 Excretion
2.9 Nervous System and Behaviour
2.10 Reproduction

Scypha is calcarious sponge which was formerly called *Sycon* or *Grantia*. It is somewhat more complicated anatomically than *Leucosolenia*. *Scypha* has numerous species which are widely distributed.

2.1 Systematic Position, Habit and Habitat

2.1.1 Systematic Position

The sponge described below belong to the:

Phylum		Porifera
Class	:	Calcana
Order	:	Heterocoela
Family	:	Sycettidae
Genus	:	*Scypha (Sycon)*

2.1.2 Habit and Habitat

Scypha is a small, marine sponge found permanently attached to submerged solid objects like rocks, shells of molluscs and corals. It inhabits shallow waters near the coasts just below the low tide-marks. It is especially abundant in places where wave action provides with an adequate food supply and well oxygenated water by constant renewal of water. *Scypha* is branching, colonial sponge, though solitary individuals are also found. The branches are joined together at the base. It feeds on minute organisms and small particles of organic matter Reproduction takes places asexually as well as sexually. Dispersion of the progeny occurs by free-swimming flagellated larvae. It shows good degree of power of regeneration.

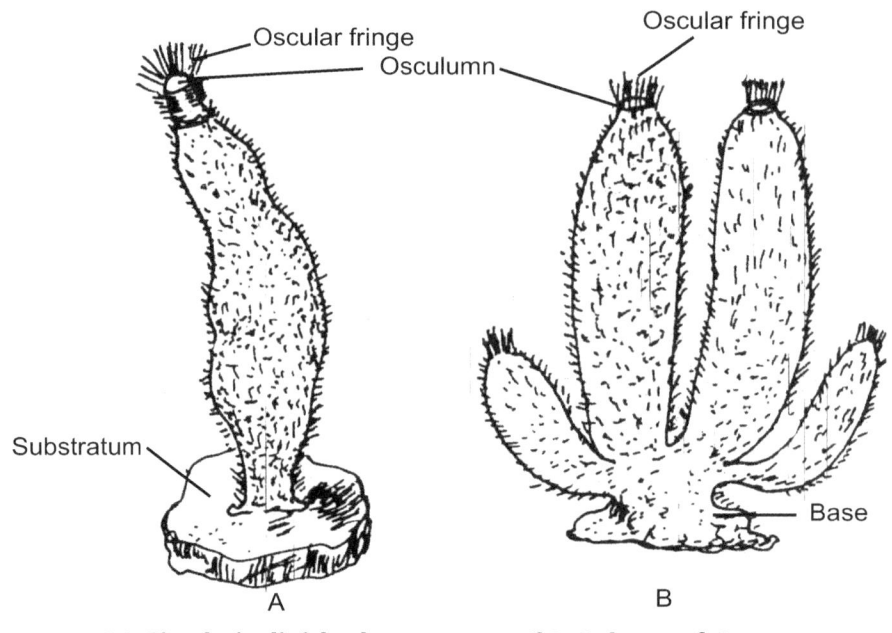

(a) Single individual   (b) Colony of *Sycon*

Fig. 2.1: *Sycon*

2.2 External Morphology

Shape and Size: The body or the branch of *Scypha* is vase-shaped which is slightly wider at the middle than at the ends. It measures 20-25 mm in height and 5-6 mm in diameter.

Colour: The sponge shows different shades of grey or light brown.

Osculum: The distal free end of the body is perforated by a large terminal opening called osculum. It is also called as exhalent or excurrent pore. The osculum is guarded by a funnel like collar formed of long, upright needle like spicules called oscular fringe. It prevents small animals from entering the sponge body.

Collar: Below the osculum, the distal end of a cylinder shows somewhat short and narrower region called collar.

Body Surface: The body surface, when seen under lens shows polygonal elevations separated off from one another by grooves. From the elevations protrude groups of neeedle-like and spear-like spicules that gives the sponge a bristly appearance. The grooves bear groups of minute pores called dermal ostia, which are inhalent or incurrent pores. These are intra cellular apertures.

2.3 Cell Types: Histology of the Body Wall

All sponges are diploblastic that is, their body wall consists of two layers, the dermal layer or epidermis and gastral layer or gastrodermis separated by a gelatinous mesoglea or mesenchyme.

(1) Dermal Layer: The dermal layer or epidermis covers the outer surface and lines the incurrent and excurrent canals as well as the spongocoel. It is composed of a single layer of large, flattened, polygonal ectodeinial cells called pinacocytes. Hence, this layer is also called pinacoderm. The cells are closely cemented together by their thin margins. Each pinacocyte contains a nucleus at the centre which is much thicker than the periphery. These cells are highly contractile and they can greatly reduce or increase the surface area of the sponge.

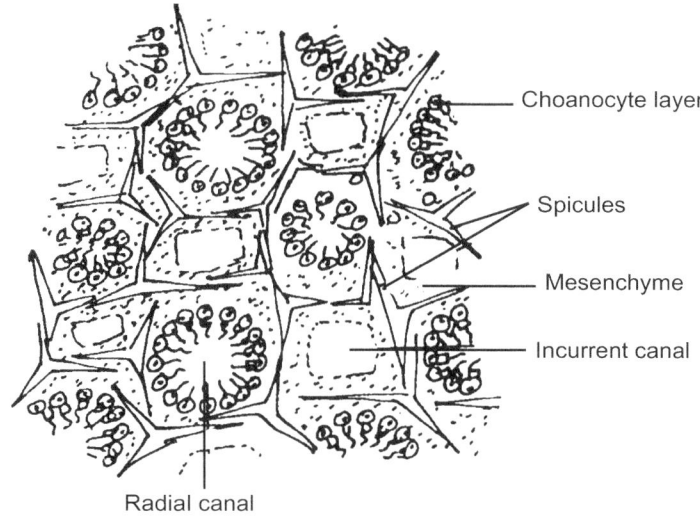

Fig. 2.2: Diagrammatic V.S. through the wall of *Scypha*

The dermal layer is protective in function. It prevents mechanical injuries and checks the entry of the micro organisms. It also holds the semifluid mesoglea in position, preventing its dispersion into water. The cells of the dermal layer surrounding the openings namely oscula, dermal ostia and apopyles are elongated and contractile. They are called myocytes. These cells work like sphincters to close the apertures between them.

(2) Gastral Layer: The gastral layer of choanoderm, lining the radial canals, consists of a single layer of large flagellate or collar called the *choanocytes*. A choanocyte is a somewhat oval or round in shape and contains a single nucleus, one or more contractile vacuoles, food vacuoles and reserve food particles. The cells bears at its inner end a long whip-like, vibratile flagellum, partly surrounded by a delicate, transparent contractile collar. The flagellum arises from the basal granule which is joined with a centriole forming a *centroblepharoplast*. The latter controls the movement of flagellum. It is connected by a thread, the *rhizoplast* with another organelle, the *parabasal body*, lying on the nucleus.

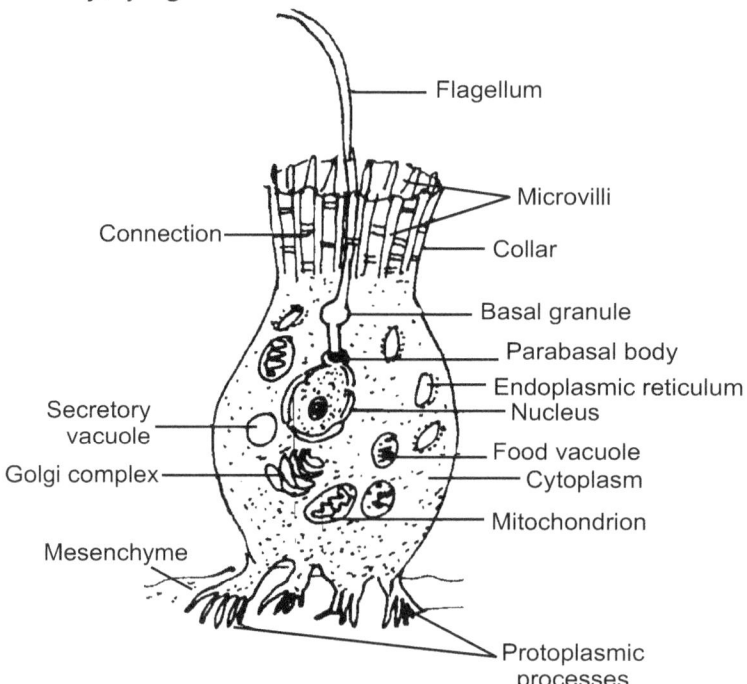

Fig. 2.3: Ultra structure of *choanocyte*

Electron microscopy has revealed that a choanocyte contains all the intracellular organelles such as Golgi bodies, mitochondria, endoplasmic reticulum, ribosornes etc. The collar is formed by highly contractile, 20 to 30 protoplasmic tentacles or microvilli, which are often joined together by side branches. The flagellum shows the usual pattern of 9 + 2 contractile fibres

The choanocytes set up a water current so important for the sponge, ingest and digest the food particles, and secrete the mesoglea.

(3) Mesoglea or Mesenchyme: It is the intermediate layer lying in between dermal and gastral layer. The mesoglea consists of a clear, non-living, gelatinous matrix, presumably of a protein nature. This layer is secreted by the choanocytes. It is thin in between canals but thicker outside the radial canals and inside the incurrent canals. These thickened parts of the mesoglea are respectively called the dermal cortex and the gastral cortex.

Cells Found in Mesoglea: The cells found in the mesoglea are of two main types.

(1) Scleroblasts: These cells migrate from the dermal layer and give rise to the spicules of various types. These cells are also called spicule forming cells and in *Scypha* the cells are called *calcoblasts* because they secrete calcarious spicules.

(2) Amoebocytes: These cells are with pseudopodia and show free movement in the body of sponge. The amoebocytes differ in size, shape of pseudopodia and function. Following are the chief forms of amoebocytes.

- (i) **Collencytes or Connective tissue cells:** These cells are with slender branching pseudopodia which may anastomose forming a sort of loose network.
- (ii) **Chromocytes or Pigment cells:** These cells are with lobose pseudopodia and contain pigment granules and impart colour to the sponge.
- (iii) **Trophocytes or Nourishing cells:** These cells collect partly digested food from the collar cells, digest it and later distribute it. These cells also possess lobose pseudopodia.
- (iv) **Thesocytes or Storage cells:** They have lobose pseudopodia and store reserve food materials in the form of glycogen or gjycoprotein.
- (v) **Phagocytes:** These cells engulf excreta and damaged tissues.

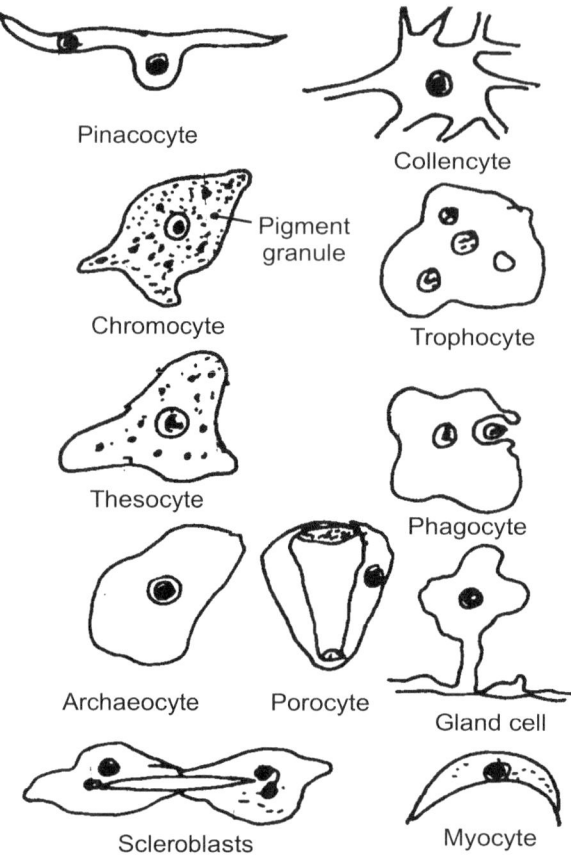

Fig. 2.4: Types of cells found in sponge

- **(vi) Archaeocytes or Embryonic cells:** These are large reserve cells, having blunt pseudopodia, large nucleus with a conspicuous nucleolous and often cytoplasmic inclusions. They give rise to sex cells, that is ova and sperms and when required change into other types of cells. These cells also play an important role in regeneration. Such cells are termed *totipotent* which can convert into any other kinds of cells within an animal.
- **(vii) Gland Cells:** These cells send an extension to the dermal layer and secrete a sticky material for attachment of the sponge to the substratum.
- **(viii) Myocytes:** These are fusiform and highly contractile cells similar to the smooth involuntary muscle cells of other invertebrates. These are arranged circularly to form sphincters surrounding the osculum, apopyles and other openings which can be opened or closed by them.

2.4 Skeleton

The body of the *Scypha* is internally supported by endoskeleton of calcarious spicules which are situated in the mesoglea. Spicules are minute, calcarious bodies of clear glossy appearance, consisting in general, simple spines or of spines radiating from a point. They are of three types: rod-like or monaxons, three-rayed or *triradiate* and four-rayed or *tetra-radiate*. The monaxon spicules further show three types such as long, short and spear-like or club-like. The spicules are arranged in the body of sponge in a definite manner.

Long one rayed needle like monaxon spicules are arranged in a circle around the osculum. The short monaxons mostly lie parallel to the radial canals. The spear-like or club-shaped monaxon called the oxeotes are grouped in the dermal cotex and partly project out over the polygonal elevation giving the sponge a bristly appearance.

Triradiate spicules are present along the flagellated canals, with one ray, pointed towards the closed distal ends of the canals. Four rayed or triradiate spicules in the thick gastral cortex surrounds the spongocoel.

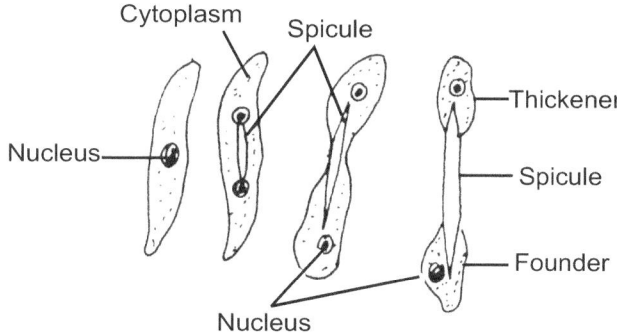

Fig. 2.5: Secretion of monaxon spicule

A spicule is enveloped by an organic sheath. It is calcarious and the calcium carbonate forming it is largely crystalline. Besides, it also contains magnesium sulphate, sodium, water etc.

Spicules are secreted by cells, called scleroblasts, that migrate into the mesoglea from the dermal layers of cells. Single scleroblast give rise to one ray of a spicule only. Thus for triradiate and tetraradiate spicules, three and four sclerobalsts are required. During the formation of spicule, the scleroblast first secretes inside it, a slender axial filament of organic material. Then calcarious matter ($CaCO_3$) is deposited around this thread. Later, the whole spicule is ensheathed by an envelope of organic matter.

Prior to the spicule formation, the scleroblast becomes binucleate by the division of its nucleus. The spicule formation begins between the two nuclei. As the lengthening of spicule occurs, the two nuclei move apart and finally the cell divides into two cells or *sclerocytes*. The cell situated at the inner end of the spicules is termed the *founder*, the other lying at the outer end is called the thickner. The spicule is chiefly laid down and shaped by the founder cell, whereas the *thicker* cell only deposits additional layers of calcium carbonate. After complete formation of spicule, both the cells leave it and wander into the mesoglea, the founder first and the thickener later.

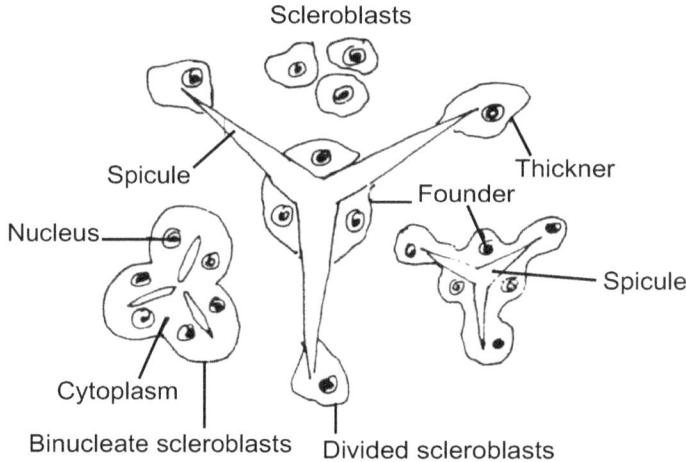

Fig. 2.6: *Scypha*. Secretion of triradiate spicule

The spicules form the endoskeleton which gives support and definite shape to the body of the sponge. They protect it from being torn by the wave action and prevents collapsing of canals with external pressure of the water.

2.5 Canal System

Scypha, like other sponges, possesses the characteristic peculiarity the canal system. The sponge body is traversed by numerous intercommunicating canals of several types which together form the canal system. The type of canal system found in *Scypha* is known is *syconoid type* which is more advanced than asconoid type.

The canal system includes cavities such as spongocoel, radial or flagellated canals, excurrent canals and incurrent canals.

(i) Spongocoel: If the cylindrical body of the *Scypha* is cut open longitudinally, it shows that the osculum leads into a narrow tubular cavity called *paragastric cavity* or *spongocoel*. It is lined by algae, flat polygonal cells, contractile cells called *myocytes* forming a sort of spincter. The remaining cavities of canal system are small and radially arranged in a regular manner in the thick wall of spongocoel.

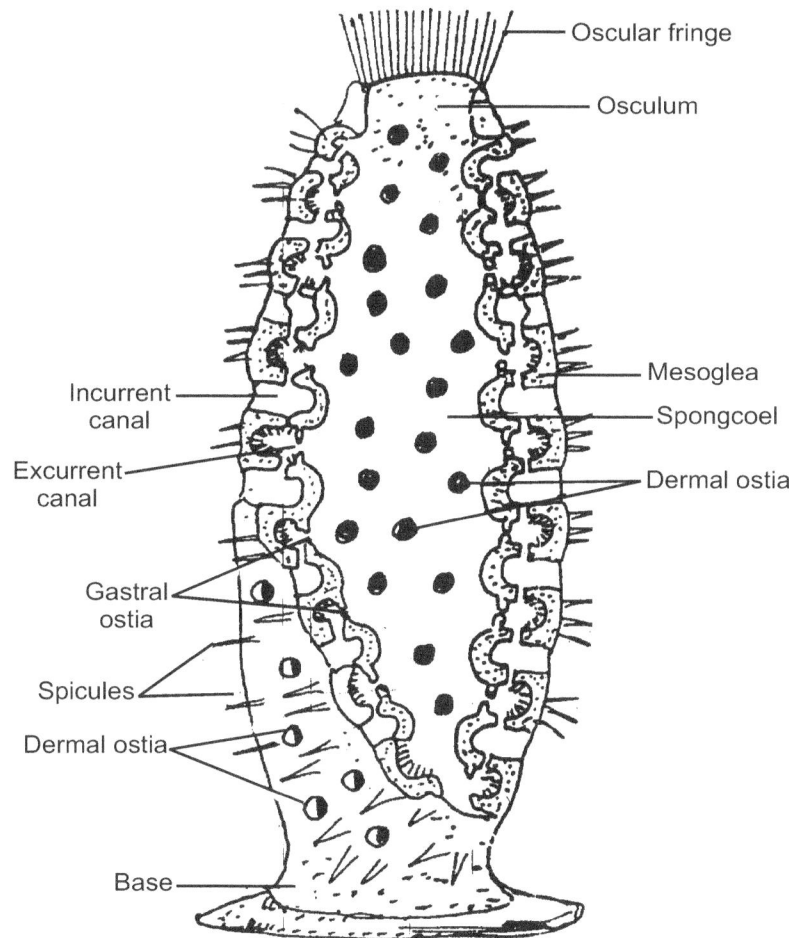

Fig. 2.7: *Sycon*: V.S. of body showing canal system

(ii) Radial or flagellated canals: The thick body wall lining the spongocoel contains many finger-like, straight out pushing at regular intervals called *radial* or *flagellated* canals. The radial canals are relatively wide and polygonal (octagonal) in cross section. They are closed at their outer ends which lie some distance inside the polygonal surface elevations. Internally, they open into excurrent canals by apertures called *apopyles*, which joins the spongocoel. An apopyle is a large circular opening in the centre of a thin partition, the *diaphragm*, the stretches between the adjoining radial and excurrent canal. It can be contracted or dilated by *myocytes* which border it. The radial canals are lined with loosely arranged, flagellated collar cells known as the *choanocytes* hence also called *flagellated canals*. The incurrent canals communicate with the radial canals by the short narrow canals called *prosopyles*.

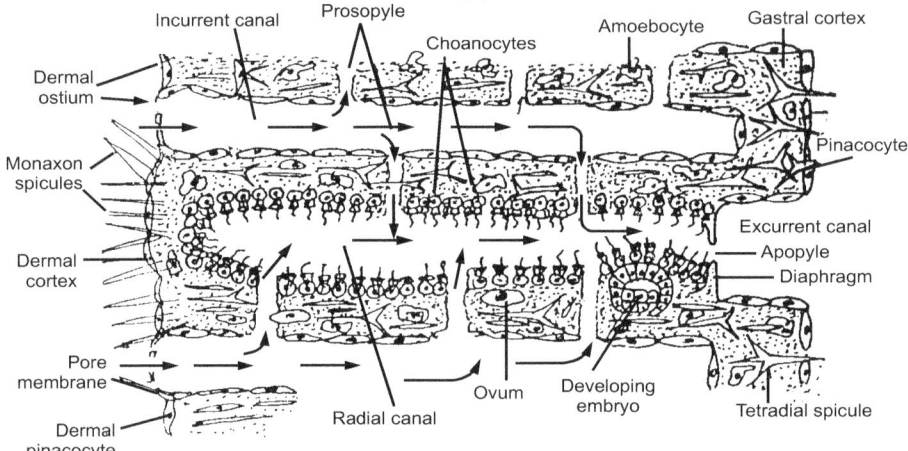

Fig. 2.8: *Sycon*: Radial or flagellated canal

(iii) Excurrent canals: The excurrent canals are short, wide chambers that lie inside the radial canals and communicate internally with spongocoel by very wide aperture termed the *gastric ostium*. They are lined by flat *ectodermal* pinacocytes like the spongocoel. Between the radial canals and excurrent canal is then diaphragm perforated by large hole called *apopyle*, which is surrounded by highly contractile sphincter like cells called *myocytes*. Due to these cells apopyle can be contracted or expanded to some extent.

(iv) Incurrent canals: In between the two successive radial canals, a tubular space called incurrent canal is present. Thus radial canals and incurrent canals are arranged alternately. They appear squarish in cross-section. The incurrent canals open to the exterior between the blind out ends of the radial canals by apertures termed dermal *ostia*. Externally an incurrent canal is covered by a pore membrane with 3 or 4 ostia which are intercellular. The pore membrane also contains contractile cells or myocytes some of which surround the dermal ostia and serve as sphincters for them.

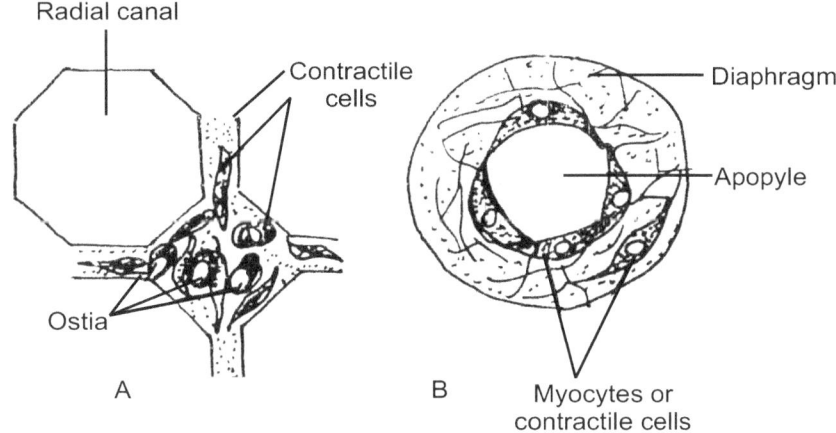

Fig. 2.9: *Scypha*
(a) Magnified pore membrane
(b) Apopyle surrounded by its diaphragm

The incurrent canals are lined by flattened ectodermal cells called *pinacocytes* similar to those lining the spongocoel. The incurrent canals end blindly, at their inner ends, not reaching the spongocoel. Between the incurrent canal and spongocoel, the mesoglea is specially thickened to form the *gastral cortex*. The wall between the incurrent and radial canals is pierced by numerous minute pores called *prosopyles*. These are perforations in *porocytes*. The porocytes are tubular contractile cells, formed from modified pinacocytes.

Circulation of water: The flagella of the radial canals create, by their uncoordinated but constant beating, a water current that circulates through the canal system. Water enters the incurrent canals through the dermal ostia, passes through the prosopyles into the radial canals and then through the apopyles into the excurrent canals, from where it passes, by way of the gastric ostia, into the spongocoel and finally out through the oscultim.

2.6 Nutrition

Scypha shows holozoic type of nutrition. Its food consists of minute planktonic organisms like protozoans, diatoms, bacteria and tiny particles of organic matter. Only small sized food particles which can enter the dermal ostia or pass through the prosopyles are taken by the animal. Dissolved nutrients are also utilized by the animal.

(i) Ingestion or Feeding Mechanism: *Scypha* is a filter feeder. There is no mouth and digestive cavity, however the choanocytes are the feeding organs of the sponge. The constant uncoordinated beating of choanocytes flagella sets up a water current that draws the food particles into the radial canals through the dermal ostia, incurrent canals and prosopyles. Each flagellum of the choanocyte beats in a spiral fashion from its base to tip and this creates a current which starts from the base of the flagellum and passes towards its tip. Because of this situation, the water with food-particles passes towards the collar. The food-particles adhere to the outer, sticky surface of the collar of the choanocytes, while water escapes into the collar between the processes composing the collar, that is, microvilli of the collar acts as a filter for trapping, food particles which move towards its base. These particles are then engulfed by pseudopodia arising from the choanocyte at the base of its collar.

(ii) Digestion: Digestion is entirely intracellular and occurs in food vacuoles as a Protozoa. In *Scypha*, the large choanocytes perform the function of digestion. The enzymes are secreted in the food vacuoles from the surrounding cytoplasm which gradually digest the food materials. Contents of the food vacuoles are first acidic and later become alkaline. This is similar to acidic phase of digestion in the stomach and alkaline phase in the intestine of the higher animals. Several types of enzymes like proteases, carbohydrases and lipases have been isolated. However, it is not certain whether they are secreted by the sponge itself or by the bacteria present in its body.

(iii) Distribution: Digested food is distributed to the other cells of the sponge by two ways: by cell to cell diffusion and by amoebocytes called *trophocytes*. The trophocytes take up wholly or partly digested food from the choanocytes and move in the mesoglea, delivering nutrients to the various cells.

(iv) Storage: The digested food is stored as reserved glycogen, fats, glycoprotein or lipoprotein inside the amoebocytes called *thesocytes*.

(v) Egestion: Undigestd food is egested by chanocytes, and amoebocytes into the spongocoel and removed by the outgoing current of water through osculum.

2.7 Respiration

There are no special respiratory organs in *Scypha*. Respiration is aerobic. Gaseous exchange occurs by simple diffusion between the cells of sponge and the current of water. Every cell respires for itself. Oxygen dissolved in water is taken in by diffusion through the general body surface by the pinacocytes and internally by the choanocytes. Amoebocytes distribute the oxygen through the mesoglea and take away the carbon dioxide where action ensures regular supply of oxygen, sponges prefer places where water contains plenty of oxygen, it dies if water is deficient in oxygen or if its pores become packed with debris. The upper part of the body, just below the osculum, seems to consume more oxygen than the basal part. The rate of respiration may be controlled by the incurrent of water.

2.8 Excretion

The nitrogenous waste matter formed in the cells as a result of metabolic activity is chiefly ammonia. Special excretory organs are lacking. Ammonia leaves the cells by diffusion into the water, filling spongocoel and surrounding the sponge. From the spongocoel, the waste matter is eliminated by outgoing current of water and from the vicinity of the sponge, it is carried away by wave action. According to some investigators, nitrogenous waste matter is taken up by amebocytes, which pass into the spongocoel to escape with the outgoing water current.

2.9 Nervous System and Behaviour

In *Scypha*, there are no nerve cells or sensory cells, therefore the animal is unable to react to a stimulus as a unified whole. In the absence of a nervous system, there is no co-ordinated action of the whole body. Even a strong stimulus, like a cut or a blow, at one part, is not transmitted to other parts of the body to any appreciable extent.

Instead, each cell is sensitive and reacts individually. Specialised cells, like myocytes, however, respond to certain stimuli, though very slowly. They respond, probably with some degree of co-ordination, to stimuli such as exposure to air or polluted water by contracting and closing the openings they surround. In the sponges, power of conductivity is very slight which needs one to many minutes for completion. The oscular rim appears to be the most sensitive part of the sponge, where conductivity is best developed.

Recently, some scientists have reported the presence of a primitive type of nervous system but it lacks confirmation. According to their opinion, some collenocytes which receive and conduct stimuli, serve as bipolar neutrons and form a diffuse network connecting the choanocytes with pinacocytes ands the myocytes. Some workers found such bipolar nerve cells in mesoglea but their role is not confirmed.

2.10 Reproduction

Scypha reproduces by both asexual and sexual methods.

(1) Asexual Reproduction: The asexual reproduction takes place by external budding and regeneration.

- **(a) Budding:** A small outgrowth or bud arises from the base of the sponge and acquires an osculum at the tip of the free end. It may remain attached to the parent sponge and add to its size or become free and form a new sponge and lead an independent life, by fixing itself somewhere else.
- **(b) Regeneration:** All the sponges show high power of regeneration. It is the ability to replace the parts lost by injury. Any piece of the body of the *Scypha* is capable of growing into a complete sponge, if kept in a suitable environment.

(2) Sexual Reproduction: The sexual reproduction occurs by sperms and ova, both of which develop in the same sponge. *Scypha* is thus, monoecious that is hermaphrodite. There are no special organs like testis and ovaries. Both the sperms and ova are produced from the undifferentiated amoebocytes called *archeocytes* which are present in the mesoglea. The sperms and ova however, do no mature simultaneously to ensure cross-fertilization. The ova ripen earlier then the sperms. This condition is called *protogyny*.

Oogenesis: The egg mother cell or oogonium is first derived from an enlarged amoebocyte with large nucleus and conspicuous nucleolus. The amoebocytes migrate in the cavities of radial canals and undergo mitosis, each producing four oocytes. The oocytes traverse choanocyte layer and enter the mesoglea layer where they grow considerably in size by engulfing or fusing with other similar cells or by receiving nourishment from nurse cells called trophocytes. After completion of the growth, each oocyte changes into ovum by undergoing a meiotic division. in which polar bodies are extended. During the developments, egg mother cell shows amoeboid movement. A ripen ovum is large oval or spherical cell with a large nucleus having prominant nucleus in it. It lies in the wall of a radial canal, ready for fertilization by a sperm from another sponge.

Spermatogenesis: The sperm-mother cell or spermatogonuim is described as an enlarged amoebocyte which is supposed to be a modified choanocyte. The spermatogonium is surrounded by one or more flattened cover-cells. The cover-cells are derived either by the division of the mother cells or from other amoebocytes. The spermatogonium undergoes two or three divisions and form spermatocytes which give rise to spermatozoa by meiosis. The whole structure that is cover cell and spermatocytes is called the *sperm nest* or *spermatocyst*. A mature sperm consists of a round nucleated head and long slender vibratile tail. Tail is useful for movement so that it can reach to other sponges.

Fertilization: Fertilization is internal and the ova or eggs are fertilized in-situ. When sperms mature, the spermatocysts rupture discharging the sperms into the radial canals. From here they are carried by the outgoing current of water to the exterior through the osculum. With the incoming water current, the sperms enter the body of another sponge through its dermal ostia and reach to the radial canals. Here, each sperm enters a wandering amoebocyte or a choanocyte. The choacnocyte loses its collar and flagellum and becomes amoeboid and migrate into mesoglea. The cells penetrated by the sperms are known as the sperm-transit cells because they serve to carry the sperms to the ova through mesoglea. The *sperm transit cell* remains in close contact with ovum and forms a conical depression to receive it. The sperm also loses its tail and its head swells up. The swollen head becomes surrounded by a capsule. The capsule with the sperm head enters the ovum. Thus, the act of fertilization is completed and fertilized egg or zygote is formed. The sperm transit cell now departs. There are *amoebocytes* form the blood capsule in which the zygote gets enclosed. Early development occurs within the broad capsule of the parent sponge.

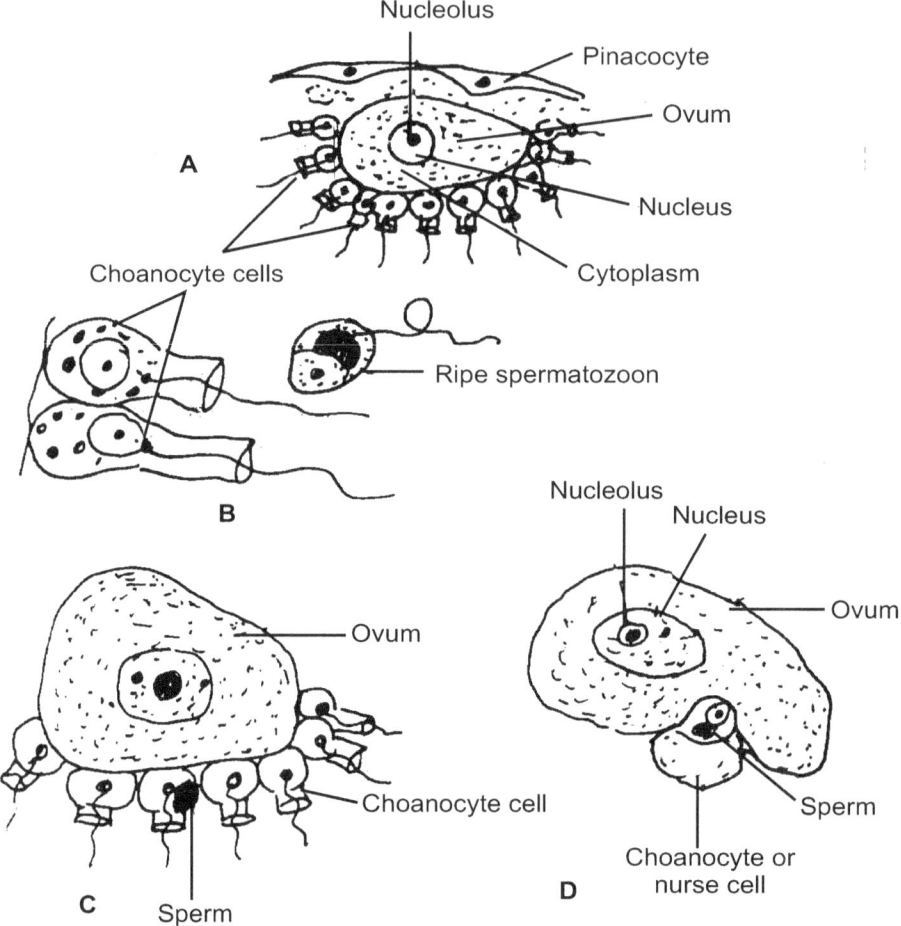

Fig. 2.10: Gametes and Fertilization
(a) Egg situ, (b) A ripen spermatozoan near two choanocytes,
(c) Sperm entered in a choanocyte adjacent to ovum in Grantia,
(d) Nurse cell giving sperm to ovum

Development: The zygote undergoes holoblastic cleavage and develops in situation into a blastula. The first three cleavages are vertical and produce a disc of eight pyramidal cells or blastomeres. The next cleavage is horizontal which divides *blastomeres* unequally, yielding two tiers of 8 *blastomeres* each. The blastomeres of upper tier are small and are called *micromeres* which form the future choanocytes. The blastomeres of the lower tier are large called *macromeres* which produce the future epidermis. A small cavity appears amongst the blastomeres called blastocoel and the embryo with it the *blastula*. The small cells multiply rapidly and elongate, each acquires a flagellum on its inner end, facing the blastocoel. The large cells remain undivided for some time, become rounded and granular and develop in their middle, a large opening that functions as a mouth to ingest adjacent maternal cells. This stage of the embryo is termed *stomoblastula*.

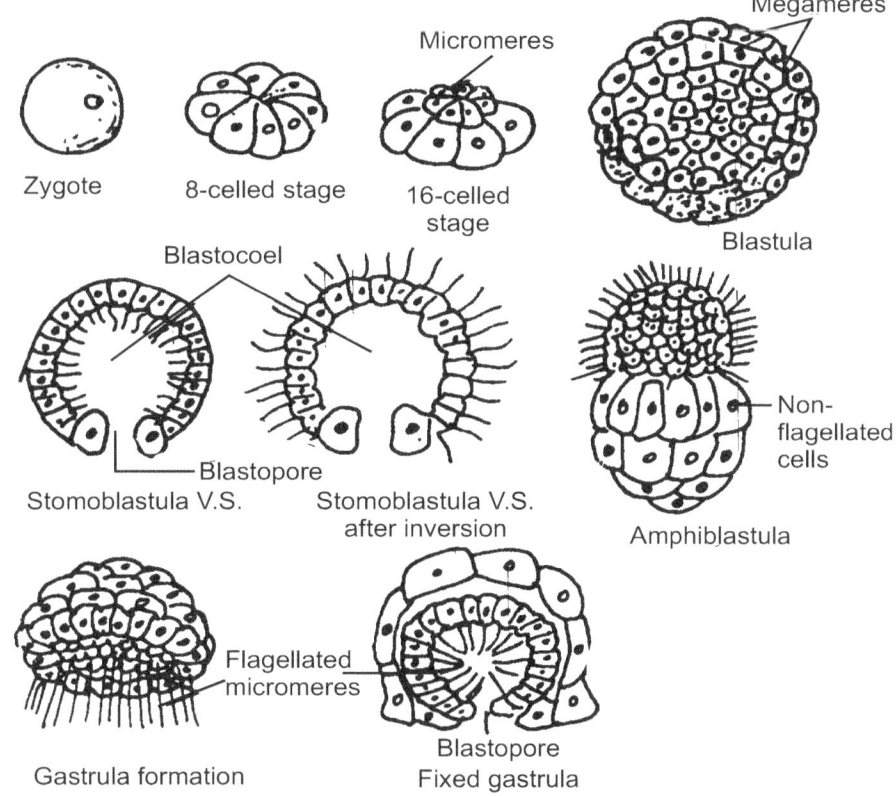

Fig. 2.11: Development stages of *Scypha*

Larval Development: The stomoblastula soon undergoes a process of inversion in which it turns its inside out through the mouth. As a result the flagellar ends of the micromere are brought to the outside. Now the macromeres also multiply slowly and as they progress on all sides, the mouth of the stomoblastula crosses. By further cell division, the embryo elongates and becomes ready for free life. After inversion, the embryo is termed the amphiblastula larva because it is partly flagellated and partly non-flagellated.

The *amphiblastula larva* which is enclosed in broad capsule then ruptures and makes its way into the radial canal and finally leaves the parent body by way of the osculum, with the outgoing water current. It swims about freely in the sea with the flagellated half directed forwards.

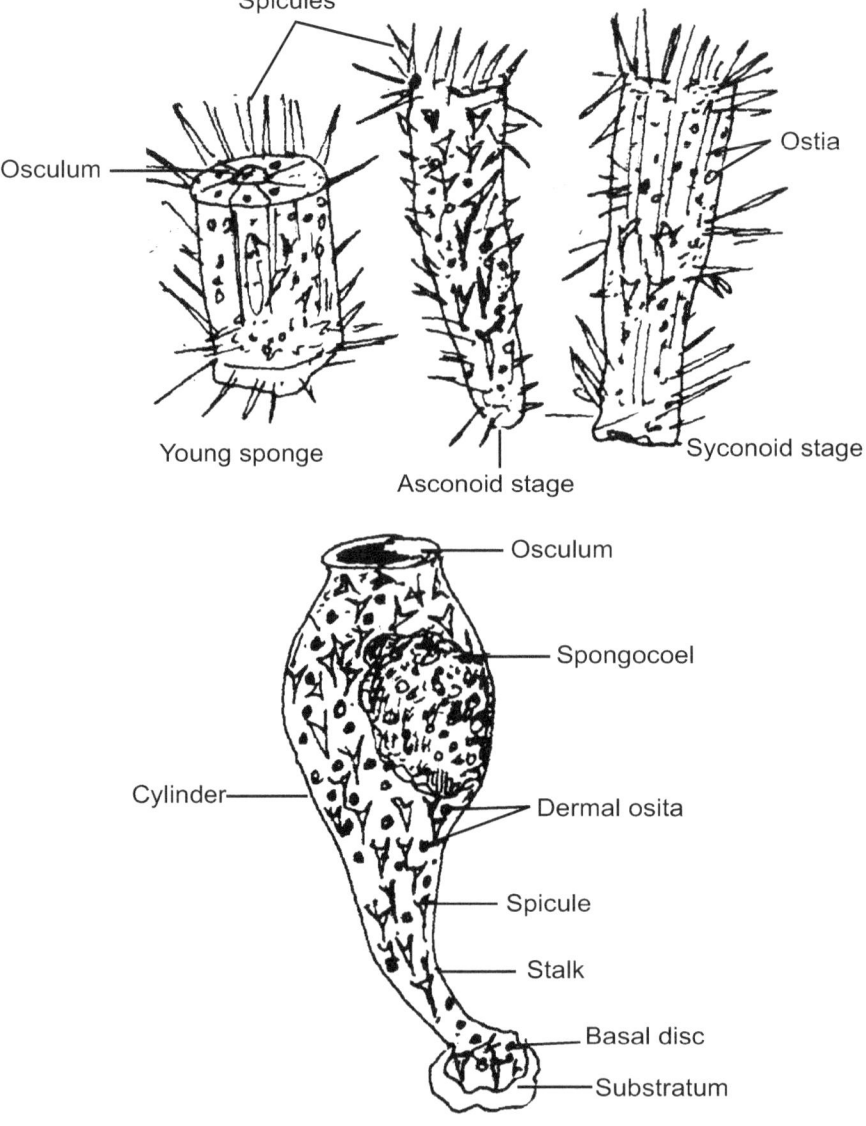

Fig. 2.12: Development Stages

After swimming for some time the flagellated half of the larva invaginates into or is overgrown by the large non-flagellated cells. With this process, the single layered amphiblastula larva changes into a two two-layered *gastrula* with an opening, the *blastopore*, at the invaginated end. The outer layer of gastrula in made of the non-flagellated granular cells while the inner layer of the flagellated cells. Gastrulation, thus, in a way reverses the inversion that takes place at the stomoblastula stage.

Metamorphosis: The gastrula soon fixes itself to some substratum by its blastoporal end and lengthens into a cylindrical structure. At the basal end the blastopore closes by the growth of cell layers. While at the free end, develops a perforation which becomes the osculum. Several small perforations in the cylinder become the dermal ostia. The outer non-flagellated cells flatten to form the dermal layer or pinacoderrn. The inner flagellated cells develop collars and give rise to choanoderm, archeocytes and other amoebocytes. The future spongocoel is lined by choanocytes. At this stage the young *Scypha* resembles adult asconoid sponge, *Lucosolenia*. This is known as *olynthus* stages. The wall of the cylinder gradually thickens due to the formation of mesoglea between the two layers of cells. The invagination of dermal layer forms the incurrents canals, while envagination of spongocoel gives rise to the radial canals. The radial canals are lined by flagellated choanocytes. Meanwhile, spicules, and various types of amoebocytes are differentiated in the mesoglea. The non-flagellated cells give rise to scleroblasts and myocytes while the archeocytes and other amoebocytes develop from the flagellated cells.

It is interesting to note that in sponges, the flagellated and non-flagellated layers of larva, produce the gastral and dermal layers respectively, whereas in other Metazoa they are derived from non-flagellated and flagellated layers of the larva, respectively. Thus, the two layers of a sponge gastrula can not be named the ectoderm and endoderm and neither the two layers of the adult sponge can be termed epidermis and gastrodermis as it is done in the metazoa.

(B) COELENTERATE - *HYDRA*

2.11 Coelenterata - *Hydra*
2.12 Systematic Position; Habit and Habitat
2.13 External Morphology and Internal Structure
2.14 Epidermis - Ultrastructure
2.15 Locomotion
2.16 Nutrition
2.17 Respiration and Excretion
2.18 Nervous System and Behaviour
2.19 Reproduction and Development
2.20 Regeneration

2.11 Coelenterata - *Hydra*

Hydra is a small freshwater commonest polyp which lives solitary life in ponds and lakes. It is the best representative of coelentrates to study the fundamental characteristics of Metazoa and Coelenterata. *Hydra* is simple in form and structure. Its body organisation corresponds roughly to the gastrula stage of the higher animals. Hence it may be considered as the living counter part of some remote ancestor of the higher metazoa.

Leeuwenhoek in 1702 first described *Hydra* to the Royal society of London. But its real discover was Abraham Trembley (1744) a Swiss biologist who recognised its animal nature. Reaumur called it a polyp. The name *Hydra* was given it by Linnaeus because of its special power of regeneration. Actually *Hydra* was a nine-headed greater serpentine dragon of the ancient Greek mythology. When one of its head was cut off, two new ones immediately appeared in its place. Thus, the name hydra is, an old Greek word for 'Water-serpent' was given to this animal because of its ability to regenerate its lost or injured parts. There are large number of species of hydra- found in the different parts of the world. The most common freshwater species of hydra is *Hydra vulgaris* which is orange-red in colour found in America and Europe. The *Hydra fusca*, *Hydra oligactis* which now belong to the genus *Pelmato-hydra* called brown hydra are distributed chiefly in Punjab in India, North America and Europe. The green hydra formerly called *Hydra viridis* is now known as *Chlorohydra viridissima* is common in America and Europe. Its green colour is largely due to the presence of the symbiotic green algae *Zoochlorellae* in its endodermal cells. There are also whitish and pinkish species belong to Hydra proper. They are without *Zoochlorellae*. *Hydra gangetica* is found in the ponds and reservoirs along the river Ganges. The following account applies in general to all the species.

2.12 Systematic Position, Habit and Habitat
2.12.1 Coelenterata - *Hydra*
Systematic Position

Phylum	-	Coelenterata
Class	-	Hydrozoa
Order	-	Hydroida
Suborder	-	Anthomedusae
Genus	-	*Hydra*

2.12.2 Habits and Habitat

Hydra is the simple and solitary coelenterate found in fresh water pounds, pools, lakes streams and ditches. They are not found in polluted and hot waters. They prefer and flourish in cool, clear and stagnant water. *Hydra* usually remains attached to submerged vegetation or with any solid object. When it is undisturbed its body remains extended with tentacles spread out and shows expansions and contractions without any apparent region. When animal is hungry, its body and tentacles are stretched to the maximum limit and captures any food that comes in contact with it. It is carnivorous in habit and feeds on small insects, insect larvae and small crustaceans.

Collection and Culture of *Hydra*

Hydras are usually abundant near surface of water where there is more light and oxygen. They can be collected from freshwater lakes, ponds etc. usually during winter months by filling a glass jar with pond water and aquatic weed like *Hydrilla* plants and leaving them undisturbed in some lighted place.

After sometime number of *Hydra* can be observed either attached to the wall of glass jar or with the leaves of *Hydrilla* plant. The microscopic observation can be done by putting them on a glass slide with the help of dropper. *Hydra* can be cultured in the laboratory. The isolated hydra may be transferred in aquarium and adequate food must be supplied daily to them. The food consist of *Daphnia* which are readily available in stagnant water. The population of *Hydra* increases by budding.

2.13 External Morphology and Internal Morphology

2.13.1 External Morphology

Shape and Size: Body of the hydra is like an elongated cylinder. It is easily visible to the naked eyes when fully extended it becomes elongated and slender. It shows distinct radial symmetry. The fully expanded *hydra* is about 2 to 20 mm in length but diameter is about 1 mm. The great variation in the length is due to its remarkable power of contraction and expansion. When *hydra* contracts the body becomes somewhat globular and measures only a few millimeters.

Body Form: The body of the hydra is tubular and shows the following parts.

(i) Pedal disc: *Hydra* is sessile but its proximal or aboral end of the body is flattened and closed called pedal disc or basal disc. It is useful for temporary attachment to the object. It also helps in locomotion. The pedal disc is provided with large number of gland cells which secrete a sticky substance for attachment to the substratum and also secrete in gas bubble enclosed by a film of mucus, for floating.

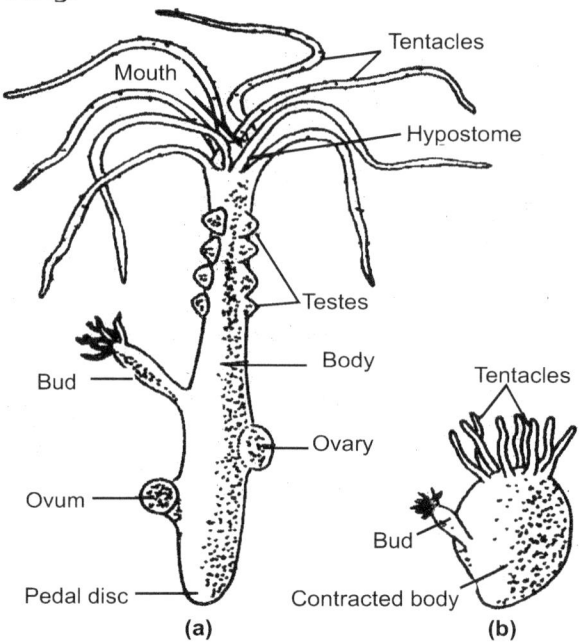

Fig. 2.13: *Hydra.* External features, (a) Expanded body bearing bud and gonads. (b) Contracted body bearing bud

(ii) Hypostome: The free distal end or oral end of the body bears a circular opening the mouth which is situated at the apex of the conical projection of the body called oral cone, hypostome or manubrium. The mouth which opens into the gastrovascular cavity or enteron.

(iii) Tentacles: The hypostome is encircled by a circlet of 6 to 10 slender, contractile and hollow thread like process called the tentacles. They are primarily food gathering devices but can also be used for locomotion. The tentacles are hollow, their cavity is communicated to the gastrovascular cavity. The tentacles possess nematocysts. The fully extended tentacles may measure upto 7 cm or more with extremely thin diameter. The fully extended body may attain a length of 30 mm. The tentacles can be greatly extended at the time of feeding or locomotion. When body contracts it forms very small, spherical mass of jelly with tentacles looking like minute, blunt knobs.

(iv) Buds: Frequently, the side of the body may bear one or more lateral buds in various stages of development. They are more at the proximal end. A well developed bud bears its own mouth, hypostome and tentacles. When the fully formed buds are detached from parent body, they give rise to new individuals.

(v) Gonads: During breeding season, temporary gonads may also be seen projecting from the side of the body of mature individuals. The testes occur near the oral end which are conical projections, while ovaries are situated towards the proximal end and these are oval projections.

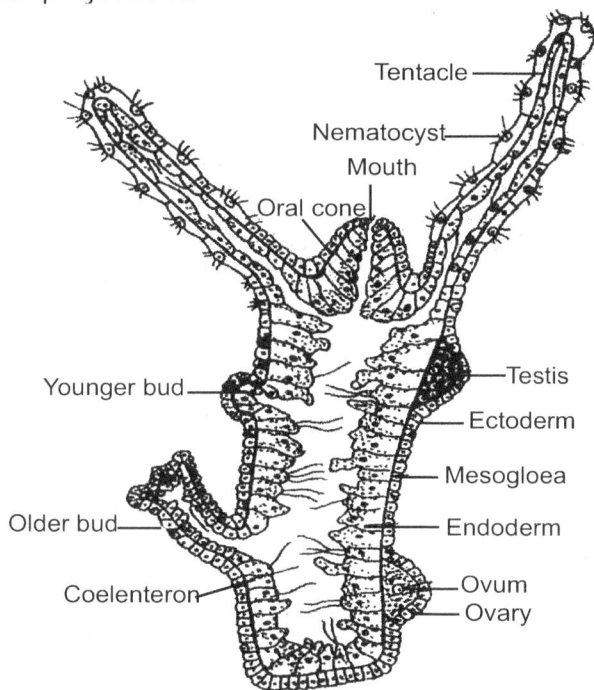

Fig. 2.14: *Hydra* **L.S.**

2.13.2 Internal Structure

The internal structure of *hydra* can be well studied with its longitudinal and transverse sections. The internal structure shows body wall which surrounds a large central cavity extended into the tentacles called gastrovascular cavity or coelenteron (Greek Koilos = hollow, enteron = gut) or enteron. In longitudinal section the gastrovascular cavity is seen to open to the outside through the mouth. There is no anus or an excretory pore.

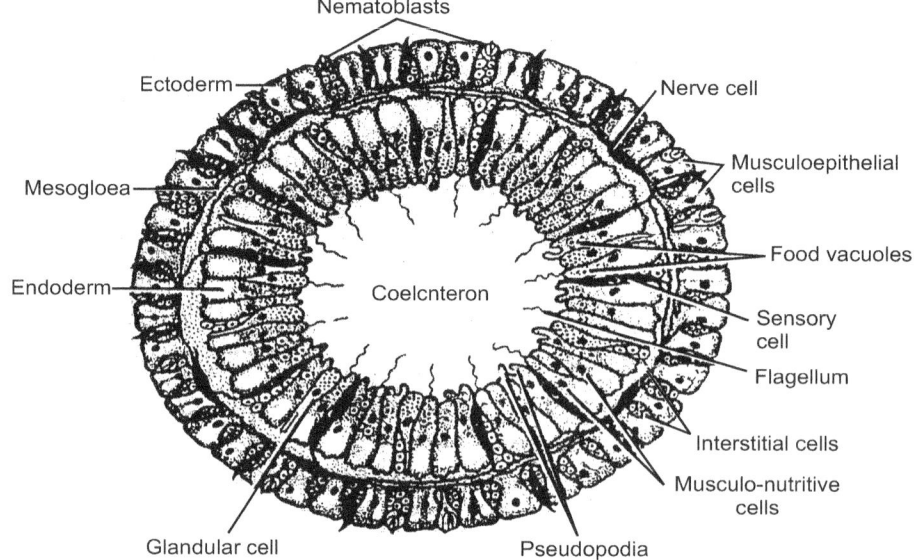

Fig. 2.15: *Hydra* T.S.

2.14 Epidermis

The epidermis is the outer cellular layer composed of small cuboidal cells. It is covered externally with a thin and delicate cuticle. The epidermis forms a thin layer about one-third of the thickness of body wall. Epidermal layer consist of the following of different seven types of cells:

1. Epithelio-muscular cells.
2. Interstitial cells
3. Gland cells
4. Cnidoblast cells
5. Sensory cells
6. Nerve cells and
7. Germ cells.

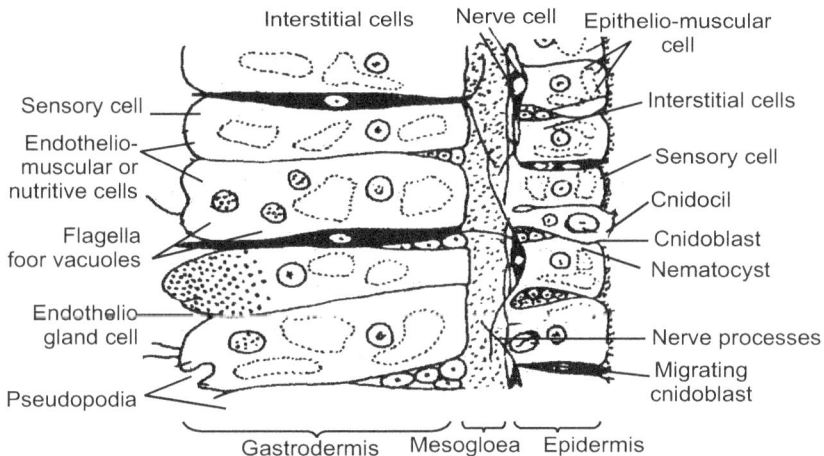

Fig. 2.16 (a): *Hydra*: A portion of the section of body wall magnified.

The epidermis is protective, muscular and sensory in function.

1. Epitheliomuscular cells: (Fig. 2.17) The major part of the epidermis is formed by epitheliomuscular cells. These cells are composed of both epithelial and muscular parts. The epitheliomuscular cells of the epidermis are cylindrical with their inner ends produced into two or more muscular processes which have myonemes or unstriped muscle fibres, these muscle fibres branch and branches anastomose. These fibres are contractile fibres. The muscular processes or muscle tails and myonemes run parallel to the longitudinal axis of the body. They are outside or embedded in the mesogloea. When muscular processes contract the body and tentacles become shortened. These cells show outer wider ends cemented together in weavy borders to form the continuous external epidermal surface of the body. The epitheliomuscular cells has a large nucleus and along the border of wider end there is a row of mucous granules which secrete cuticle. There are also pair of supporting fibrils in the body of cell. The epidermal cells of the pedal or basal disc are granular and they secrete mucus of attachment. These cells also posses pseudopodia which help in gliding movement. Some of the epidermal cells located on the basal disc are specialised for gas secretion which forms the bubble by which the hydra breaks from its attachment and is lifted up. The detailed structure of epitheliomuscular cells is revelaed by electron microscopy.

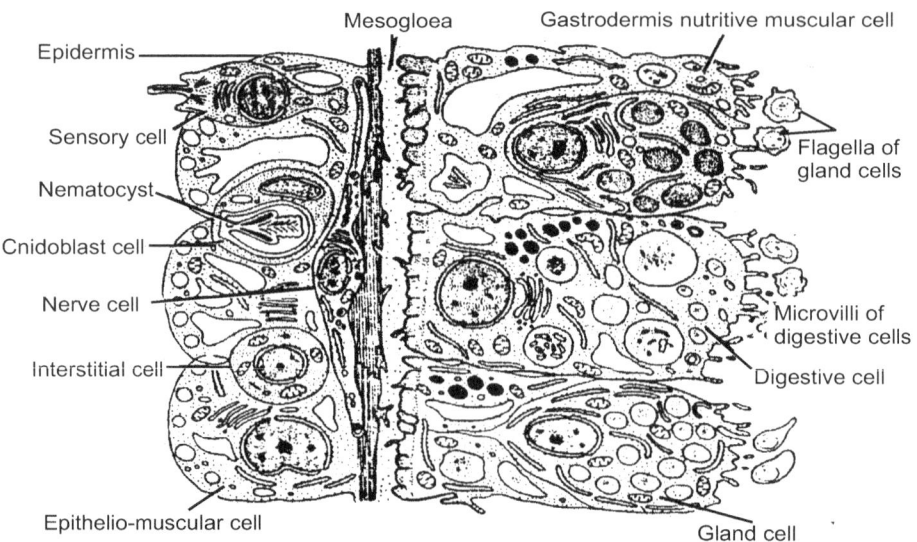

Fig. 2.16 (b): *Hydra*. **Diagrammatic representation of an electron micrograph of a section of a portion of body wall to illustrate the relationships of cells layers and cell types**

Ultrastructure of epithelio-muscular cell: Under electron microscope these cells appear large columnar or cuboidal in shape. Each cell contains a centrally or basally placed nucleus. The nucleus is large and irregular in outline and contains granular material and a large dense, central nucleolus. The cytoplasm contains rough and smooth endoplasmic reticulum. In the ground substance of the cytoplasm many free ribosomes and mitochondria are present. The Golgi complex lie parallel to the long axis of the cell, which are composed of parallel lamellae, vesicles and vacuoles. The opical portion of the cells contains a large number of spherical mucous granules with 0.5 to 1.0 µ in diameter. These secrete a finely granular material which forms a thick protective mucous layer covering the cell surface. The intracellular spaces provide a spongy appearance to the cell. There are large vacuoles present near the Golgi complex. The cell membrane gives out a few minute projections or microvilli at the outer free surface. At the junctions of two cells, an intercellular space about 120 A° wide is left between the two adjacent cells membranes. Regularly spaced transverse bars called septate desmosomes are present in these spaces.

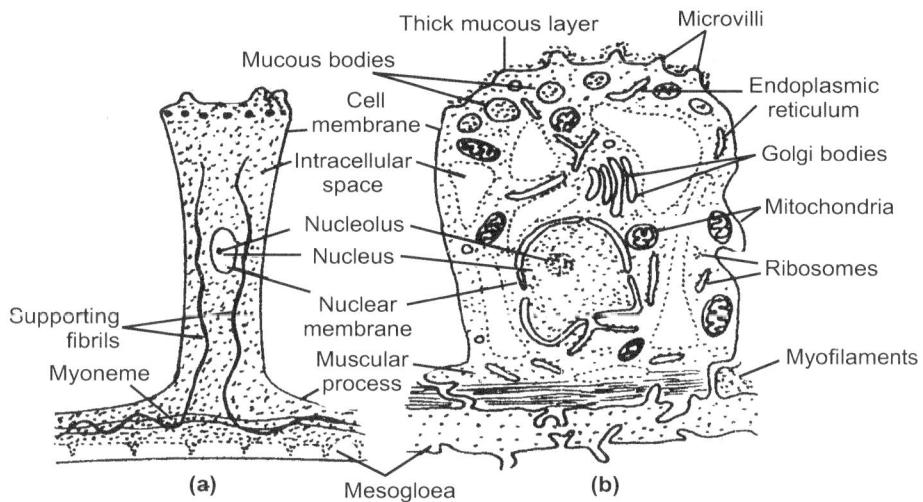

Fig. 2.17: *Hydra*. An epithelio-muscular cell. (a) Under light microscope, (b) Under electron microscope

The muscular process of the cell are filled with two types of myofibrils. The myofibrils with 50 A° diameter are more in number while myofibrils with diameter with 200A° diameter are less in number and are scattered in them. There are microtubules with 200A° diameter which run parallel to the muscular processes and they are useful to carry water or ions and may, therefore, involved in changes in the electrical potential of muscular processes.

The epitheliomuscular cells show regional variation. The cells of tentacles are large and equipped with numerous cnidoblasts, more mucous granules and more elaborate endoplasmic reticulum. The cells of penducle region contians are cuboidal and small with few intracellular space and mucous granules. The basal cells are called glandulomuscular cells and are filled with mucous granules. They have well developed endoplasmic reticulum.

1 µ or mu	= 0.001 mm	= 10^{-3} mm
1 mg or milli mu	= 0.001 µ	= 10^{-6} mm
1 A° or Angstrom	= 0.1 mµ	= 10^{-7} mm

Functions: The epitheliomuscular cells form the protective covering to the body. They bring about contraction, shortening, extention and bending of the body. These cells help in locomotion. They are also useful for attachment to the substratum. They also help in respiration through mucous layer at the cell surface.

2. Interstitial cells

These cells lie in the spaces between the inner ends of cells of the epidermis and between outer ends of cells of gastrodermis. They occupy the spaces between the narrow basal ends of the epithelia musuclar cells. These are simple, small, oval or round cells with large nucleus. Just below the tentacles the interstitial cells form the growth zone from which all types of new cells are given and old worn out cells are pushed out and shed at the proximal and distal ends. The nematocysts and germ cells are also formed from the interstitial cells. These cells also give rise to epitheliomuscular cells. The interstitial cells renew all the cells of the animal once every 45 days. Thus, they are totipotent.

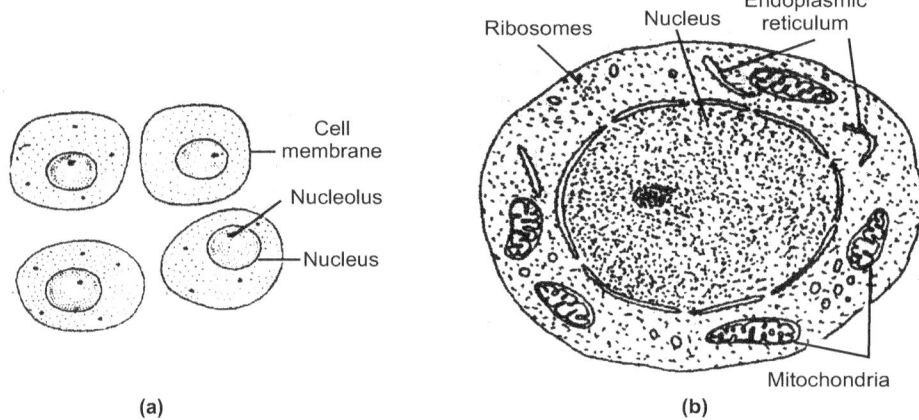

Fig. 2.18: *Hydra*. Interstitial cells: (a) Cells under light microscope (b) A cell under electron microscope

Ultrastructure: Each interstitial cell is small, oval or round with 5μ in diameter and contains clear cytoplasm and relatively large nucleus with small nucleolous. The cytoplasm is filled with free ribosomes, smooth endoplasmic vesicles and mitochondria.

Functions: Following important functions are performed by interstitial cells.

(i) These cells give rise to different types of cells thus, these cells play an important role in rebuilding tissues during growth, budding and regeneration.

(ii) They also give rise to germ cells during breeding season.

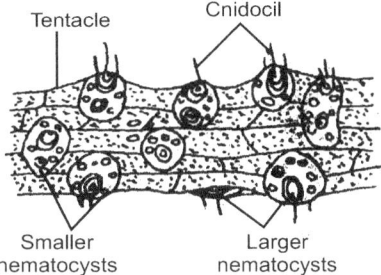

Fig. 2.19: A portion of tentacle of *Hydra* showing epidermal cells with batteries of nematocysts

    (iii) They replace the old wornout cells of gastrodermis and also form new nematocysts.

    (iv) These cells are also called reserve cells because they are capable of developing into any kinds of cells.

  3. Cnidoblasts: (Fig. 2.19) These cells are found throughout the epidermis but they are abundant on the tentacles. Some of the interstitial cells of the epidermis give rise to highly specialised cells called cnidoblasts. These cells are also called nematoblasts or stinging cells. Presence of these specialised cells is the characteristic of all cnidarian coelenterates.

  4. Structure of Cnidoblasts: (Fig. 2.20) These cells are somewhat oval in shape and cytoplasm contains large crescentic nucleus with incospicuous nucleolus lying to one side the cells contians a oval or pyriform bladder like sac called nematocystor stinging cell.

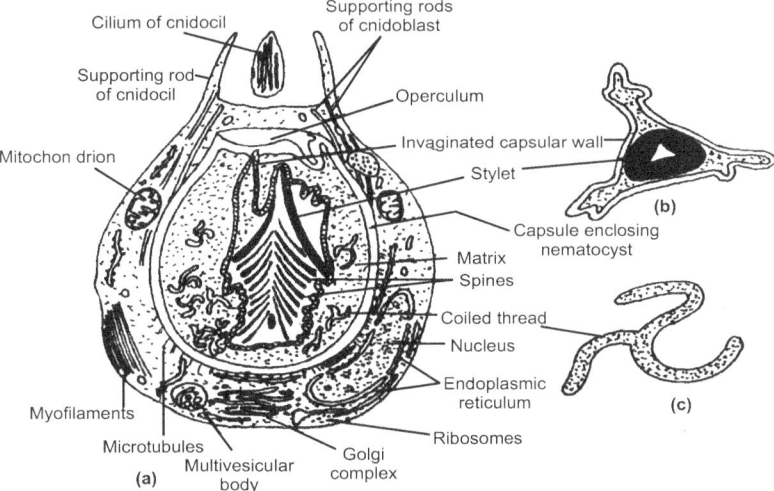

Fig. 2.20: *Hydra*. Diagrammatic representation of an electron micrograph of a cnidoblast containing a nematocyst

The nematocysts is made up of capsule encloses a coiled tube or thread which is continuous with the wall of the capsule. The sac is filled with proteinous poisonous fluid called hypnotoxin. It is a mixture of proteins and phenols.

Nematocyst is not a cell because it is chitinious and non-living. In the space of chidoblast cell secretes a double walled chitinous capsule with lid or operculum. One end of the capsule forms a tube lying coiled in the capsule. The tube has basal swelling called a butt and long coiled thread which may be close or open at the tip. There may be spines inside the tube. At the base of the thread pointing inward, are three large spines called barbs or stylets and three spiral rows of minute spines, called barbules. The arrangement and number of spines are constant in a particular species and of great taxonomic value. The outer end of nematoblast projects a pointed spike like structure called cnidocil. On the wall of the capsule are contractile fibrils running into the cnidoblast. In some nematocysts the cytoplasm of the chidoblast forms contractile muscular fibrils. Some nematocysts have a lasso or spring like thread attached to the base of the cnidoblast which prevents certain nematocyst from being thrown out of the body of an animal.

Ultrastructure of cnidoblast: The nucleus of cnidoblast contains inconspicuous nucleolus. The cytoplasm contains endoplasmic reticulurn, free ribosomes, basally located Golgi complex, mitochondria, lipid droplets and multivesicular bodies. A bundle of small myofilaments is present in the basal region of the cnidoblast extending from the capsule of the nematocyst. Fine microtubules are attached to the base of capsule which is double walled. The cnidocil is composed of central core surrounded by large rods. The core contains smaller fibrils. From the capsule about 20 hollow rods extend upward. Converging around the core appears to be modified cilium and it contains smaller fibrils in 9 + 2 pattern.

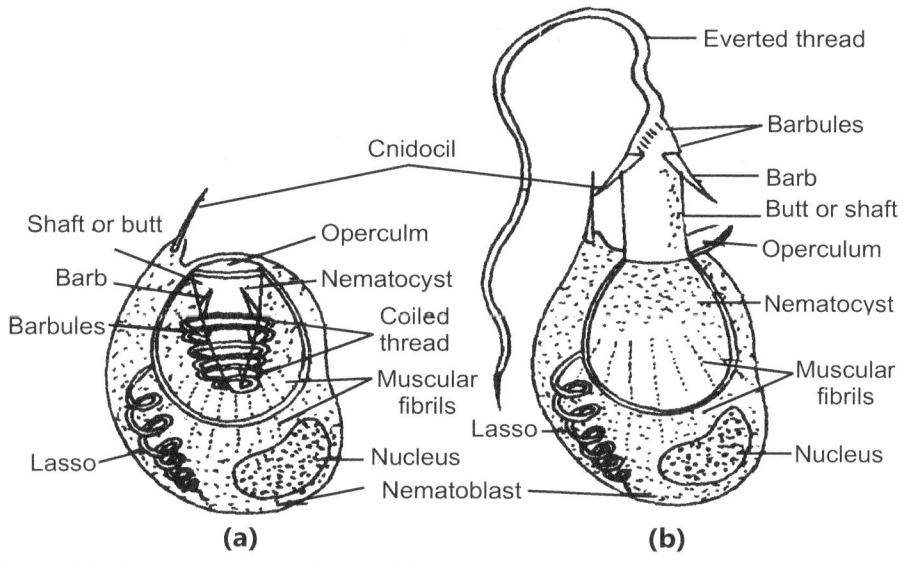

Fig. 2.21: *Hydra*: Cnidoblast with nematocyst. (a) A cnidoblast at rest (b) A cnidoblast with nematocyst discharged

Origin of nematocysts: The nematocysts develops in the interstitial cell of the epidermis of the trunk region which is called cnidoblast cell. Then the cnidoblast with developing nematocyst migrate through the body wall or into the enteron. Then they are taken up by endoderm cells and transferred to the mesogloea through which they travel and penetrate outwards again through the body wall and reach to their ultimate position where development is completed. The cnidoblast gets fixed in the ectoderm with its base reaching the mesogloea. The cnidocil bores through cuticle and projects outside.

Types of Nematocysts: (Fig. 2.22): There are four types of nematocysts found in *Hydra*. They are:
   (i)   Penetrants or stenoteles.
   (ii) Desmonemes or volvents.
   (iii) Small glutinant or atrichous isorohizas.
   (iv) Large glutinants or isorhizas.

1. Penetrants or stenoteles: These are largest and complex nematocysts. They have large capsule, the butt is stout with their spiral rows of spines on its distal half. The lowest spines of each row is a large stylet. The thread is long hollow tube coiled transversely with three rows of small spines. The thread opens at the tip. The penetrants are weapons of defence and offence. Their thread penetrates the body or chitinous exoskeleton of the prey and inject the poisonous fluid called hypnotoxin. The poison either anaesthetizes or paralyses the victim or kills prey outright. They are also used for obtaining food.

2. **Desmonemes or volvents:** They are small and oval in shape. There is no butt, the thread is thick with no spines and it is closed at the tip. The thread is smooth, elastic forming a single loop. When discharged they tightly coil around small projections such as the hairs or bristles of the prey. Thus prey is unable to move. They are also used for obtaining food.

3. **Small glutinants or atrichous isorhizas:** They are oval or elongate with no butts. Thread is open at tip and it has no spines. They fix the tentacles to an object when animal walks to it tentacle.

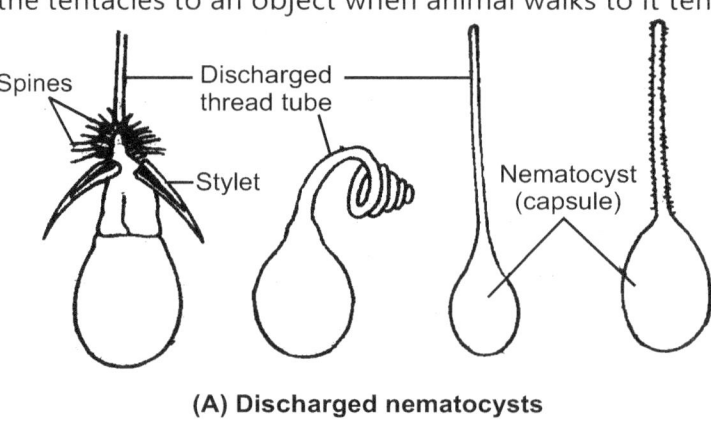

(A) Discharged nematocysts

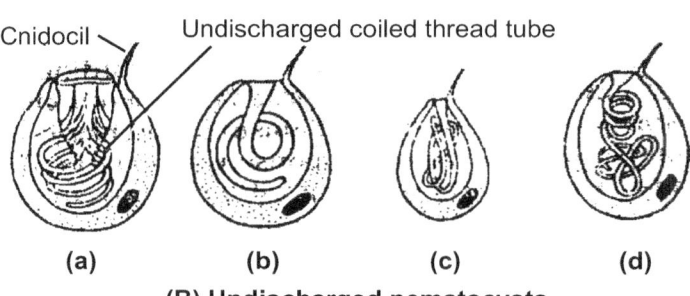

(B) Undischarged nematocysts

Fig. 2.22: *Hydra*: **Four types of nematocysts**

(A) Discharged, (B) Undischarged,
(a) Penetrant, (b) Volvent, (c) Small gluitnant, (d) Large glutinant

4. Large glutinants or holotrichous isorhiza: These nematocysts have oval capsule. The butt is narrow and thread open at the tip. The thread and butt are with small spines. The thread is long with narrow butt and forms three or four transverse coils. Their function is doubtful but they stick to the surface of the prey. The glutinants secrete a substance possibly used in locomotion by fastening the tentacles of hydra to solid object while somersaulting as well as in food capture.

Distribution of nematocysts: The nematocyts are scattered in the epidermis but are absent on the basal disc. They are abundant on the tentacles and body. Large number of all four kinds of nematocysts are present on the tentacles. The holotrichous isorhizas are present on the hypostome. Whereas stenoteles and some holotrichous isorhizas are found on the body.

Mechanism of discharge of Nematocyst: The discharge of nematocysts takes place from proper stimulation of cnidocil by food, prey or enemy. However, the exact mechanism of discharge of nematocyst is not clear. They are not under the control of nervous system, hence they are independent effectors. There are different opinions and views regarding their discharge. The cause of discharge was formerly supposed to be mechanical contact with cnidocil. But direct mechanical stimulation as by the commensal protozoans swimming near *Hydra* has no influence on the nematocysts. Some animals swimming near a *Hydra* will cause the nematocysts in the usual way when stimulated. The nematocysts separated from the body can also shoot out their thread if an adequate stimulus is applied. **Chun** (1881), **Lendenfeld** (1887) and **Murbach** (1893) supported the view based on nervous control of discharge of nematocysts.

There is another view which is recent and more advanced, supported by **Iwanzoff** (1896) and Warren (1960). According to this view nematocysts are independent effector organs and both chemical and mechanical factors are involved in mechanism of discharge. There is no nervous control, because discharge response is wholly local and never transmitted. But exact nature of discharge still remains uncertain.

For discharge of nematocysts following explanations are given:

1. There are two factors responsible for discharge of nematocysts. First, the presence of chemicals in liquid form in water and second, a mechanical contact of cnidocil and cnidoblast by prey or food animal. Thus, both chemical and tactile stimuli are present then the nematocysts are discharged.

2. There is hollow thread in the capsule of nematocyst which is gelatinous. On suitable stimulation the operculum of the nematocyst opens and water enters the capsule. The gelatinous thread is liquified and forced out like a jet to set of liquid when comes in contact with air solidifies and becomes the external thread of the nematocyst.

3. The nematocysts are present in the cnidoblast cell and it has both receptor and effector parts, which discharge the nematocyst on cnidoblast under combined influence of chemical and mechanical stimuli received by the cnidocil and transmitted to the cnidoblast. During the discharge of the nematocyst the operculum opens, water enters the capsule, the tube is turned inside out and shot out with a force, the eversion causes the spines to come to the outer surface of the tube. The thread of the nematocyst either sticks to the prey (glutinants), or coils around its bristles (volvents) or it penetrates its body (penetrants), and injects a powerful toxin which paralyses even such large animals as water flea or small worms.

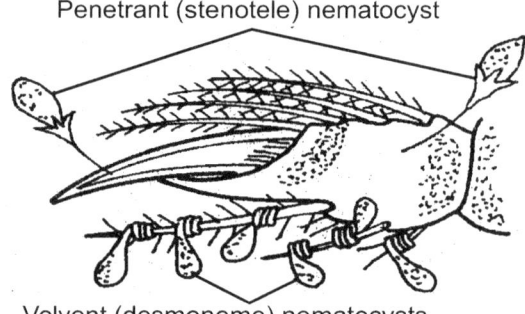

Penetrant (stenotele) nematocyst

Volvent (desmoneme) nematocysts

Fig. 2.23: Volvent nematocysts holding a small acquatic crustacean by coiling around the bristles of its leg

The thread of the nematocyst once discharged cannot withdrawn so that the discharged nematocyst cannot be used again. Such nematoblasts migrate to the gastrovascular cavity and are digested to be replaced within 48 hours by fresh nematoblast developed from the interstitial cells.

Functions of Nematocysts

(i) The nematocysts or cnidoblasts are the organs of offence and defence of *Hydra*.

(ii) They also serve in food-capture.

(iii) The nematocysts help in locomotion and anchoring with the substratum.

5. Sensory cells: (Fig. 2.24): These cells are scattered throughout the epidermis deeply situated among the epithelio-muscular cells. They are abundant on tentacles and hypostome. Sensory cells are long narrow cells with a large nucleus and one projecting flagellum or sensory hair. Their basal or inner ends are connected to fine modulated processes which join the nervous system.

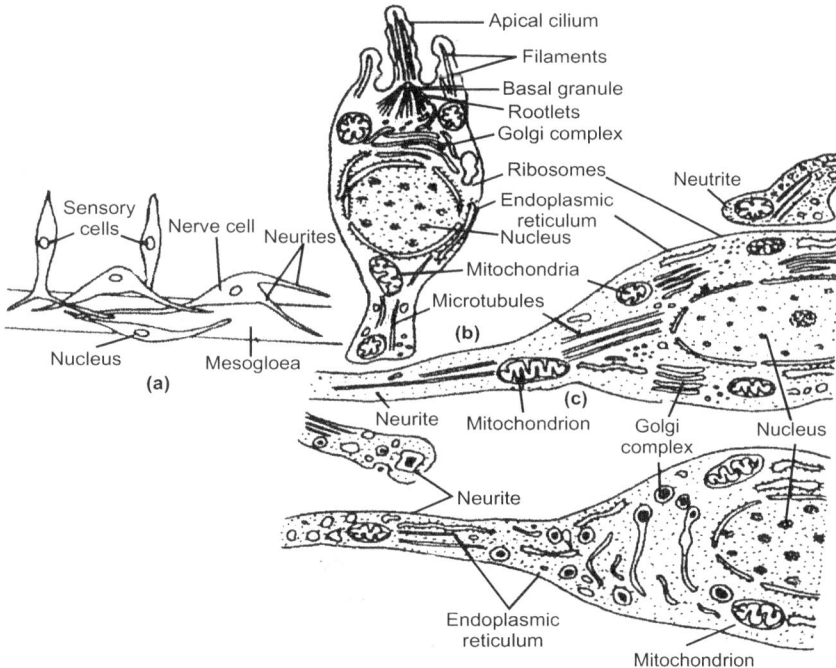

Fig. 2.24: *Hydra*. Sensory and nerve cells. (a) Under light microcope (b) Sensory cell under electron microscope; (c) Nerve or ganglion cell under electron microscope; (d) Neurosecretory cell under electron microscope.

Ultrastructure: The cell is situated perpendicular to the long axis close to the apices of epithelial cells. From the apical end of the cell modified cilium emerges. The plasma membrane of the cell forms notched surface which forms a collar and a single cilium extends from the base of the notch. The cilium contains nine peripheral and more than two central fibres. All these fibres arise from the basal body from which small rootlets extend into the cytoplasm. Typical cytoplasmic inclusions like mitochondria and small vesicles are present. Microtubules also extend into the apical collar. Golgi complex lies above the the nucleus. The basal end of the cell is situated above the ganglion cell or gives rise to a process.

Functions:

1. These cells are sensory to touch, light, temperature changes and chemicals.

2. The sensory cells act both as receptors and as a sensory neuron, i.e. cells both receive and transmit impulses.

6. Nerve cells: (Fig. 2.24). These are also called as ganglion cells and located beneath the epithelio-muscular cells just above their muscular processes. They are originated from epidermis, probably from interstitial cells. Each nerve cell has small, elongated cell body with nucleus and one or more processes, called neurites. They show resemblance with multipolar neurons of higher animals but they are very primitive because their processes are differentiated into axons and dendrites. The nerve cells remain separate and their processes do not fuse.

Ultrastructure: The electron microscope reveals that the nucleus of nerve cell is bounded by a nuclear membrane bearing pores. Nucleoli may or may not be present. Cytoplasm contain smooth and rough endoplasmic recticulum, mitochondria, Golgi complex, small and large vesicles. There are highly developed microtubules which extend long distances in the neurites. The neurites are about 10 µ in length and they contain ribosomes, small and large vesicles, mitochondria and microtubules.

7. Neurosecretory cells: (Fig. 2.24). These cells contains membranes bounded dense granules. The Neurosecretory cells are deeply situated and contain cilium that extends towards the surface. The cilium is originated from the base. There are rootlets of cilium which extend in the cytoplasm. These cells, resemble with nerve cells except presence of the membrane bound granules. The size of the granules is about 1000 to 1200 A° in diameter. The granules are also present in neurties. Mitochondria and Golgi complex are also present in the cytoplasm.

8. Germ cells: During summer, the interstitial cells undergo repeated divisions in certain restricted regions of the body of the *Hydra*. These cells form the gonads which latter differentiate either into testes or ovaries.

GASTRODERMIS

The inner layer called endoderm or gastrodermis lining the coelenteron has very much similar plan to the epidermis. This cell layer forms about two–third of the body wall and performs sensory, secretory digestive and muscular functions. The gastrodermis is mainly composed of large columnar epithelial cells. This layer has not cuticle. The gastrodermis consists of the following cells:
  (i)   Nutritive muscular cells or digestive cells.
  (ii) Interstitial cells.
  (iii) Gland cells.

1. Nutritive cells: (Fig. 2.25). These are epithelio-muscular cells, which are numerous and conspicuous forming major bulk of the gastrodermis. These cells are long and club shaped cells resting perpendicularly on the mesogloea. The base end of these cells form muscle processes but arranged tranversely inside the mesogloea. They form the circular muscles which on contraction reduces the diameter of the body. Thus, they have opposite action to that of the epidermal muscle tails. Some of them around the mouth and the bases of the tentacles act as sphincters to close off their openings. The cells are highly vacuolated and often filled with food vacuoles.

The free end of the nutritive cell usually bears two flagella and they are projecting into the gastrovascular cavity. The flagella are useful to keep liquid food in motion inside the gastrovascular cavity. Besides flagella, blunt pseudopodia like those of *Amoeba* may also extend from the cell to engulf the food particles. In green *hydra* (*Chlorohydra*) gastrodermal cells bear green alage *Zoochlorella* which give green colour to *Hydra*. The nutritive cells also secrete digestive enzymes into the coelenteron for the digestion of foods.

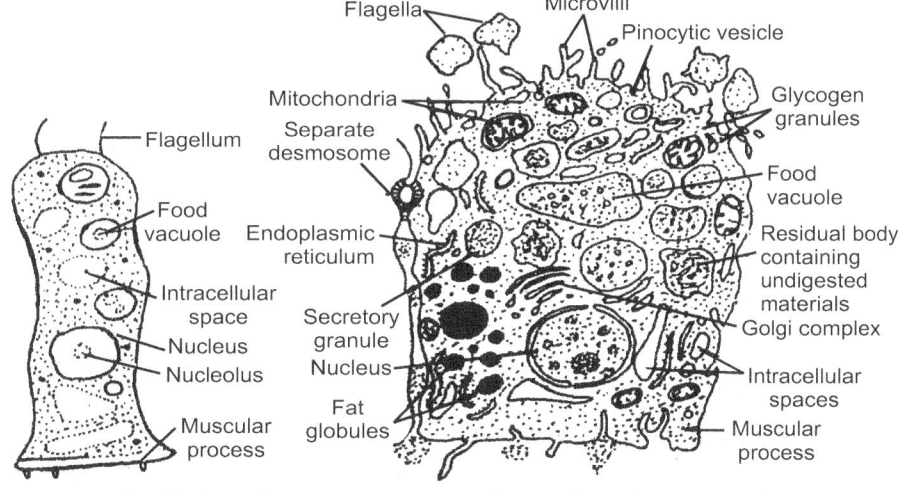

(a) Under light microscope   (b) Under electron microscope
Fig. 2.25: *Hydra.* **Nutritive muscle cell**

1. **Ultrastructure:** The nutritive cell has central or basal nucleus with nucleolus. There are large number of membrane bounded vacuoles present in the cytoplasm. The vacuoles located at the apical regior called digestive vacuoles and those present at the basal region contain undigested food material. In the cytoplasm both smooth and rough endoplasmic reticulum, free ribosomes and Golgi complex occur abundantly. In addition to these mitochondria, intracellular spaces glycogen granules and liquid droplets are present in the cytoplasm. The apical border or the free end of the cell shows varying lengths of microvilli projecting in the digestive cavity. There are two flagella which show the typical structure having 9 + 2 fibres. There are pinocytotic invaginations located at the bases of microvilli. The pinocytotic channels and separate desmosome junctions between adjacent cells are also present.

The nutritive cells of the tentacles are pyramidal in shape and contain a large intracellular space surrounded by cytoplasm. The cytoplasm contains lipid droplets and food vacuoles. The shape of the digestive cells of hypostome is irregular. Whereas cells of peduncle are small and cuboidal. The digestive cells of the base are large, cuboidal with large intracellular spaces. There cells are with few microvilli and pinocytotic vesicles but with more lipid droplets. Depending on the location the digestive cells perform different functions. The digestive cells of stomach, budding and hypostome regions perform ingestion and digestion. The peduncle and tentacle cells carry out storage function. The basal cells provide energy for mucous secretion because these cells are full of lipid droplets.

2. **Interstitial cells:** Among the bases of the nutritive cells few interstitial cells are scattered. These cells can be converted into other type of cells when the need arises. Hence these cells are called totipotent in nature.

3. **Gland cells:** (Fig. 2.26). These are club-shaped cells with broader base and projecting into the coelenteron. They are located separately between the nutritive cells. The base of these cells is narrow and tappering which extends towards the mesogloea but do reach it.

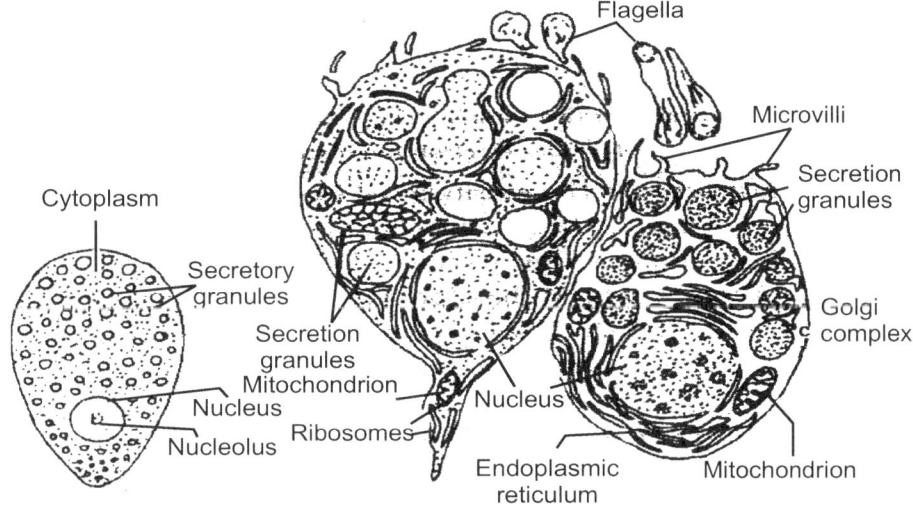

(a) Under, light micropscope (b) Under electron microscope showing different types of secretory granules

Fig. 2.26: *Hydra*. Gland cells

There are two types of gland cells namely:
1. **Mucous gland cells** which are found in the mouth of hypostome. They secrete mucus which helps in swallowing solid good.
2. **Enzymatic gland cells** are found in the stomach where they secrete different digestive enzymes useful for digestion of the food. The stalk and tentacles regions are without gland cells. Since in *Hydra* there is extracellular digestion, the gland cells discharge their secretions into the coelenteron. These cells are not under the control of nervous system but they have their independent effectors.

Ultrastructure: The gland cell has basal nucleus with nucleolus. The secretory granules, mitochondria, endoplasmic reticulum and golgi complex are present in the cytoplasm of the cell. The plasma membrane of the cell bears few microvilli and flagella. The large number of secretory granules are found around the apical region. These granules are also distinguishable histochemically into mucus and enzyme secreting types. Gland cells are numerous in hypostome, many in stomach and budding zone, they are very few in peduncle and virtually absent in the tentacles and the base.

MESOGLOEA

The mesogloea (Greek, meso = middle; glea = glue) lies between the epidermis and gastrodermis and is attached to both layers. It is a thin homogenous, gelatinous or jelly-like material. There are no fibres or cellular material in the mesogloea. It serves as a basement membrane and a place of attachment for epidermis and gastrodermis. Mesogloea forms a continuous layer which extends over both body and tentacles. It forms thicker layer in the stalk region while thin in the tentacles. Due to this arrangement basal region can tolerate great mechanical strain and gives tentacles more flexibility. Mesogloea as gives support and rigidity to the body of the hydra thus it works as a elastic skeleton.

Ultrastructure: The mesogloea layer is about 0.1 μ in thickness consisting small filaments of 100 A° thickness. The filaments are with transverse striation and they lie parallel, or obliquely, or scattered in the mesogloea randomly to the longitudinal axis of the body. There are also small dense granules of glycogen present in the mesogloea. The intercellular spaces of the epitheliomuscular and digestive cells are filled with mesogloea. The process of these cells may extend into the mesogloea; which sometimes interlocking with one another. It also contains the network of nerve fibres produced by the nerve cells of the two layers.

Gastrovascular Cavity

The transverse and longitudinal section of *Hydra* shows a central cavity in its body called coelenteron (i.e. hollow gut) which is called as gastrovascular cavity. It is also known as enteron, gut or coelenteron. Mouth opens in this cavity and there is no other opening in it. The gastrovascular cavity is continuous in the tentacles and they are also hollow. The gastrovascular cavity is the place of digestion and circulation of good.

2.15 Locomotion

Hydra remains attached to the suitable object with its basal disc in the water. Sometimes it remains stationary but also show considerable locomotion due to changes in the environment. The tentacles and body show twisting movements in response to various stimuli like light or chemicals and for the capture of good. All these movements are caused by the contraction or expansion of the

contractile muscle processes of the epitheliomuscular cells of the epidermis and gastrodermis. *Hydra* shows locomotion by several ways which are as follows:
1. Spontaneous movement
2. Looping
3. Somersaulting
4. Gliding
5. Cuttle fish like movement
6. Floating
7. Climbing
8. Swimming.

1. Spontaneous movement: (Fig. 2.28). This is the body movement which takes place at intervals of several minutes. During this movement the tentacles and body contract suddenly and rapidly becoming like a small barrel. The adverse stimulus is also responsible for sudden contraction of the body.

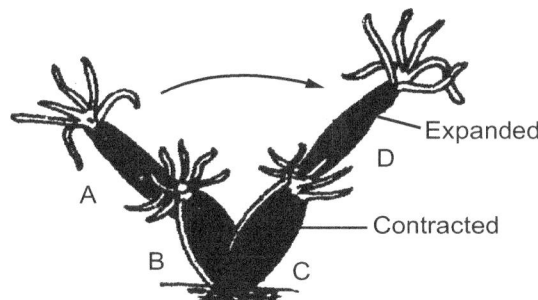

Fig. 2.27: *Hydra* **showing spontaneous changes of position**

After sometime the body and tentacles gradually extend in a new direction. This movement helps the animal for food collection from new site where more food is available. When extension of body takes place the animal becomes very long and slender. Bending of the body and tentacles also takes place due to contraction of one side and elongation of other side. This helps in the capture of prey.

2. Looping: (Fig. 2.28). *Hydra* can also move from place to place in search of food. Therefore, animal repeatedly use its base and tentacles in looping movement. It is common type of walking similar to the looping of caterpillar. During looping usually the body first extends and then bends over, so that tentacles attach to the substratum by means of the small glutinant nematocysts. It then releases the attachment of the basal disc and brings up closer the ring of tentacles and attached. The tentacles now loosen their hold, the body becomes erect and repeats the process.

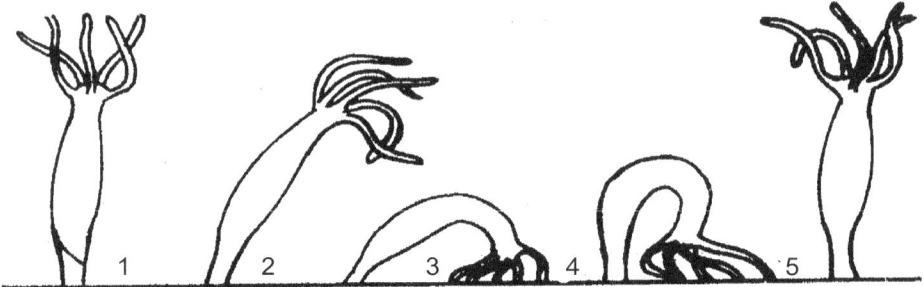

Fig. 2.28: *Hydra* showing looping movements

3. **Somersaulting** (Fig. 2.29). It is similar to the looping movement with slight modifications. *Hydra* extends its body and is bend to one side to place the tentacles on the substratum. The glutinant nematocysts assist for the fixation of tentacles. The basal disc is freed from its attachment and animal remains erect on its tentacles. After this position the body of the *Hydra* contracts strongly and becomes a small ball. Then body of *Hydra* extends and bend to place the basal disc on the substratum. The tentacles loosen their hold and the animal again assumes an upright position. These movements are repeated and animal moves from place to place.

Fig. 2.29: *Hydra* showing somersaulting movements

4. **Gliding:** This is very slow movement exhibited by the *Hydra*. Gliding movement is used by the animal in moving a short distance along a smooth surface. *Hydra* simply slides or glides slowly along its attachment by alternate contraction and expansion of basal disc.

Actually gliding takes place due to creeping amoeboid movements of the cells of the basal disc. Which project the pseudopodia like projection. In this manner considerable distance can be covered by the animal.

5. Cuttle fish like movements: (Fig. 2.30). Occasionally *Hydra* shows this type of movement in which only tentacles are used in movement. The tentacles are fixed to the substratum and pedal disc remains up. *Hydra* moves on the substratum with the help of tentacles using them as legs.

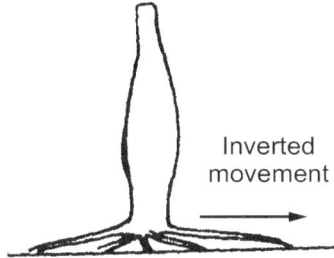

Fig. 2.30: *Hydra* **showing cuttle-fish-like movements**

6. Floating: (Fig. 2.31). For this movement sometimes *Hydra* can produce a bubble of gas which is secreted by epidermal mucus cells of the basal disc. This bubble assist the animal to float on the surface of the water and carried from one place to another by water current or waves. Sometimes *Hydra* attaches to a floating leaf or twig by its basal disc.

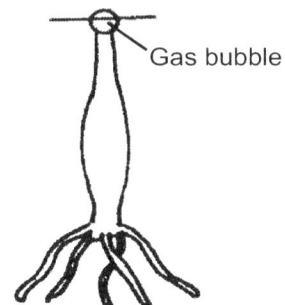

Fig. 2.31: *Hydra* **showing floating**

7. Climbing movement: (Fig. 2.32). In climbing movement again tentacles play an important role. *Hydra* can climb by attaching its tentacles to some object and then releasing the basal disc and by contracting the tentacles the body of the animal is lifted up to a new position. Among the aquatic weeds this movement is employed by *Hydra*.

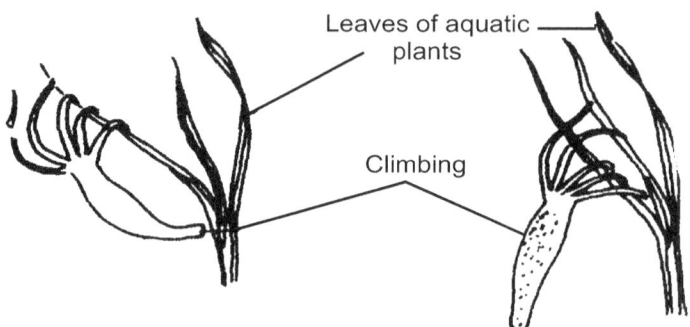

Fig. 2.32: *Hydra* showing climbing

8. Swimming: Sometimes *Hydra* frees itself from the substratum and swims in water by the undulating wave-like movements of body and tentacles.

2.16 Nutrition

Food: *Hydra* is carnivorous animal and its food consists of small crustaceans like *Cyclops* and *Daphnia*, small annelid worms and insect larvae. It may swallow prey larger than itself. Such as young fish and tadpoles.

Ingestion of good: Coelenterates are the first animals which capture the food with the help of special structures called nematocysts. When prey comes in contact with tentacles, the stenoteles nematocysts from the tentacles are projected towards the prey and they penetrate the body of it. They inject the poison and paralyse the prey.

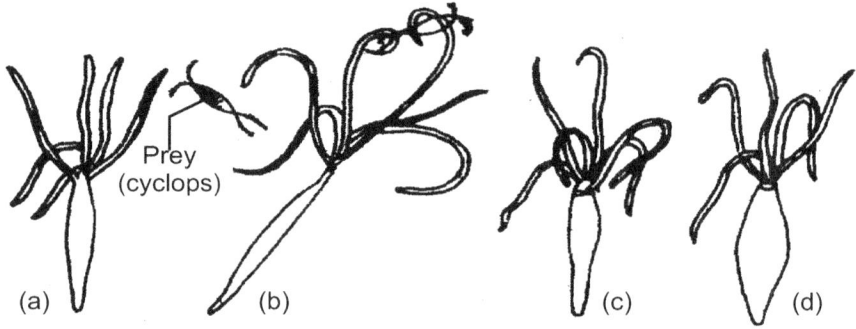

Fig. 2.33: *Hydra* capturing and ingesting the prey

The volvents coil around the bristles and appendages of the prey to hold it. The tentacles holding capture prey now contract and bend inward bringing the paralysed prey towards mucus lined mouth which opens widely to swallow the prey. The contraction of hypostome, mouth and body wall force the food into the coelenteron where digestion takes place. *Hydra* generally feeds on living prey. It feeds or engulfs only those animals which contains the chemical glutathione. This chemical is present in the tissue fluid of the animals. When body of the prey is punctured by stenoteles nematocysts of glutathione is released. Thus, this chemical is necessary to evoke feeding reaction of *Hydra*.

Digestion: At the time of swallowing the mucus secreted by the mucus gland cells of the hypostome cover the engulfed food. The gland cells of the gastrodermis secrete the digestive juice containing only trypsin like proteolytic enzymes. The food is digested in two stages. First the prey is killed by the action of digestive juices. The contraction and expansion of body of *Hydra* brings about the churning movements which help in through mixing of digestive juices with the food. The larger food particles are converted into smaller particles. The digestive enzymes then act on the disintegrated food in the coelenteron. The proteolytic enzyme trypsin partly digests the proteins into polypeptides in an alkaline medium (pH 8 to 8.2). The fully digested materials like proteins and fats are absorbed by gastrodermal cells. This type of digestion, occuring in the coelenteron outside the gatrodermal cells, is called extra cellular digestion. Some endodermal cells produce pseudopodia which engulf the semidigested food particles into the food vacuoles. The food vacuoles are first acidic, then become alkaline and the food present in the food vacuole is digested. This type of digestion which occurs within the cell is called intracellular digestion. Thus, in *Hydra* both types of digestion occur. It combines the digestive procedures of both lower (protozoa) and higher (vertebrates) forms.

The soluble products of digestion (especially glycogen) absorbed by the gastrodermal cells are distributed by the process of diffusion from cell to cell to all the parts of the body. Some endoderm cells after taking the food into food vacuoles detach from the body wall and wander about in the enteron to the parts where food is needed. *Hydra* can digest proteins, fats and some carbohydrates. Digested food is assimilated to endoderm cells and transferred to ectoderm or into the enteron from where it is distributed to all body parts. Thus, enteron cavity plays dual role of digestion as well as circulation of the food. The digested food forms of oil globules are stored in the ectoderm.

Egestion: The indigestible residues, like exoskeleton of crustaceans are egested from the mouth by the contraction of the body. The mouth, thus functions also as an anus. Egestion occurs by a sudden quit due to contraction of the body, so that the indigestible material, debris are thrown out to some distance.

2.17 Respiration and Excretion

There are no special organs for respiration and excretion in *Hydra*. The blood and blood vessels are absent. The body wall of the *Hydra* is very thin and water is easily circulated in the gastro-vascular cavity, thus most of the cells of the body remain freely exposed to the surrounding water. Therefore, the exchange of oxygen and carbon dioxide occurs through the general body surface. Nitrogenous wastes are chiefly ammonia which also diffuses through the general body surface. It is also believed that the gastrodermis of basal disc is said to accumulate some excretory matter which may be eliminated through the pore.

Osomoregulation

Since animal is aquatic the water continuously enters the body cells by endosmosis. It is finally collected into the gatrovascular cavity. From this cavity collected water is expelled out through the mouth by wave of contraction passing from the basal disc region to the hypostome region.

2.18 Nervous System and Behaviour

2.18.1 Nervous System

The nervous system of the *Hydra* is of primitive type (Fig. 2.34). The nerve cells are also primitive with two or four branching nerve fibres. These nerve fibres are simple and primitive because they do not form axon or dendrites. They are connected with the fibres of other nerve cells. When two nerves are connected to each other but there are no synapses. They form a continuous nerve net or plexus. In *Hydra* there are two nerve nets, one in connection with the ectoderm which is more highly developed. Another nerve net is present near the endoderm.

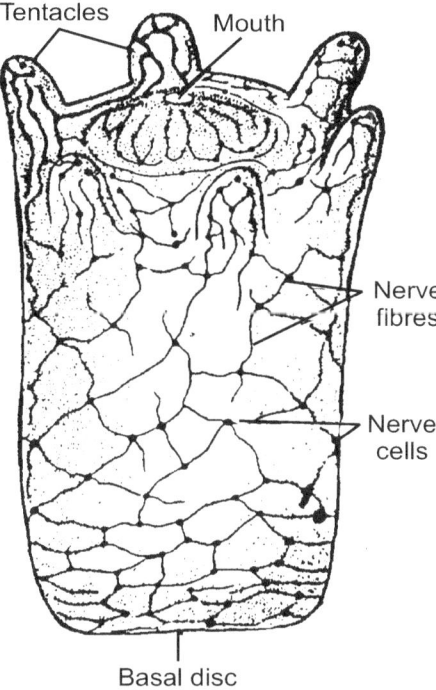

Fig. 2.34: *Hydra*. Nerve net

Thus, the nerve nets are on each side of the mesogloea. Among these two nerve networks, the ectodermal nerve net is very well developed and it is concentrated around the mouth and basal disc regions. Near the hypostome nerve fibres running circularly form a sort of loosely organised nerve ring. A similar concentration of nerve fibres occurs at the basal disc region. Both the nerve nets are connected to each other through nerve fibres. The nerve net is connected with the sensory cells on one hand and with the muscle processes of the epitheliomuscular cells on the other hand. Thus, providing a sensory neuromotor mechanism. The sensory cells are receptors for touch, light and chemicals and stimuli pass from them through the nerve nets to muscle processes which act as effectors. The nerve cells are non-polarised, it means there seems to be little directional control of nerve impulses, because there is no brain or nerve centre. Hence, the impulses are conducted in all directions through the nerve fibres and may travel all parts of the body. Thus, a stimulus in one region usually bring about a reaction in the whole animal. The nervous system of *Hydra* is diffused and works as a receptor → conductor → effector system. Between receptors and effectors the nerve cells form the conducting chains. The messages radiate in all direction from the point of stimulation but there is no evoke responses equally in all the effectors.

The sensory neuromotor system of *Hydra* provides the first and the simplest neural mechanism in the animals. Due to presence of the nerve net and sensory nerve cells make the *Hydra* a much more sensitive and well co-ordinated animal.

2.18.2 Behaviour

Hydra shows movements concerned with feeding are automatic and they are under the control of external environment. It gives response to the contact stimulus. If one tentacles is touched, the other tentacles and even body may contract. Which indicates that the stimulus is transmitted in all directions through never net. It is proved that animal gives more response at the point of stimulus and it becomes weak in more distant regions, because each nerve net offers some resistance to the conductor of impulses. The resistance is more at the site of nerve cells. *Hydra* generally prefers the shallow places instead of great depth where it gets more oxygen. It always remains horizontal with the hypostome lower than the foot. It also hangs with head down and foot up with the help of a gas bubble. It can also change the body shape becoming full extended narrow cylinder like or like a barrel or ball shaped with contraction.

The behavioural pattern of the *Hydra* depends on the physiological state of the animal. Well fed *Hydra* gives slow and slugish response to the stimulus, whereas hungry animal respond to various stimuli in the following way:

  (i) **Light:** *Hydra* gives positive response to the mild light, but it gives negative response to the intense light and dim light. It generally avoids darkness and becomes restless.

  (ii) **Temperature:** Moderate temperature is preferred by the *Hydra* for its life activities. It likes 20 to 25°C temperature. High and low temperatures are avoided by *Hydra*.

  (iii) **Chemicals:** Hydra gives negative response to toxic and injurious chemical but shows positive response to food.

  (iv) **Electricity:** *Hydra* reacts to weak constant electric currents by bending towards anode and it contracts entire body. If current is given to the basal disc the oral ends bend towards the anode and if applied to the tentacles the basal disc bends towards the anode side.

2.19 Reproduction and Development
2.19.1 Reproduction

Hydra reproduces by both asexual and sexual methods.

1. Asexual Reproduction

Hydra reproduces asexually by two methods namely, Budding and Fission.

(1) Budding (Fig. 2.35): The budding is the common method of asexual reproduction which occurs during the warmer months of the year. The well-fed and healthy *Hydra* show the budding. A bud develops as a simple evagination of the body wall. The bud is formed at some point in a definite 'budding zone' of the trunk about midway or near the base of the cylinder. The interstitial cells of the epidermis multiply rapidly forming slight swelling or protuberance. The ectodermal cells also increase in number below which endoderm cells acquire reserve food. Then both ectoderm and endodern are pushed out to form a bud which contains a diverticulum of the enteron. One or several buds may be formed at the same time. The bud at the distal end of the bud one by one tentacles are formed and also mouth is developed. According to **Kanajew** (1930) budding is initiated by the dividing epithelio-muscular and nutritive cells rather than interstitial cells. As bud elongates, a mouth opens at its free distal end and soon a ring of tentacles is formed at the base of hypostome. At this state, the bud resembles a little hydra, complete with stalk, tentacles and mouth. Its gastrovascular cavity remains basally continuous with that of the other *Hydra* to obtain nourishment. The fully grown bud is constricted at the base and separates itself complete from the mother *Hydra*. The new *Hydra* after separtaion migrates towards the surface of water for dispersal. The new inidividual gets fixed by its basal disc so that it becomes a solitary individual and begins its independent life. Budding generally occur during the summer months when food is ample in water.

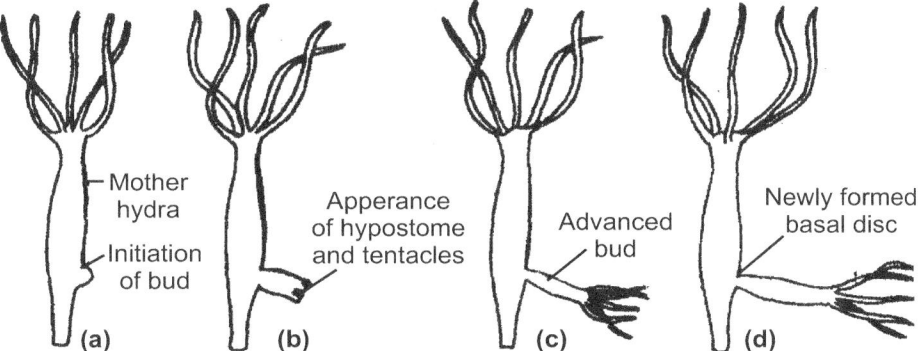

Fig. 2.35: Hydra. Bud formation. A - After 3 hours, B - After 24 hours, C - After 48 hours, D - After 72 hours, (After Ganguly, et. al.)

2. Fission: Fission is not the normal or regular method of reproduction in *Hydra*. Longitudinal and transverse fissions have been reported as the mean of reproduction in *Hydra*. It usually follow accidental breakdown or for regaining normal shape from some a typical condition such as abnormal regeneration or presence of buds. When an individual with two head or two pedal discs or fully grown bud then it undergoes longitudinal fission forming two separate individuals.

2. **Sexual Reproduction**

Hydra also reproduces sexually by the fusion of gametes. Actually sexual reproduction occurs during unfavourable conditions like excessive high and low temperatures of the water or due to increase in the amount of free carbon dioxide in the surrounding water where *Hydra* lives. Sexual reproduction is rare and seasonal in *Hydra* and it begins with the development of temporary structures called gonads during autumn. The gonads are not true gonads are formed temporarily due to the repeated proliferation of the interstitial cells of the epidermis which form bulgings on the body wall. The bulgings of gonads are different from those of buds in which there is no involvement of mesogloea and gastrodermis in gonad formation. Most of the species of *Hydra* are dioecious i.e. sexes are separate. The individual bears either male or female gonads. For example: *H. oligactis* is dioecious or unisexual. The male in smaller in size with one to eight testes, whereas female is larger in size with one or two ovaries. But some species, for example, *H. vividissima* are bisexual or monoecious or hermaphrodite, i.e. male and female gonads occur in the same individual. Usually testes develop towards the distal part of the body, while ovaries develop towards the proximal part of the body. Even in the hermaphrodite species, self fertilization is avoided because the spermatozoa and ova mature at different times. As a rule, the testes mature earlier than the ovaries.

Testes and Spermatogenesis: (Fig. 2.36). The testes produce spermatozoa and they are usually formed in the upper part of the body near hypostome. A testis is slight conical and it is easily recognisable from the spherical ovary. Each testis is formed by the interstitial cells of the epidermis which multiply rapidly to increase in number and finally push out the other epidermal cells and form the bulging or swelling. The testes are rounded or spherical in shape in dioecious forms whereas they show blunt or conical shape in monoecious forms. After formation of testes the interstitial cells play a role of sperm mother cell or spermatogonia. They undergo the process of spermatogenesis. They divide to form secondary spermatogonia which develop into spermatocytes. The spermatocyte undergo two maturation divisions, one being reduction division to form spermatids.

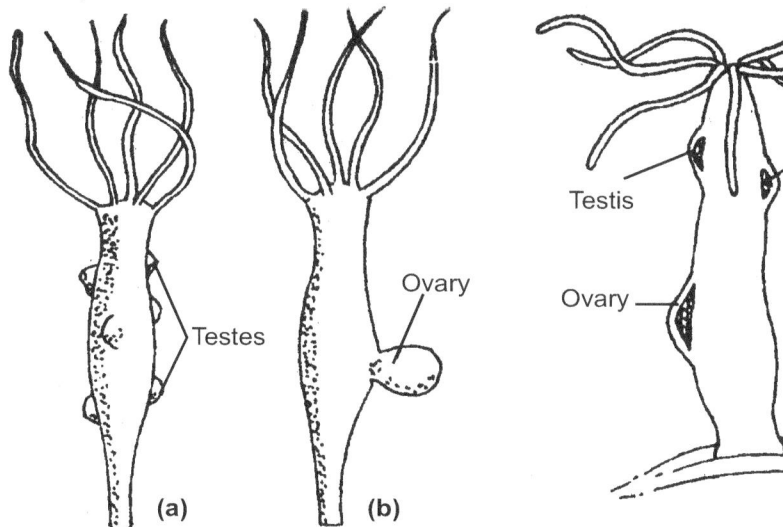

Hydra. (a) Male, (b) Female

(c) *Hydra viridissima*
A monoecious form showing male and female reproductive organs

Fig. 2.36

The spermatids undergo differentiation and are transformed into spermatozoa. A mature spermatozoon consists of three parts, a swollen head containing the nucleus, a narrow middle piece or body containing the centriole and a long, slender, vibratile tail. Each spermatozoon is haploid male gamete with 15 chromosomes in *H. oligactis*. The large number of spermatozoa are formed in the testis which exert pressure on testis, its wall ruptures and large number of spermatozoa are released in the surrounding water. They remain viable for 1 or 2 days only.

2. Ovary and Oogenesis: (Fig. 2.37). The interstitial cells also play an important role in the development of ovary like testis. The ovaries are formed towards the lower end of the body and they are generally singly. However, in *H. oligactis* about 8 ovaries are observed. The interstitial cells multiply forming the germ mother cells or oogonia. But later on, only one Oogonium which is centrally located becomes larger and is called oocyte. The remaining oogonia are used for nourishment and formation of the reserve food material called yolk. The oocyte is amoeboid in shape with large nucleus. The oocyte undergoes two maturation divisions in which one is reduction division to form a large yolk lade ovum and two polar bodies. In case of *H. oligactis* the ovum is haploid containing 15 chromosomes. Since ovum is large, yolk laden, it occupies major space inside the ovary. One ovary usually contains a single ovum but in some cases (*H. vividis*) or even, move *(H. dioecia)* are present. Because of large size of ovum, the epidermal wall bursts and freely exposing the ovum to water. The ovum is not released but remains attached to the parent by a broad base. A gelatinious protective sheath is secreted by the ovum around itself.

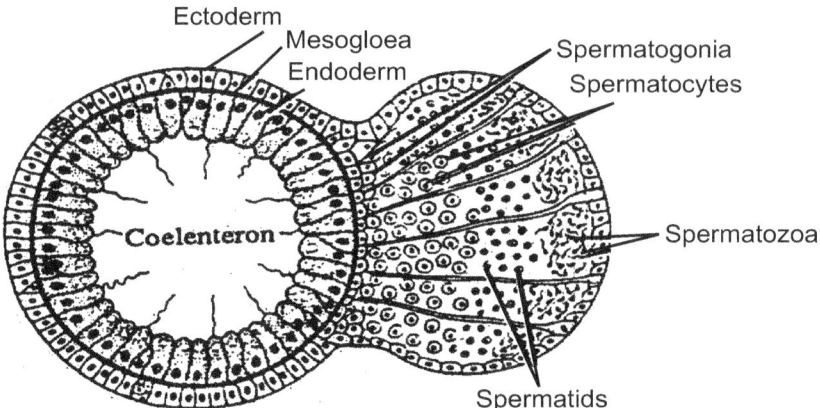

Fig. 2.37: *Hydra*. T.S. through testis showing stages of spermatogenesis

Fertilization: Different species of *Hydra* show the cross fertilization which occurs as a rule. To avoid self fertilization, even in hermaphrodite animal, the testes mature earlier than ovaries. This is called protandrous condition. However, fertilization takes place when mature sperms discharged from the a testis swim about in water and approach randomly to the naked ovum surrounded in the gelatinuous sheath. Several sperms may penetrate the gelatinuous covering but only one enters the ovum and fuses with it completely to form the zygote. This process is called fertilization. The zygote which is formed by fusion of male and female gametes contain diploid number of chromosomes i.e. 30 chromosomes. The process of fertilization takes place effectively only when the sperm reaches the ovum within its viable condition. The ovum remains viable for two hours from its being exposed to naked otherwise it perishes.

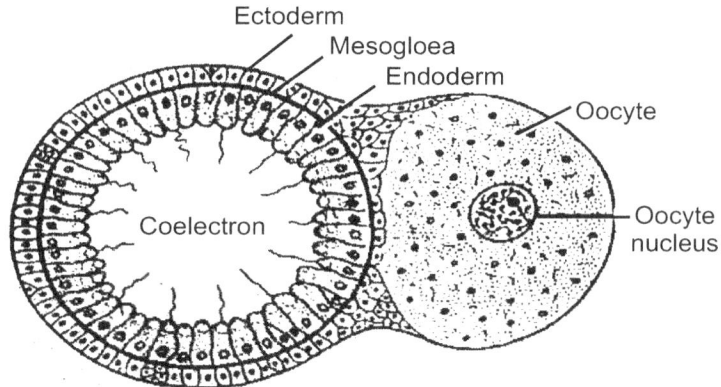

Fig. 2.38: *Hydra*. T.S. through ovary showing mature ovum

2.19.2 Development

The development begins soon after fertilization, while zygote is still attached to the parent body. The zygote undergoes total and equal clevage i.e. holoblastic to form a hollow ball of cells. The cells formed during cleavage are called blastomers which form a single layered embryo with a central cavity called blastocoel. At this stage the embryo is called blastula.

The cells of blastula divide rapidly and some of the cells delaminate into the blastocoel to completely obliterate it. Now at this stage the embryo is called gastrula which forms outer layer called ectoderm and inner layer called endoderm. The blastocoel of the blastula is completely filled by cells so that the hollow blastula is converted into a solid gastrula.

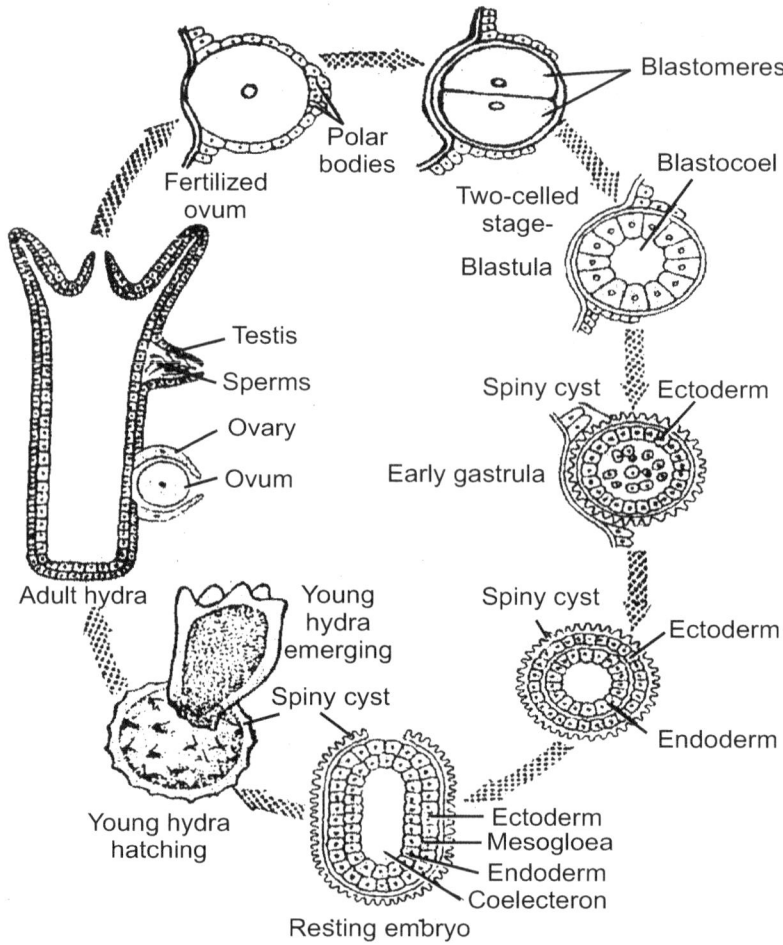

Fig. 2.39: *Hydra*. Stages in development and hatching

The solid gastrula is neither ciliated nor free swimming because it is still attached to the parent body. This is called stereogastrula which represents the planula stage of *Hydra*. Soon a new cavity called gastrocoel or archenteron, appears in the central solid mass of endodermal cells. Meanwhile, the ectodermal layer of the embryo soon secretes some secretion which hardens to form a protective covering called shell or cyst or theca around the gastrula. The theca is two layered, outer layer is thick, horny or chitinoid and spiny while the inner layer is a thin gelatinuous membrane. In case of *H. oligactics* the theca is smoth or spiny and it may be oval or round in shape. At this stage, the embryo gets detached from the parent body and settles at the bottom and remains dormant till the favourable environmental conditions return. The embryo may adhere to with its spines to the solid object or to aquatic plants by its sticky gelatinuous coat.

Hatching: Under unfavourable conditions the embryo remains dormant and unchanged for several weeks until the next spring. The embryo is tolerent to drying and freezing. This resting stage is also useful for disperal, as it can be carried by currents or by wind or by animals with their feet to other ponds where water is present.

After the approach of favourable conditions of water and warmth the embryo again becomes active and development starts. The ectodermal cells get arranged into a layer beneath the ectodermal layer and thus, a new cavity called coelenteron or gastro-vascular cavity appears. Interstitial cells arise in the ectoderm and mesoglea is secreted in between ectoderm and endoderm. The embryo elongates, the two germ layers i.e. ectoderm and endoderm give rise to their diferent derivatives like a circlet of tentacles, hypostome and mouth. Thus in theca a young *Hydra* is formed.

As the embryo increases in size theca thus becomes soft and ruptures to release young *Hydra* which fixes itself by its pedal disc and grows into an adult. There is no free swimming larval stage in the development of *Hydra* because embryo directly hatches out into the adult directly without any metamorphosis.

2.20 Regeneration

Regeneration may be defined as the ability of certain animals to restore or replace the lost or damaged parts of their bodies. *Hydra* shows this remarkable power of generation. Regeneration (Fig. 2.40) usually occurs naturally after an accident but it can be induced artificially by mutation. **Trembley** (1744) first reported the power of regeneration in *Hydra*. He demonstrated that an individual *Hydra* can be cut into several pieces and each will regenerate the lost part, developing a whole new individual. The parts usually retain their original polarity, with oval ends developing tentacles and aboral ends, basal discs.

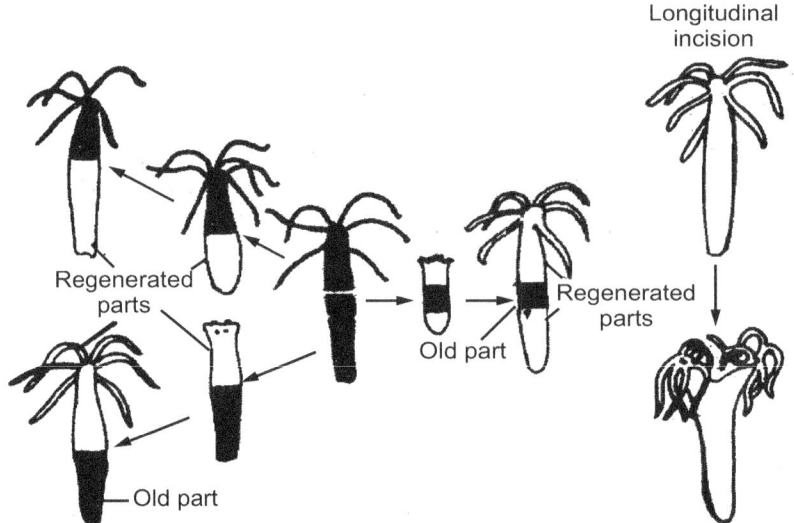

Fig. 2.40: *Hydra*. **Diagrams to show the processes of regeneration**

He demonstrated different experiments of regeneration in *Hydra*. In one experiment parts of two different individuals of different species, if brought together and grafted together in various arrangements. It was observed that the germ layers do not show mixing. The ectoderm will fuse with the ectoderm and gastrodermis with the gastrodermis.

In another interesting experiment **Trembley** showed that if head end of the *Hydra* is split into two parts by longitudinal cut and two parts are kept separted which form Y-shaped *Hydra* or two headed individual with two mouths and two sets of tentacles. (Fig. 2.41). Each head of this individual may be again split in a similar manner. In this way, **Trembley** produced seven headed *Hydra*.

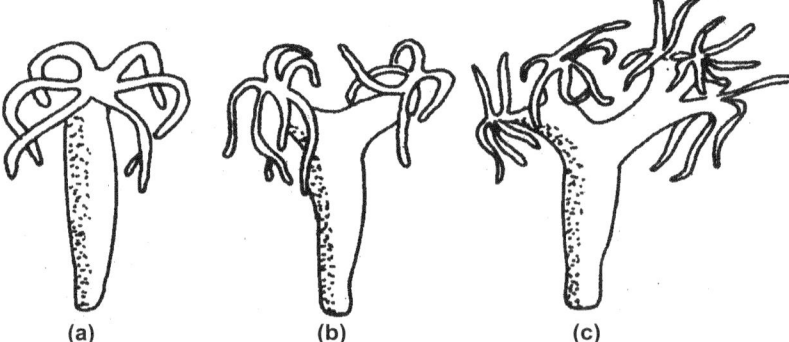

Fig. 2.41: *Hydra* **showing the formation of multihead specimen by regeneration. A - Single head Hydra; B - Two headed Hydra, C - Four headed *Hydra***

In a classic experiment, he turned *Hydra* inside out by pushing a knotted thread through the mouth occasionally, even in nature a *Hydra* becomes turned inside out. In laboratory this can be achieved mechanically or by overdoses of glutathione. After this reversal according to **Trembley**, within a short period the gastrodermal cells migrated to inside and epidermal cells to outside of the mesogloea. But recent studies in this connection revealed that this phenomenon does not occur. Generally *Hydra* turns itself right side again and if it is not possible, then the layers switch location by migration of cells through mesogloea.

Immortality of *Hydra*

According to Brien (1955) and other *Hydra* is at least potentially immortal. *Hydra* shows a growth zone just below the base of tentacles (Fig. 2.42). In the growth zone the interstitial cells are active and they give rise to new body cells of all types. As these new cells are formed the original cells are pushed towards the end of the tentacles or towards the basal disc region where old cells are shed. In this manner all the old cells are renewed once in about 45 days. This cell renewal process is continuous indefinitely. Experimentally, it is proved that if the growth zone of *Hydra* is destroyed or damaged by X-rays, the *Hydra* survives only for few days.

Symbiosis in *Hydra*

Hydra exhibits an interesting association between a plant and animal called symbiosis. Symbiosis is an association of two different species of individual in which both the partners are benefited. The green *Hydra chlorohydra viridissma* shows a classic example of symbiosis. The gastrodermal nutritive cells of this *Hydra* contain unicellular green algae *Chlorella* called *Zoochlorella* in the form of small, rounded green bodies. The algae are passed from one generation of *Hydra* to the next through the eggs. The algae multiple by binary fission and their green pigment is chlorophyll. The chlorohydra cannot separated from its *zoochlorella* because they are mutually benefited. The algae gets shelter and protection and also at the sametime gets CO_2 from respiration of *Hydra*. It also gets nitrogenous substances from its excretory wastes. *Hydra* gets oxygen and carbohydrate food material from algae due to its photosynthetic activity. Algae also synthesize proteins by combination of carbohydrates and nitrogen.

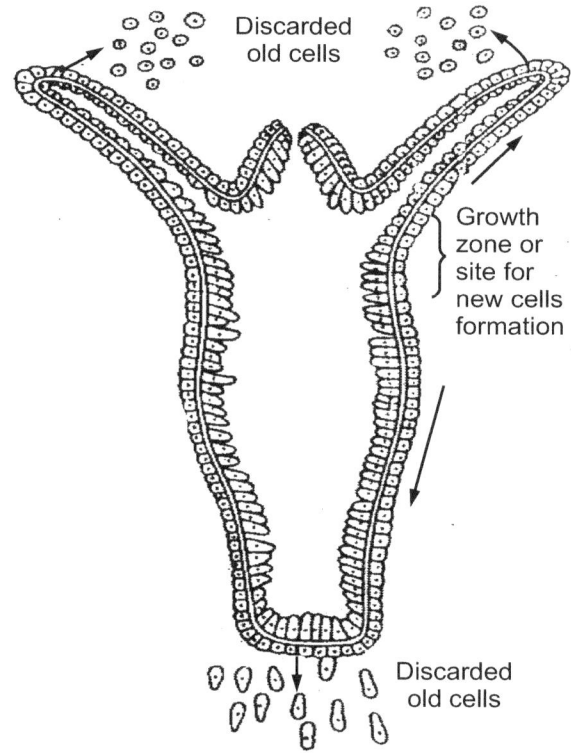

Fig. 2.42: *Hydra*. Diagram to show cell replacement

The dead or dying algae cells also form food for *hydra*. Thus, the association between the algae and *Hydra* represents partnership in which both are mutually benefitted. Such an association is called symbiosis or mutualism in which both the species get benefit from each other. In this association one individual in which other lives called host and symbiont respectively. Similarly, the yellowish or brownish algae *Zooxanthellae* live in the gastrodermal cells of the brown *Hydra. Pelmatohydra oligactis*.

Physiological Division of Labour

The primitive multicellular animals show physiological division of labour like metazoa and human society. In human society we see highly specialised people like carpenter, blacksmith, potter, farmer, doctor, engineer etc. perform different function for the society. Likewise in multicellular animals different specialised cells are present which perform that type of function for the animal. In lower metazoa similar cells performing similar functions from tissue, while in higher metazoa similar tissues together form organ and organs performing similar functions form systems. The specialised organs, or cells do the job efficiently. This is called physiological division of labour in which different cell types are specialised structurally and physiologically to perform different functions. The Coelenterates exhibit this phenomenon very well. *Hydra* is primitive form of coelenterates but still ectoderm of *Hydra* is protective, muscular and sensory in function. Nematocysts are useful for defence and for obtaining food. The ectoderm of basal disc is glandular useful for fixation of animal to the substratum. The cells also forms gas bubble for floating. The endoderm also peforms different functions like digestion, secretion. The interstitial cells are useful for replacement of ectodermal and endodermal cells. The coelenteron or gastrovascular cavity carries the function of digestion and circulation. Mouth is for both ingestion of food and egestion of indigested food. The tentacles help in obtaining food and locomotion. *Hydra* shows all division of labour and it is possible in *Hydra* because it shows beginning of differentiation of its parts. Thus it can be said that the physiological division of labour is correlated with the morphological differentiation of structure.

Review Questions

1. Give an account of histological structure of the body wall of *Hydra*.
2. Describe locomotion in *Hydra*.
3. Give an account of food and feeding and nutrition in *Hydra*.
4. Give an account of ectodermal cells found in *Hydra*.
5. Describe different types of endodermal cells in *Hydra*.
6. Describe the structure of cnidoblast of *Hydra* and give detail account and function of nematocysts.
7. Give an account of reproduction in *Hydra*.
8. What do you mean by physiological division of labour ? Explain it with reference to *Hydra*.

9. Write short notes on:
   (i) Epitheliomuscular cell
   (ii) Nematocysts
   (iii) Locomotion
   (iv) Behaviour
   (v) Budding
   (vi) Regeneration in Hydra.
   (vii) Immortality of Hydra.
   (viii) Mesogloea
10. Draw labelled diagrams only
   (i) T.S of *Hydra*
   (ii) L.S. of *Hydra*
   (iii) Electron structure of epitheliomuscular cell.
   (iv) Electron structure of cnidoblast.

Chapter 3...

Platyhelminthes and Nemathelminthes

(A) PLATYHELMINTHES - TAPEWORM - *TAENIA SOLIUM*

- 3.1 Systematic Position, Habit and Habitat
- 3.2 Morphology
- 3.3 Reproductive System
  - 3.3.1 Male Reproductive System
  - 3.3.2 Female Reproductive System
  - 3.3.3 Fertilization
  - 3.3.4 Life Cycle
- 3.4 Pathogenecity and Treatment
- 3.5 Parasitic Adaptations

Cestodes are highly specialised flatworms. They are commonly called as '*tapeworms*' because of their long, flat, ribbon-like form. These endoparasites show excellent adaptations to the parasitic mode of life and therefore various changes are exhibited in their structure. These animals are headless and limbless with no coelom, no circulatory system, no skeleton, no excretory system and food canal. The pork tapeworm, *Taenia solium*, a common intestinal parasite of man is described here.

3.1 Systematic Position, Habit and Habitat
3.1.1 Systematic Position

Phylum   – Platyhelminthes
Class   – Cestoda
Sub-class – Eucestoda
Order   – Taenioidea or Cyclophyllidea
Family   – Taenidae
Genus   – *Taenia*
Species – *solium, saginata (Beef tapeworm)*

Geographical Distribution:

Taenia solium is cosmopolitan in distribution. It is commonly found at the places where raw and inadequately cooked pork is consumed by man. Its infection is abundant in Yugoslavia, Czechoslovakia, other Slavic countries, Germany and India.

3.1.2 Habits and Habitat

The adult worms are commonly found in the intestine of man, who is the final host. The worn lies attached to the intestinal mucosa by means of head or scolex and it soaks up the food digested by its host. The larval stages are commonly found in the pig and ox.

3.2 Morphology

The body of *T. solium* is long, dorso-ventrally flattened and ribbon or tape-like, hence it is called *tapeworm*. It measures about 2 to 3 metres in length. The body of the animal is extremely narrow anteriorly and gradually it becomes broader posteriorly. The body of the animal is divisible into three regions:

(a) *Scolex* or *head*, (b) *Neck*, (c) *Strobila*.

(a) Scolex or head: The anterior end of the body possesses a small, globular knob-like head or scolex. It bears four circular suckers and they are adhesive organs. There is conical part situated anteriorly known as *rostellum*. The rostellum is armed with a double circle of alternating large and small hooks. In each circle, 28 to 30 curved chitinous and outward pointing hooks are present. Each hook consists of three parts: *blade, handle* and *base*. The scolex is useful for attachment to the intestine of host. The hooks and suckers of scolex help in attachment. However, in case of beef tapeworm (*T. saginata*) rostellum and hooks are absent.

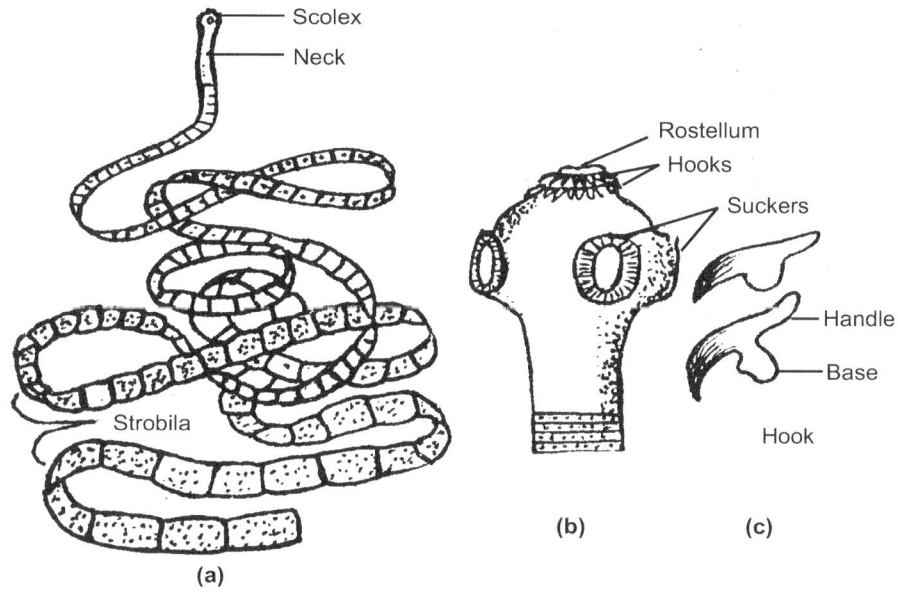

Fig. 3.1: (a) *Taenia solium* entire, (b) The scolex magnified, (c) Hooks

(b) Neck: Behind the scolex, narrow, flattened and unsegmented region is called *neck*. This is also called as area of segmentation or proliferation. New segments or proglottids are formed from neck region by asexual transverse division or budding.

(c) Strobila: It is the flattened, ribbon-like body after the neck region. The strobila is distinctly segmented, consists of a linear series of segments called *proglottids*. An adult tapeworm may contain 800 to 1000 proglottids. Since the proglottids are budded off from neck, hence those at the anterior end are youngest and at the posterior end are the oldest.

Tapeworm is hermaphrodite animal, i.e. male and female reproductive organs are present in the same individual. A proglottid is a unit part of the body enclosing a complete set of male and female organs. Each proglottid is independent and self-contained units, having a full set of sex organs and portion of excretory and nervous systems. There is no coelomic cavity and digestive system. The reproductive system is well developed and male reproductive organs develop before the female organs.

Depending on the maturity of the reproductive organs, there are three types of proglottids:

1. **Immature:** These are youngest proglottids in which sex organs are not differentiated. They are about 200 in number and broader than long.

2. **Mature:** They attain sexual maturity and produce eggs. These are found in the middle region of the body. Male and female reproductive organs are well developed. These proglottids are usually squarish or rectangular and are enclosed by a layer of tegument. Towards each lateral margin of proglottid contains longitudinal nerve and longitudinal excretory canal. In each segment, a transverse excretory canal is also present towards the posterior part of the segment.

3. **Gravid or ripe:** These proglottids are towards the posterior end containing branched uterus with full of fertilized eggs. Other organs are degenerated. These segments are longer than broad. They are regularly cut off from posterior end of strobila and this phenomenon is known as *apolysis*. They are passed to the outside with the faeces of host during defaecation.

3.3 Reproductive System

T. solium is a hermaphrodite animal. Both male and female reproductive organs are present in each mature segment.

3.3.1 Male Reproductive System

Male reproductive system consists of *testes, vasa efferentia, vas deferens* and *cirrus*. The male reproductive organs are lying on the dorsal surface of the animal.

1. **Testes:** Testes are small, follicular or round bodies and are multiple in number. Their number is about 15 to 200 and are scattered in the parenchymatous tissue of the proglottid. Testes form two lateral zones. They are degenerated in the gravid segments.

2. **Vasa efferentia:** These are the minute capillary-like ducts originating from the follicles of the testes, which join together and form common duct vas deferens.

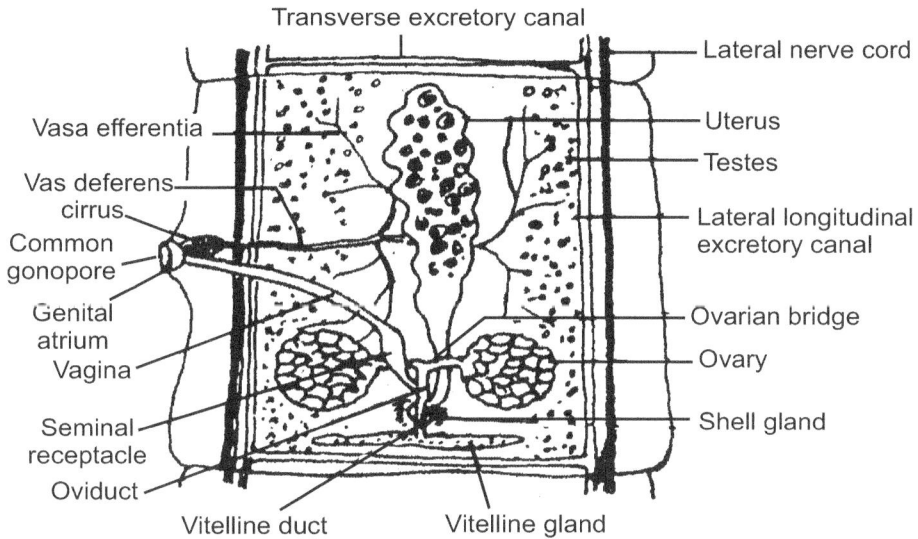

Fig. 3.2: *T. Solium*, Reproductive organs in a mature proglottid

3. Vas deferens: It is broad, thick and convoluted tubule which runs transversely and joins the laterally placed *genital atrium*.

4. Cirrus sac: The vas deferens at the terminal end becomes muscular and it forms cirrus sac.

The cirrus sac contains retractile, muscular *penis* or cirrus which is armed with spines, bristles or hooks and is irreversible through the male genital aperture into the common cup-like *genital atrium*.

5. Genital atrium: It opens outside through a common *gonopore* or *genital pore*.

3.3.2 Female Reproductive System

Female reproductive system lies on the ventral surface and consists of a pair of *ovaries, oviduct, ootype, vagina, uterus*, and *vitelline gland*.

1. Ovaries: There are a pair of ovaries situated towards posterior border of the proglottid. Both the ovaries are dorsoventrally flattened, of equal shape and size and they are connected together by means of *isthmus*. It is believed that both the ovaries are two lobes of single ovary.

2. Oviduct: It is single duct, originates from the middle of isthmus and joins with ootype. Ovary discharges eggs in oviduct.

3. **Ootype:** It is a small rounded chamber formed by the union of oviduct, uterus and vitelline duct. Ootype is surrounded by numerous unicellular glands, known as *Mehli's glands* or *Shell glands*.

4. **Vagina:** It is a narrow tube begins from female genital pore into the genital atrium. Towards the inner end before opening into the oviduct, it dilates to form the seminal receptacle in which sperms received from the other tapeworm are stored. The narrow region of vaginal duct between seminal receptacle and the oviduct is known as *spermatic duct* or *fertilization duct*. The vagina performs the function of receiving the sperms.

5. **Uterus:** It is wide, long and straight tube arising from the ootype. It lies anteriorly in the middle of the proglottid and its terminal end is blind. The uterus is simple and unbranched in mature proglottid, whereas, it is more developed and branched in gravid proglottid and is filled with fertilized eggs.

6. **Vitelline gland:** It is compact mass lying posterior to the ovaries. It contains numerous follicles which secrete yolk cells. There is a single median *vitelline duct* from the gland joins the ootype.

The yolk cells enclose the fertilized eggs inside ootype and also form the egg shell.

3.3.3 Fertilization

In the tapeworm fertilization is of two types. If sperms fertilize the eggs of same proglottid, it is called *self-fertilization*. Each proglottid is self-fertilizing during which the *penis* or *cirrus* is inserted into the vagina of the same proglottid. But in the intestine the worm remains folded back on itself so that copulation between different proglottids of the same tapeworm is also common and it is known as *cross-fertilization*. However, cross-fertilization between two different worms is impossible.

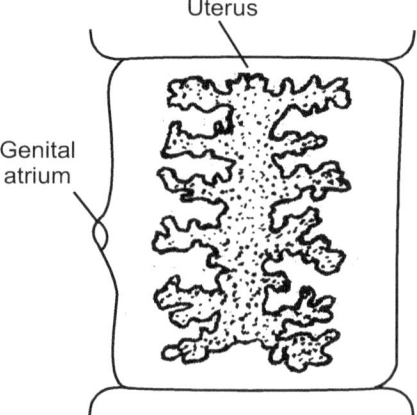

Fig. 3.3: Gravid proglottid

The sperms received by vagina are stored in the seminal receptacle. From there sperms enter the fertilization duct and fertilize the eggs. The fertilized eggs pass through ootype, where they are surrounded by yolk cells, secreted by vitelline glands. The cell becomes enclosed in a thin egg shell. The egg shell is formed by material exuded by the yolk cell. They are called capsules which pass into uterus. Large number of capsules enter the uterus, hence it enlarges forming 7 to 10 lateral branches.

3.3.4 Life-Cycle

T. solium passes its life-cycle in two hosts:
1. **The definitive host:** Man, harbours the adult worm.
2. **The intermediate host:** Pig, harbours the larval stage. (In case of *T. saginata* i.e. beef tapeworm, cattle, cow or buffalo harbours the larval stage.)

Life-cycle in Man:

The adult worm lives in the small intestine of man. The eggs or gravid segments are passed out with the faeces on the ground. By this time the embryo has reached the hexacanth stage.

Development of Hexacanth:

The development starts when egg or zygote is in uterus. The first cleavage divides the zygote into two unequal cells, a larger *megamere* and smaller *embryonic cell*. The megamere further undergoes cleavage forming several similar megamere. The embryonic cell divides repeatedly and forms larger outer *mesomeres* and smaller inner *micromeres*. The vitelline cell transfers its yolk to the megameres. The *micromeres repeatedly divide* to form a compact solid ball called *morula*. The mesomeres secrete a thick hard chitinous case or cyst called *embryophore* surrounding the morula. The micromeres form the the embryo proper. The morula at the morphiologically posterior end, develops three pairs of chitinous hooks. The embryo with 6 hooks is called as *hexacanth embryo*. The whole structure, i.e. embryo, surrounding membranes is called as *onchosphere*. Upto this stage, the embryo remains in the uterus and the proglottids become gravid.

The gravid proglottids break off in small groups, 4 or 5 at a time and pass out with the human faeces. The proglottids remain alive on the ground for some time and show slight movements, but later they die and disintegrate and releasing the onchospheres. They remain alive for longer period. Thousands of onchospheres are now scattered by wind and may settle on grass and vegetables. They are now ready to infect the intermediate host or pig (or cattle) in which further development takes place.

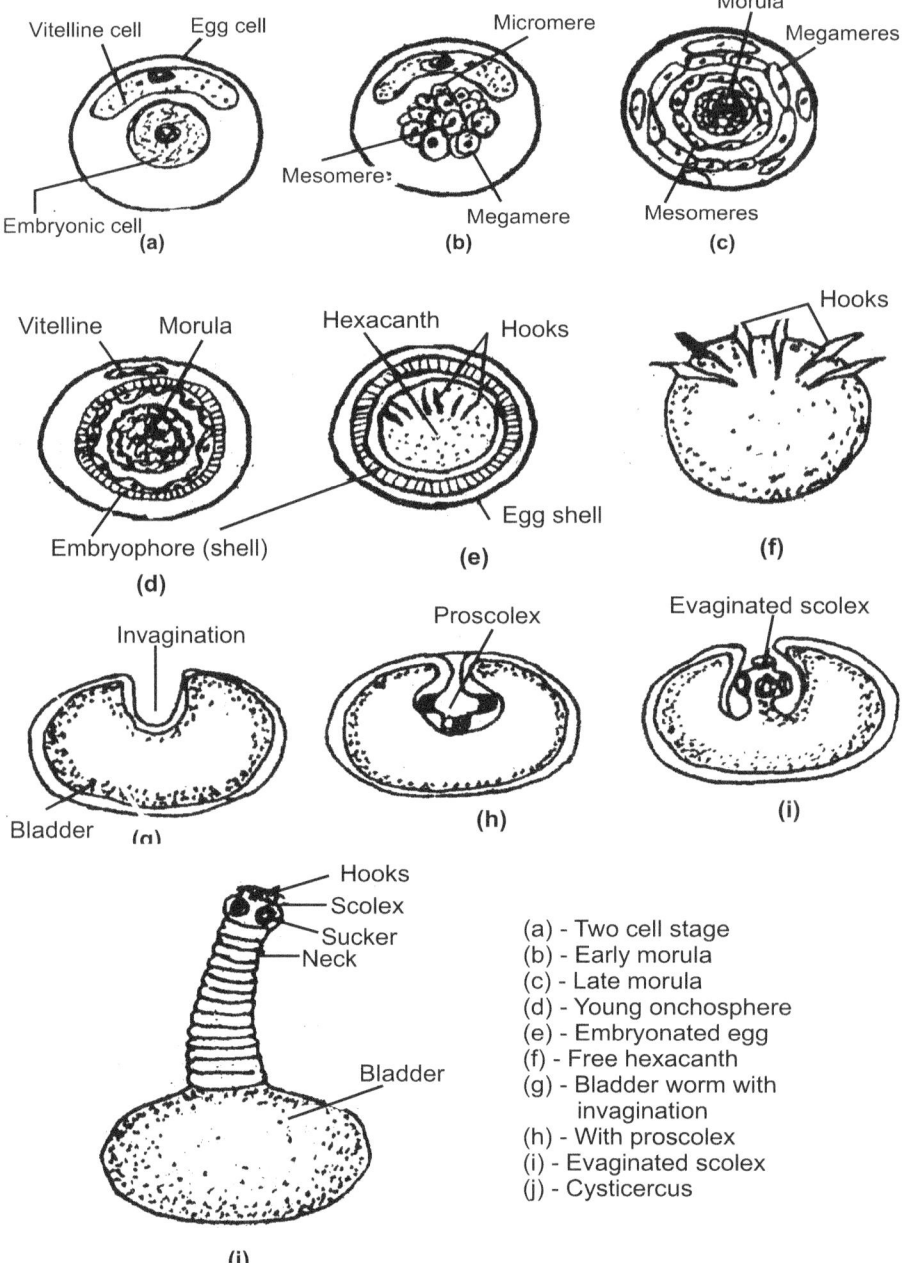

Fig. 3.4: *T. solium* Stages of Development

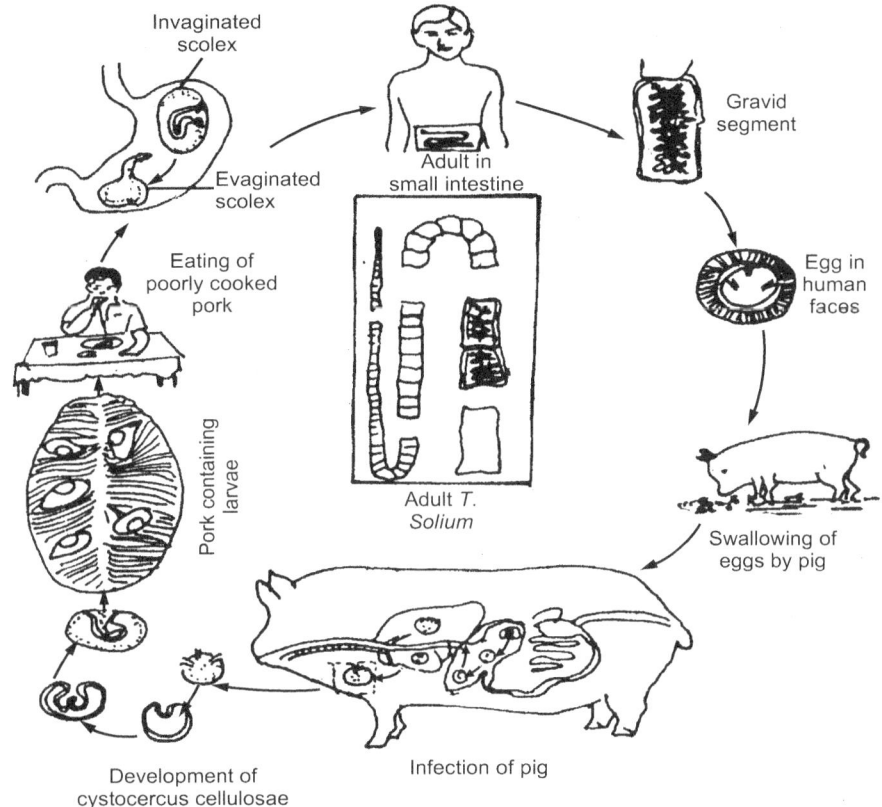

Fig. 3.5: Life-cycle of *T. solium*

Life-cycle in the Pig:

The gravid proglottids or onchospheres are eaten by pig along with the human faeces. Cows and buffaloes get infected by grazing. The ingested onchospheres reach the stomach and the embryonic membranes are dissolved by the action of gastric juices and the hexacanths are released free in 24 to 72 hours after ingestion. With the help of six chitinous hooks, the hexacanth bores the gut wall and enters the blood circulation. Usually they travel via the portal vein and successfully reach the organs like liver, heart, lungs and the systemic circulation. The naked hexacanths reach into the muscular tissues where they settle down and undergo further development. They loose their hooks on reaching their destination. They generally select the muscles of tongue, neck, shoulder, heart and liver. Then the cells in the centre are liquified and in about 8 days after infection each onchosphere forms an oval vesicle or cyst in which at the bottom the larva is present. This stage is called *cysticercus or bladder worm*. The cysticercus at this stage is fluid-filled bladder-like structure. As bladder increases, an inpushing takes place at a point morphologically the anterior end. The inpushing shows formation of scolex, suckers and hooks. For the development of the bladder worm stage from hexacanth requires period of 60 to 70 days. Many cysticerci are found in the flesh of pig and giving spotted appearance, therefore, it is called *measly pork*.

Transmission to Definitive Host:

When man eats the infected, under cooked pork or beef, the infection is effected. The cysticercus larva becomes active in the intestine and develops into adult stage. The scolex turns inside out and attaches by means of hooks and suckers to the intestinal mucosa. The larva develops into an adult worm by gradual strobilisation. The worm attains sexual maturity in 2 to 3 months and starts producing eggs and cycle is repeated.

3.4 Pathogenicity and Treatment
3.4.1 Pathogenicity

Adult worms while living in the intestine usually do not give rise to any symptom. Occasionally, they may be responsible for vague abdominal discomfort, chronic indigestion, anaemia and intestinal disorders, such as diarrhoea alternating with constipation. The proglottids may be observed in the faeces or on the body or on clothings of the patient. Nervous discomforts such as convulsions, nervousness, insomnia, nausea and epileptic fits are also seen. The effects due to adult tapeworms are collectively called as *Taeniasis*.

The larval worms in case of *T. saginata* are not found in man but of *T. solium* may occasionally be found. The larva of *T. solium* is called *cysticercus cellulosae*. Man occasionally serving as the larval host of *T. solium*, becomes infected in the same way as the pig, i.e. either by drinking contaminated water or by eating uncooked vegetables infected with eggs. Besides this, a man harbouring the adult worm may auto-infect himself either due to unclean and unhygienic personal habits or by a reversal of peristaltic movements of the intestine whereby the gravid segments are thrown back to the stomach, equivalent to the swallowing of thousands of eggs. They may develop in any organ however, they occur more in the subcutaneous tissues and muscles causing palpable or visible nodules. They may be found in the brain leading to the epileptic attacks. In the eye, the larva can be easily detected. They have a tendency to become calcified and obsolete in the course of 5 to 6 years. Larval infection is quite serious when they live in eye, liver or brain.

3.4.2 Treatment

For the control of adult worms the drugs such as *mepacrine* (atebrin), *dichlorophen* and yomesan are effective in expelling the worm. For cerebral cysticercosis, hetrazan may be administered.

Scolices and cysts of cysticerci can also be removed by surgery.

Prophylaxis:

The preventive measures include the following:
1. Individual prophylaxis consists of avoidance of eating raw or undercooked meat of intermediate hosts, i.e. pig and cattle.
2. Adequate meat inspection in the slaughter house.
3. Proper sanitary control of sewage disposal.
4. Faeces of infected persons should be properly disposed off and destroyed.

Effective treatment of infected persons to prevent infection of the intermediate hosts.

3.5 Parasitic Adaptations of Tapeworm

1. The tegument (body-covering) is freely permeable to water and nutrients. It is also resistant to the digestive enzymes of the host.
2. The internal osmotic pressure is lower than that of host fluid.
3. The pH tolerance is high, 4 to 11.
4. Hooks and suckers are present for fixation.
5. The power of anaerobic respiration enables it to live in the O_2 free intestinal contents.
6. Mouth and alimentary canal is absent because parasite is immersed in digested food.
7. Long flattened body provides a large surface area for saprozoic nutrition.
8. Enormous power of reproduction balances loss of embryos during transference from man to intermediate host. Tapeworm can survive more than 30 years, so produces large number of eggs.

(B) Nemathelminthes - *Ascaris*

3.6 Nemathelminthes - *Ascaris*
3.7 Systematic Position and Geographical Distribution
3.8 External Morphology
3.9 Reproductive System
    3.9.1 Male Reproductive System
    3.9.2 Female Reproductive System
    3.9.3 Life Cycle and Development
3.10 Pathogenicity
    3.10.1 Laboratory Diagnosis and Treatment
    3.10.2 Prevention and Control
3.11 Parasitic Adaptations

3.6 *Ascaris Lumbricoides* (Round Worm)

Ascaris lumbricoides is one of the most common or giant intestinal round worms of human being. The species of *Ascaris* are also found as intestinal parasites in vertebrates like pig, horse, cattle and chicken. *A. suum* is found in pig which is very closely related species of *lumbricoides* as both of these are morphological but are physiologically distinct. *A. galli* is found in chicken *A. megalocephala* is the endoparasite of horse.

3.7 Systematic Position, Habits and Habitat

3.7.1 Systematic Position

Kingdom	:	Animalia
Subkingdom	:	Metazoa
Phylum	:	Nematoda
Class	:	Secernentea or Phasmidea
Order	:	Ascaridida
Superfamily	:	Ascaridoidea
Family	:	Ascarididae
Genus	:	*Ascaris*
Species	:	*lumbricoides*

Geographical Distribution

It is cosmopolitan, having a world wide distribution being specially prevalent in tropics, such as China, India and South–East Asia. The parasite is most common in agricultural areas where warm moist climate exists and the regions where personal and community hygiene are lacking.

3.7.2 Habits and Habitat

The adult worm is an endoparasite of human host which lives freely in the lumen of the small intestine (jejunum). It do not show anchoring to the wall of mucosa. It is more common in children than adults. Their number may be 1000 to 5000 adult worms in single host. The worm feeds on the semi digested food (chyme) of the host in the intestine which is sucked by the sucking action of its pharynx. It is also suspected that the worm may suck the blood and tissue fluid by biting to intestinal mucosa. The worm feeds on partially digested fluid food, hence there is no stomach and oesophagus and it directly leads to the intestine which is long, straight and ribbon like. The mechanism of food digestion in parasite is not clear but various enzymes like amylase, lipase, esterase and proteases have been identified in its intestine.

They protect themselves from being digested by their host by the presence of thick cuticle on their body and also they secrete antienzymes which make digestive enzymes of host ineffective. Therefore, these worms are not digested as a food in the gut of host. This parasite is called *microaerophilic* because it needs very small quantity of free oxygen. Adult worms generate energy anaerobically. On the other hand, the free living eggs and larval stages of *Ascaris* need more oxygen for their metabolism and development.

3.8 External Morphology

A. lumbricoides is elongated, cylindrical and tapering at both ends. The body is covered by thin, tough and protective elastic cuticle which is transparent. The colour of the adult worm is pinkish, light brown or yellowish white, but it gradually changes to white. The thin cuticle is secreted by underlying syncytial hypodermis. There are nine layers of cuticle. Below the hypodermis, well developed musculature is present. Pseudocoel is the fluid filled body cavity in which the various organs and systems of the worm lie.

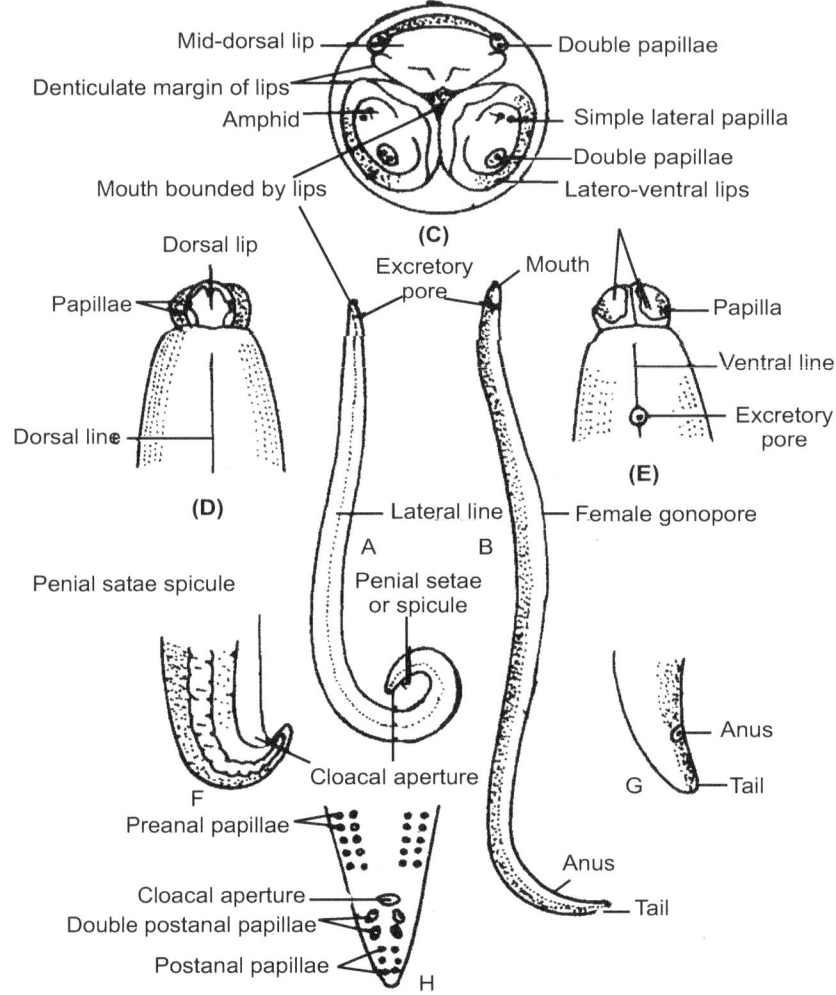

Fig. 3.6: Male and female *Ascaris*
***Ascaris lumbricoides*. A – Male, B - Female, C – Entire view of mouth and lips, D – Anterior end in dorsal view, E – Anterior end in ventral view, F – Posterior end of male, G – Posterior end of female, H – Posterior end of male in ventral view showing papilla**

The mouth opens at the anterior end and it is surrounded by three finely toothed lips, one dorsal and two ventro lateral. Each lip bears minute teeth or denticles on its oral margin. These lips bear sensory structures called labial papillae. The dorsal lip has two double sensory papillae and each ventrolateral lip has one double sensory papilla. The ventrolateral lips possess single *amphidial gland* or *amphid* which is olfactory chemoreceptor. Behind the lips, there is a pair of *cervical papillae* or *deirids* one on each lateral line at about level of excretory pore. Excretory pore is situated midventrally behind the lips. At the posterior end, anus in female and cloaca in male with spicules are present. There are also glandulo-sensory structures called phasmids are present. Male has many capulatory papillae.

Sexual Dimorphism

A. lumbricoides is dioecious i.e. sexes are separate with distinct sexual dimorphic characters.

Male: The male is smaller than female and it measures about 15 to 25 cm. in length with a maximum diameter of 3 to 4 mm. The posterior tail end of the male is curved ventrally in the form of a hook having a conical tip. The genital pore opens into the cloaca from which two curved copulatory spicules protrude. The anus opens with the ejaculatory duct into cloaca. Near cloaca there are ventrally placed cuticular elevations which are 50 pairs of preanal papillae and 5 pairs of post anal papillae. These are concerned with copulation, hence called copulatory papillae.

Female: It is longer and stouter than the male worm and measured 25 to 40 cm. in length with maximum diameter of 5 mm. The posterior tail end of the female is neither curved nor pointed, but is conical and straight. The anus is subterminal opens directly on the ventral side in the form of transverse slit. The female genital aperture called *vulva* or *gonopore* is situated midventrally at about one-third of the length from the anterior end. This part of the worm is narrow and is called *vulvar waist* or *genital girdle*. The presence of girdle indicates that the mature female is ready for copulation. The female has enormous capacity of egg laying liberating about 2,00,000 eggs daily.

3.9 Reproductive System
3.9.1 Male Reproductive System

It consists of a single long genital tube with number of coils in the posterior half of body cavity. There is single long thread like coiled *testis* which joins to *vas deferens* of the same diameter. The vas deferens joins a broader *seminal vesicle* lying in the posterior one-third of the body. The seminal vesicles lead into narrow, muscular *ejaculatory* duct which opens into *cloaca*. There is pair of muscular sac called *spicules pouch* which unite to join the *cloaca*. The pouches contain spicules and they are useful as copulatory organs to open the female *genital pore* or *vulva*. They are helpful for transfer of sperms. The testis is *telogenic* i.e. terminal portion contains mitotically dividing spermatogonia. The spermatozoon is elongate, oval in shape with absence of tail and acrosome.

3.9.2 Female Reproductive System

The female organs are didelphic (double) and occupy posterior two-third of the body and consist of ovaries, oviducts, uteri and vagina.

Two long thread like *ovaries* are highly twisted, tube like join to the broader *oviducts*. Each oviduct is further continued into still broader, thicker and muscular *uterus*. The first part of uterus serves as the *seminal receptacle* where sperms are stored and where fertilization occurs, the remaining uterus stores fertilized eggs. Vagina is formed by the union of two uteri and opens by transverse *gonopore* or *vulva*. Oogonia are produced at the tip of the ovary. The final maturation of oocytes occurs in the uterus and interaction between sperms and these cells occurs in seminal receptacle. In *Ascaris* male and female has unequal number of chromosomes. Male shows 43 chromosomes where as female shows 48 chromosomes. [See Fig. 3.7].

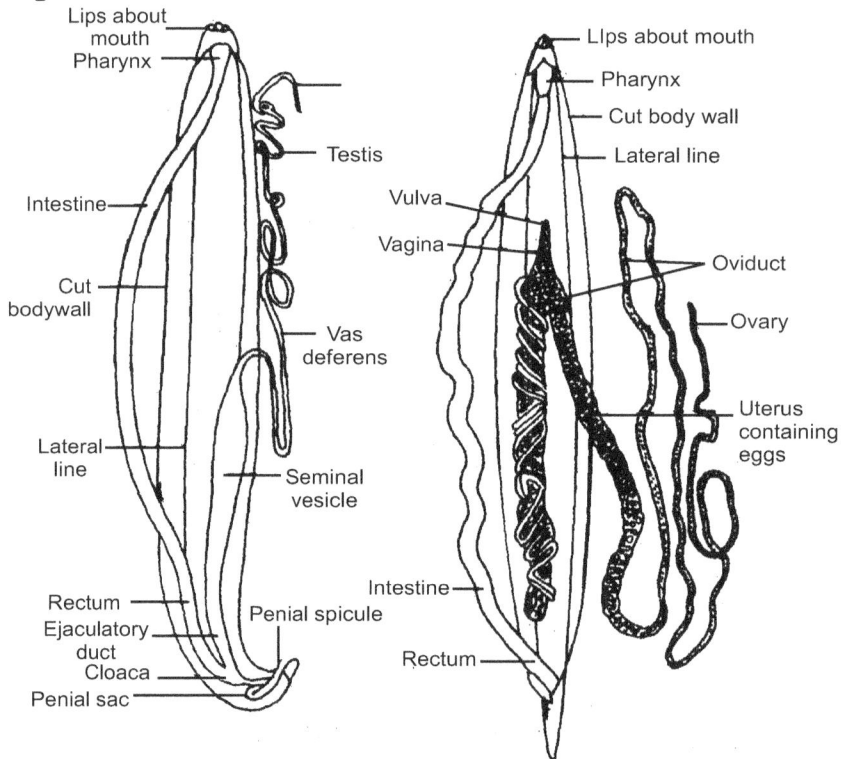

(A) *Ascaris lumbricoides.* (B) *Ascaris lumbricoides.*
Male reproductive system   Female reproductive system
Fig. 3.7: Male and Female Reproductive System

3.9.3 Life-Cycle and Development

Copulation and fertilization: Since adult worms live in the human intestine, hence mating or copulation takes place in host's intestine only. During copulation, male *Ascaris* moves in such a way that its cloacal aperture faces the vulva of the female and then male thrusts its copulatory spicules to open the vulva of the female. Then soon the cloacal wall of male contracts causing transfer of sperms into the vagina of the female and they come to lie in the seminal receptacle part of the uteri, wait for ova to come through the oviduct for fertilization.

During fertilization which occurs in seminal receptacle, entire sperm enters the ovum. This is followed by completion of meiotic division of oocyte and chromosomal pairing. Soon after fertilization, the glycogen globules of the egg migrate to the surface to form the fertilization membrane which soon hardens into a thick, clear inner *chitinous* shell. Then the fat globules of the egg form a *lipoid layer* below the chitinous shell. Now as fertilized egg passes down, the uterine wall secretes an outer thick, yellow or brown albuminous (proteinous) coat or outer shell having a characteristic wavy surface or ripplings. These eggs are known as mammiliated eggs. Such eggs are elliptical in shape measuring 60-70 µ by 40-50 µ. Female *Ascaris* also produces many unfertilized eggs which are with more elongated capsule. Its shell is also thinner and without vitelline envelope. Egg contains amorphous refractive matter.

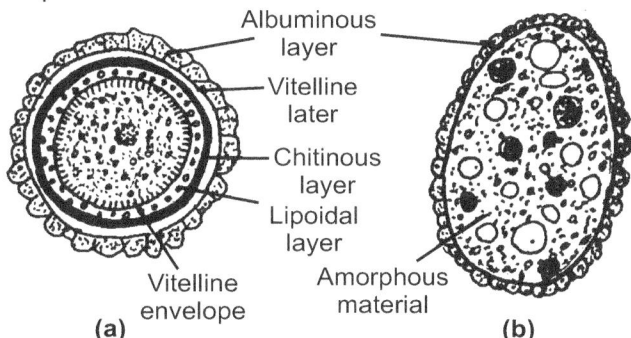

Fig. 3.8: Fertilized (a) and unfertilized (b) eggs of *Ascaris*

The female *Ascaris* lays enormous number of eggs per day. Both uteri may contain about 2.7 crores eggs and everyday female may lay 200000 eggs. The female has life span of 9 to 12 months. Thus mature female can produce at least 6 crores of eggs in this reproductive life span. Among these eggs, many eggs are infertile. Large number of fertile eggs also show high mortality rate. Very few infective larvae reach in the human intestine which is necessary environment for completion of the life cycle and continuation of the species.

Development: Life cycle begins from fertilized egg stage. Development shows metamorphosis including series of 4 larval stages to adult worm. The development of egg and first 3 larval stages occur outside the human host. i.e. in the soil where eggs are deposited. The infective larval stage when enters the human host exhibits parasitic life and develops into adult in the gut. Following are the different stages of development in the life cycle of *Ascaris*.

Eggs in Faeces: Fertilized eggs containing the unsegmented ovum are liberated in the intestine of man and then passed with the faeces. The wall of the egg capsule is permeable to water and gases but it is highly resistant to cold and warm temperatures, strong chemicals and desiccation. The eggs can even survive in 10% formalin solution and sea water. They do not survive in high temperatures above 70°C and excessive solar heat. The eggs fall on the ground and can remain alive for months in the moist soil though complete drying kills them. In order to develop they require oxygen, moisture, shade and a temperature lower than that of the human body, the most favourable temperature is 34°C. Under such favourable conditions, the embryo in the egg develops rapidly into a elongate, motile first stage larva. The eggs require a period of incubation outside human body.

Early development: The stages of early embryonic development like cleavage or segmentation etc. start in soil. The pattern of cleavage is *spiral and* determinate. Cleave shows phenomenon of chromatin diminution in which loss of chromosomal material occurs during early embryogenesis but its biological significance is not known. In the first cleavage, 2 blastomeres are formed out of which one blastomere forms ectoderm and another gives rise to endoderm and mesoderm. The embryonic cells form *blastula* at 16 celled stage having blastocoel. Then *gastrula* is formed by epiboly or overgrowth of the ectodermal cells over the endodermal cells and by invagination of stomodaeum and endodermal cells. The morula elongates into tadpole like shape. By the end of 10 to 14 days, a worm like juvenile is resulted called first stage larva which shows movements inside the egg capsule.

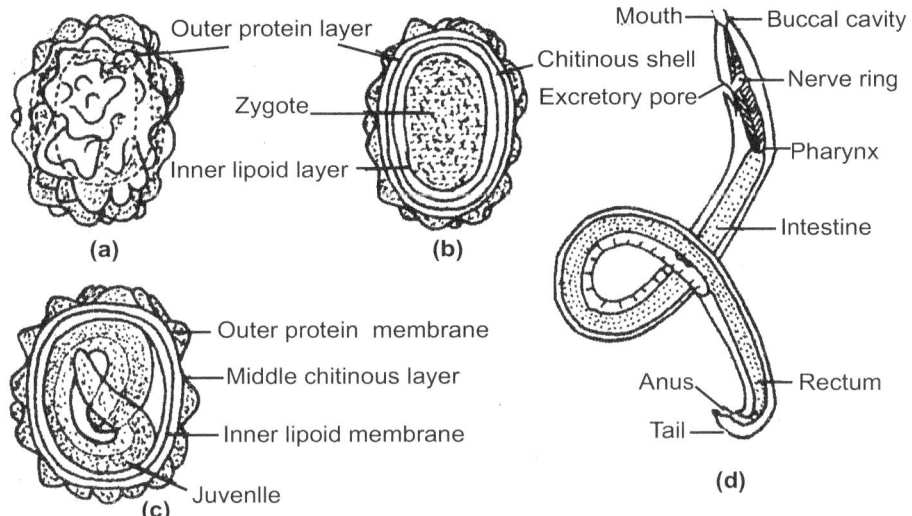

Fig. 3.9: Formation of first stage larva
Ascaris. (a) An entire mammilated egg; (b) Mammilated egg in section; (c) Embryonated egg; (d) Rhabditiform larva

First stage larva: The juvenile possesses an alimentary canal, a nerve ring and a lateral excretory system. It is elongated worm like structure with rounded anterior end and a tapering tail. Body is enveloped by very smooth cuticle and large number of granules are present in the body which are absorbed or used up after first moult. The juveniles very much similar with *Rhabditis*, a soil nematode, hence it is also referred to as *rhabditiform* larva or *rhabditoid*. This is infective to man. Before hatching, the larva undergoes a moulting.

Second stage larva: It is formed inside the egg capsule when the first instar larva moults in about 7 days and becomes the second stage *juvenile* or second stage *rhabditoid*. The larva shows digestive, excretory nervous systems as well as sense organs. The organs like excretory pore and anus are formed midventrally. The larva also exhibits appearance of labial papillae, amphids and phasmids.

The genital premordium develops on the middle of ventral side of the intestine. By the end of 7 days the larva shows 250 μm length and 14 μm diameter. It moults into the next larval instar.

Third stage larva: This larval stage becomes fully developed in 10-14 days and environmental temperature plays important role. The different organs are fully differentiated. This stage is infective to man. If this larva does not gain entry in the body of host then it can remain viable under favourable conditions of oxygen, temperature and moisture for about six years in the soil.

Infection to man: As mentioned earlier that, there is no secondary host in the life cycle of *Ascaris*, infection to man (host) occurs when he swallows contaminated or polluted raw vegetables, food or water with infectious eggs. Thus the embryonated eggs pass down to the small intestine (duodenum) of host. The egg capsule becomes weak due to the action of CO_2, pH and host's digestive juice or enzymes. The larva inside the egg shell also gets activated. The larva secretes a *hatching fluid* inside the egg capsule which contains the enzymes like esterase and chitinase. These enzymes also make the egg shell very weak and alter the structure. The larva forms the buldging at one place and the vigorous movement bursts the egg shell and larva is liberated in the intestine. This process is called hatching and it takes the period of 3 to 4 hours. The juveniles are about 0.2–0.3 mm long and 13–15 µ in diameter and have the all structures of the adults except the reproductive organs.

Development in human host: After reaching to the definitive host, the larvae do not remain in the intestine for further development, but go on a typical wandering tour of 10 days in the body of host. The newly hatched larvae bore through the intestine wall and carried along the portal vessels to the liver. Here they live for a period of 3 to 4 days. Then they enter the hepatic vein and through the post caval vein come to the right side in the heart, from where they are carried several times through the body along with the blood stream. Then they go through pulmonary arteries into the lungs. They spend about a week in lungs passing through small blood vessels. While in the lungs they grow much bigger and increase in length from 0.2 mm to 2 mm and moult (third instar) and the larvae become now 4th instar larvae. Breaking through the capillary wall they reach the lung alveoli. The time taken for such migration is on average 10-15 days.

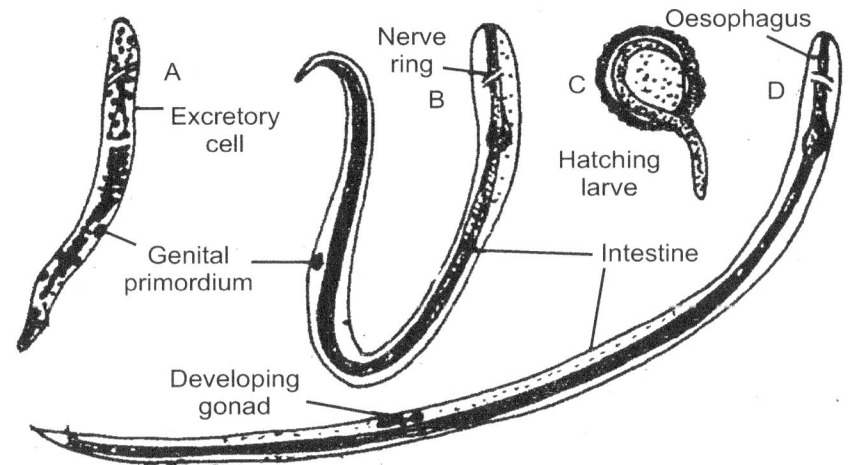

**Fig. 3.10 (a): Larval Development of *Ascaris lumbricoides*
A – Second stage larva; B – Third stage larva undergoes hatching;
C – In the Host's Intestine; D – Fourth stage larva**

Fourth stage larva: The larvae in the lungs and lung alveoli are fourth stage larvae which are now ready to reenter in the intestine. From the lung alveoli, the larvae crawl up bronchi and trachea and aided by the current caused by ciliated epithelium of the respiratory tract, they are propelled into the larynx and pharynx and are once again swallowed by the same host.

The larvae pass down the oesophagus to the stomach and finally reach to the upper part of host's intestine which is their normal place. At this time the larva is very much tolerant to the gastric juices and intestinal digestive enzymes of the host. The larva shows anaerobic metabolism. Most of the organs and systems are well developed.

The genital premordium becomes elongated and differentiated into male and female gonads. The larva also shows presence of dorsal and ventral lips with teeth and papillae.

The worm feeds on the nutritious semi-digested food in the intestine and grows to a length of about 25 mm. The worm undergoes the fourth and last moult and adult worm is formed. The moulting is induced by a ecdysteroidal hormone.

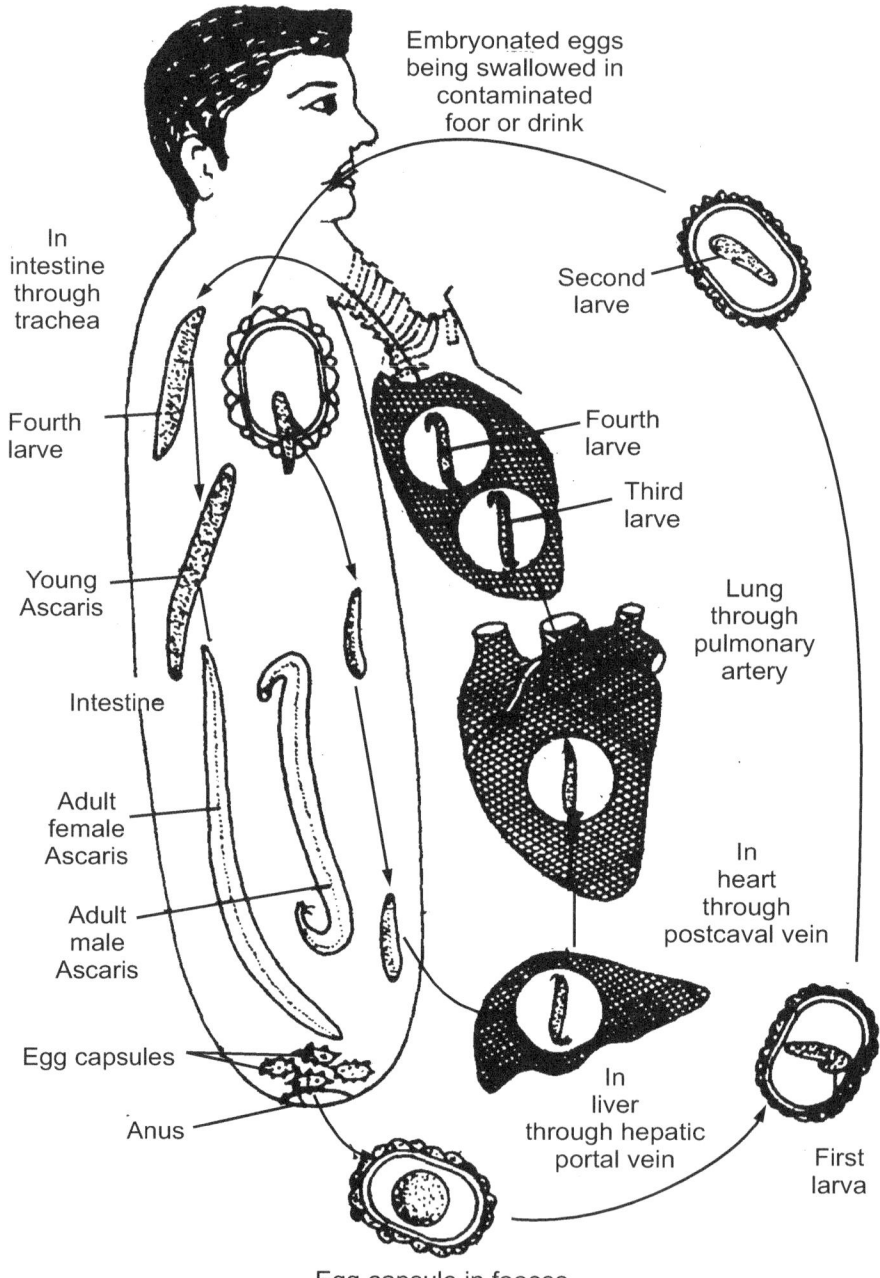

Fig. 3.10 (b): *Ascaris lumbricoides*. Life-cycle

Adult worms: The fourth stage larva undergoes fourth and final another moulting between 25th and 29th day of infection. The adult *Ascaris* is small and exhibits sexual dimorphism and in 60 to 70 days they grow into adult male and female and attain sexual maturity. The parasite feeds voraciously on the food in intestine and grows rapidly to its final size. Sexually mature adults start copulation and mating and female discharges the egg and cycle is again repeated. The average life span of the parasite in the host's body is only 9 to 12 months.

Mode of infection: The infection is effected by swallowing ripe *Ascaris* eggs with unwashed raw vegetables, tubers, salads etc. cultivated on a soil manured with human excreta containing the eggs of the worm. Water supplies may be contaminated and infection may occur by drinking polluted water. Where soil pollution is common, the eggs may directly be conveyed to the mouth by dirty fingers. Infection may also occur by inhalation of eggs in the dust reaching in the pharynx and swallowed. The areas where dust storms are common in northern parts of Asia and Africa, the infection is also very common. This dust also settles on unprotected water and food stuff and when such food or water is consumed the infection is easily acquired.

3.10 Pathogenicity or Parasitic Effects

Infection of *A. lumbricoides* in man is known as *ascariasis*. If one or few worms are present in the intestine they are not very dangerous, however, if large number of worms are present in the intestine they may obstruct the passage and consequences are very serious. They damage the intestine. The pathological effects of the parasite categorised into two types, effects produced by migrating larvae and effects due to adult worms.

1. Effects produced by migrating larvae: Due to heavy infection of migrating larvae in lungs show typical symptoms of pneumonia such as fever, cough and dyspnoea. This is called *Ascaris pneumonia* (Loeffler's syndrome). The sputum which is often blood tinged may contain *Ascaris* larvae, swollen face, utricarial rash and eosinophilia (20%) are seen in such cases. The lungs are severely affected by these larvae. When they break lung capillaries into alveoli, some trauma and localised haemorrhages occur. Due to damage of pulmonary tissue, the respiratory function of lungs is affected. Children are very susceptible and such condition may prove fatal. When there is heavy infection in liver, the necrotic damage results into hepatitis or inflammation of liver. If larvae pass beyond the pulmonary capillaries and reach the general circulation, they are filtered out to various organs such as kidney, spleen, brain, spinal cord, heart and eyeball. This may have symptoms like muscular pain, headache and inflammation of retina. The larvae may carry microorganisms from intestine to other tissues.

2. Effects produced by adult worms: Adult worms are located in the intestine, hence symptoms are mostly related to the gastro-intestinal tract. The adult worms may produce pathogenic effects in the following ways.

(1) Spoliative action: The worms feed on the intestinal food of the host and naturally host is not getting nutritive materials like proteins and vitamins which are very high in the worm. This effect is very common in hyper infected children and may contribute to protein energy malnutrition. *Ascaris* infection may cause vitamin-A deficiency resulting into night blindness. *Ascaris* worm secretes antienzymes which neutralise the intestinal enzymes of host. This results into non-digestion of food stuff by host which ultimately leads into malnutrition. Antitryptic and antipeptic enzymes play important role. Due to severe nutritional drain children suffer from stunted growth. It also affects their memory, thinking ability and general intelligence.

(2) Toxic action: The body fluid of *Ascaris* when absorbed is toxic and may give rise to typhoid like fever, also responsible for various allergic manifestations such as utricaria, oedema of the face, conjunctivitis and irritation of the upper respiratory tract. Various products of worm contain toxins such as haemolysins, endocrinotoxins, neurotoxins and awaphylaxins.

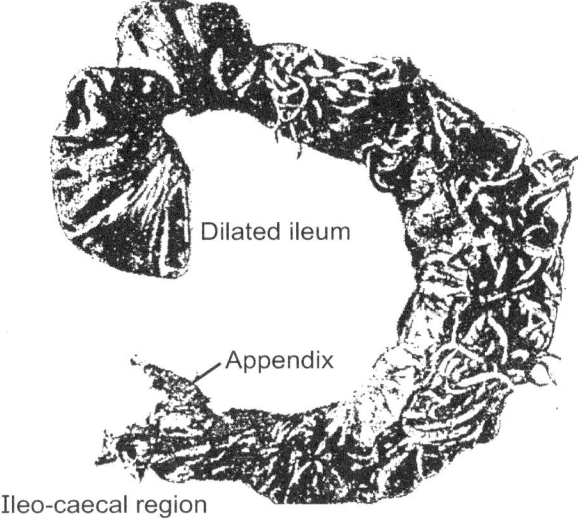

Fig. 3.11

Some people who show these parasites in their gut may become immunologically sensitised to the toxic wastes liberated by worms. These waste substances are directly absorbed by the mucosa of intestine. These foreign proteins act as poisons to host leading to systemic poisoning or *toxaemia*. Patients also exhibit nervous symptoms like general nervousness, photophobia, convulsions, meningitis, insomnia and paralysis below the waist are also evident.

(3) Mechanical effects: The presence of *Ascaris* has led to the occurrence of intussusception. It may penetrate through the ulcers of the alimentary canal. A large number of Ascaris forming a bolus has been known to produce intestinal obstruction, particularly in young

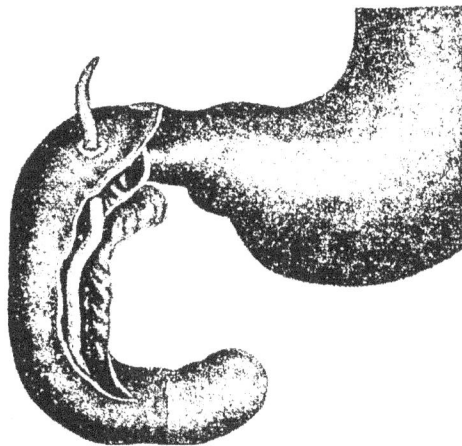

Fig. 3.12: *A. lumbricoides* **perforating through a duodenal ulcer**

children because of relative small size of the intestinal lumen. Sometimes worms block the gut lumen causing intestinal gangrene and death. The worm may enter bile duct and even liver causing obstructive hepatitis and jaundice. Sometimes when worms enter in appendix causing acute *appendicitis*. The worms may perforate the intestine and enter the body cavity causing fatal *peritonitis*. They may pass in pleural cavity and urinogenital organ. Rarely, worms may enter the larynx, lung, Eustachian tube and even the eye. The worms frequently migrate and may enter the stomach and may be vomited out or may pass up through the oesophagus at night, coming out through the mouth or nose. Thus during migration, worms may accidentally enter into the respiratory passage causing suffocation by blocking the rima glottides or may even enter into a bronchus. When worms enter in biliary passage cause haemorrhagic pancreatitis. In liver due to penetration of worms causing one or more abscesses.

3.10.1 Laboratory Diagnosis and Treatment

Ascariasis is not ignorable disease and diagnosis of the disease is also very easy and can be done by direct and indirect evidences.

I. Direct evidences:

1. The adult worm may pass out spontaneously in the stool or per anum between stools or may be vomited or escape through nose. Administration of specific anthelmintic drugs or preparation may lead to the expulsion of the worm and its detection.

2. The presence of *Ascaris* in intestine has been demonstrated by radiography (X-ray) with Barium emulsion; which being ingested by the worm within 4 to 6 hours, casts an opaque shadow.

3. Presence of eggs in the stool may be detected by direct microscopic examination of a saline emulsion of the stool. Concentration by *floation method* may be employed for the detection of eggs in the stool. It is to be noted that unfertilized eggs do not float in salt solution. Microscopic examination of bile obtained by duodenal intubation may reveal *Ascaris* eggs.

II. Indirect evidences:

In this method, blood examination is carried out. *Eosinophilia* is present only at the early stage of invasion but if present in the intestinal phase suggests associated strongyloidiasis or toxocariasis. Dermal reaction (Allergic) or scratch test is used for diagnosis. Powdered *Ascaris* antigen has often been found to be positive but the results are variable.

Treatment: There are number of ascaricidal drugs and preparation available for the treatment of ascariasis. The old remedy was use of *oil of chinopodium* and *santonin*. These were highly toxic. Later on less toxic, effective and tolerable medicine *ascaridole* was used as ascaricidal drug. *Hexylresorcinol* is very safe and effective drug given in capsule which removes upto 95% of worms from the intestine. For ascariasis the drug of choice is a *piperazine* salt (hydrate, citrate, phosphate or adipate). This is cheap, safe and ascaricide available in the form of syrup and gives best results for deworming children. This drug paralyses the worms.

Thiabendazole is used as a recent equally effective, broad spectrum anthelmintic drug which kills many other intestinal parasites. *Pyrantel pamoate* is also the effective drug. *Mebendazole* and *albendazole* are recent and extremely safe drugs with rare side effects are currently used. Tetramisole and *levamisole* are other recent ascaricidal drugs with excellent results. A single dose of these drugs gives 99% parasitological cure. There are no effective drugs which kill the larvae and worms located in different organs. For their removal, surgical methods should be used.

3.10.2 Prevention and Control

Prophylaxis (Prevention): Following prophylactic measures should be adopted against ascariasis.
1. Keeping good sanitary condition is the only way to prevent the infection of *Ascaris*. Sanitary facilities should be installed in urban as well as rural areas and people should use them.
2. Pollution of soil with human faeces should be avoided.
3. Vegetables should be thoroughly washed and properly cooked before use, raw vegetables and nuts should not be used. Avoid the vegetables grown on soil manured by human excreta.

4. Avoid the use of polluted water for drinking purpose.
5. There should be proper disposal of human faeces.
6. Use the compost manure in fields instead of night-soil as a fertilizer for growing crops or vegetable.
7. The infected individuals should be given treatment for ascariasis.
8. Education regarding importance of personal and public hygiene and sanitary laws should be given to the children in schools. Finger nails should be regularly cut to avoid the collection of dirt and eggs below them. Hands should be properly washed with antiseptic soap before touching edibles or eating.
9. Infection of *Ascariasis* should be controlled at both individual and community levels. Patients suffering from ascariasis should be detected and treated with ascaricidal drugs. Deworming can be carried out by using drug piperazine at individual treatment and mebendazole for mass treatment.

3.11 Parasitic Adaptations in *Ascaris*

Ascaris is an obligatory endoparasite of man living in the intestine. For comfortable and successful parasitic life the worm exhibits number of following adaptive features.

1. Body is long and cylindrical in shape with tapering ends.
2. The body is covered by tough and resistant elastic cuticle and it resists against the action of host's digestive enzymes.
3. The worms secrete antienzymes which protect the worm from being digested by host's digestive enzymes in the body of host.
4. There are no adhesive organs found in worm and lack of these organs is compensated very poor power of locomotion as by slight movement it maintains its position in the intestine of the host and also counteracts the intestinal peristalsis.
5. Presence of muscular pharynx for ingestion of semi digested food by suctorial action. Since it feeds on the predigested food, the digestive system is very simple and poorly developed.

6. There is no circulatory system, but pseudo-coelomic fluid serves for absorption, transport and distribution of food, oxygen and waste matter.

7. The worm shows anaerobic respiration since they live in oxygen deficient environment. However, free living larvae show aerobic respiration.

8. Sense organs are limited and very simple.

9. Female lays enormous number of eggs in faeces, hence few of them atleast survive and continue the species.

10. The eggs are provided with very protective capsule which helps survival and development of larvae outside the body of host and they remain viable for long time.

11. The eggs are very small in size, so they can be easily dispersed.

12. There is no intermediate host in the life cycle, but mode of direct infection increases the chances of larvae to reach fresh human host.

Summary

- Cestodes are highly specialised flatworms. They are commonly called as 'tapeworms'.
- The body of the animal is divisible into three regions:
  (a) Scolex or head, (b) Neck, (c) Strobila.
- *T. solium* is a hermaphrodite animal.
- *Ascaris lumbricoides* is one of the most common or giant intestinal round worms of human being.
- *A. lumbricoides* is elongated, cylindrical and tapering at both ends.
- *A. lumbricoides* is dioecious i.e. sexes are separate with distinct sexual dimorphic characters.
- *Ascaris* is an obligatory endoparasite of man living in the intestine.

Review Questions

1. Describe reproductive system of *T. solium*.
2. Explain life cycle of *T. solium* in pig.
3. Describe male reproductive system of *A. lumbricoides*.
4. Give an account of life cycle and development of *A. lumbricoide*.
5. Write short notes on:
   - (a) Parasitic adaptations of tapeworm
   - (b) External morphology of round worm
   - (c) Prevention and control of round worm
   - (d) Sexual dimorphism

Chapter **4**...

Annelida - Earthworm

4.1 Systematic Position, Habit and Habitat
4.2 External Characters
4.3 Digestive System
4.4 Blood Vascular System (Circulatory System)
4.5 Excretory System
4.6 Reproductive System
    4.6.1 Male Reproductive System
    4.6.2 Female Reproductive System
4.7 Nervous System and Sense Organs
4.8 Economic Importance of Earthworm
✎ Summary
✎ Review Questions
✎ University Questions

Introduction

- The common Indian earthworm is a burrowing animal belonging to the phylum Annelida. It serves well to illustrate the principal characteristics of the annelids.

- Although it is not the typical animal type of phylum Annelida but it is easily available and fairly large worm and hence suitable for the basic study of an invertebrate type.

- Earthworm is terrestrial and shows a number of specializations associated with terrestrial mode of life.

4.1 Systematic Position, Habit and Habitat

Phylum - Annelida	(i)	Coelom or true body cavity is present.
	(ii)	Body is cylindrical and metamerically segmented.
Class - Oligochaeta	(i)	No distinct head but clitellum is distinct.
	(ii)	Setae few in number (oligoi - a few) and arranged singly.
Order - Neo-oligochaeta	(i)	A large terrestrial worm.
	(ii)	Clitellum behind 12th segment.
Genus - *Pheretima*	(i)	Setae are in complete rings in the middle of each segments.
	(ii)	Clitellum extending over 14, 15 and 16 segments.
Species: *posthuma*	(i)	Spermathecal openings in intersegmental grooves.
	(ii)	Genital papillae on 17th and 19th segments.

Habitat
- Earthworms are distributed almost all over the world. They do not occur in the regions where soil is sandy and deficient in humus. They are also not found in mountain regions where soil is poor and scanty.
- Earthworms do not like acidic soils. They generally prefer to live in upper layers of slightly damp soil, gardens and lawns upto the depth of 30 to 45 cm. They live in burrows which protect them from enemies and unfavourable climatic conditions.
- One acre land may contain on an average about 50,000 earthworms. Earthworms generally respire by moist skin which is kept moist by mucus secreted by skin. Hence, they always prefer habitat with moisture.

Habits
- Earthworms are terrestrial animals and they make their burrows by boring with their pointed anterior ends and partly by ingesting the soil through mouth and passing it behind through the anus in the form of castings.

- These pellets of worm or worm castings are also used to line the burrows. The soil which is ingested by the worm is crushed into powder and organic matter from it is digested and residue is discharged.
- Thus, their burrowing habit makes the soil loose and brings the subsoil to the surface like a plough and due to castings the soil becomes fertile, hence they are regarded as friends of farmers. Now earthworm farming and vermicompost is very well accepted by farmers for better yield. In many countries now they are commercially tapped to convert organic wastes into manure.
- Earthworms are nocturnal animals. During daytime they lie in their burrows, but come out at night for feeding. They feed on dead organic matter.
- They lack special sensory organs yet they respond to several stimuli. They generally avoid strong light, irritating chemical vapours, mechanical vibrations.
- They generally live within a foot or two from the surface but during adverse conditions like excessive cold or heat they may go deeper parts of soil and protect themselves from drying.
- During the rainy season, large number of earthworms emerge out and may be seen crawling on the ground probably for oxygen. Many of them die due to hard rain.
- They come up on the surface because the percolating water is lacking in oxygen. When they come on the surface they are quickly paralysed by ultraviolet rays of sun or by dehydration.
- According to **Michaelsen** earthworms rarely leave burrows in other circumstances except when ill or flood out during the rainy season.

4.2 External Features

Shape and Size

- *Pheretima posthuma* has a long, elongated, bilaterally symmetrical and cylindrical body. Body is metamerically segmented.
- There is neither distinct head nor appendages. Its posterior end is more or less blunt and anterior end is tapering. Thus, the shape and size of the animal is adapted for burrowing. The mature worm measures about 15 cm in length and 5 mm in thickness.

Colouration
- The skin is soft, moist with glistering deep brown or clay coloured. The dorsal surface is darker than the ventral.
- There is dark median line on the dorsal surface which is nothing but the dorsal blood vessel running just below the skin from end to end.
- Genital openings and papillae are present on ventral surface.

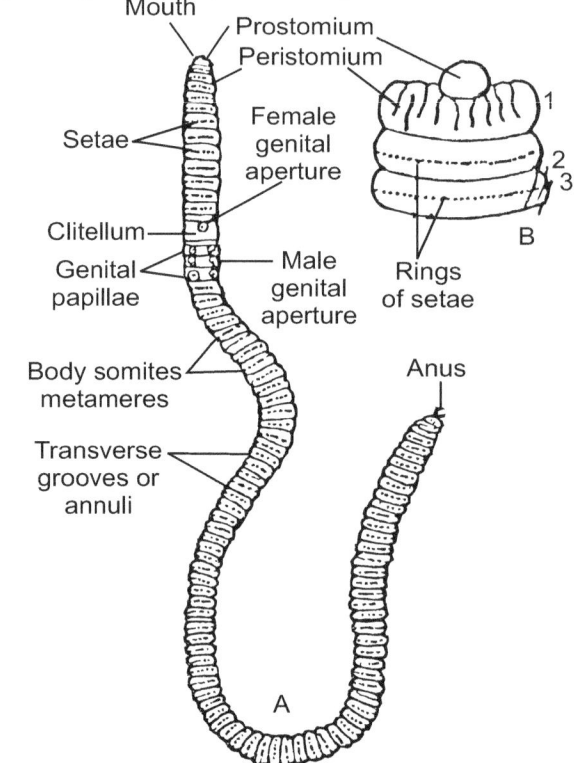

**Fig. 4.1: A - Entire worm in ventral view,
B - Anterior end in dorsal view**

Segmentation
- The body of earthworm is metamerically segmented containing 100 to 120 similar segments.
- Each segment is transverse ring like groove or annulus called *metamere* or *somite*.
- External segmentation corresponds with the internal segmentation of the body. There is no distinct head and sense organs on the anterior end of the earthworm.

- There are also no appendages in the earthworm. At the anterior end the first segment is called *peristomium* or *buccal* segment in which mouth is situated.
- In front of the peristomium is a small fleshy, rounded lobe called the *prostomium* which over hangs the mouth dorsally. It also lacks the sense organs and appendages.
- The last segment of the body is called *anal segment* because it carries the terminal anus.

Clitellum
- In a mature worm, the segments 14, 15 and 16 are modified into a girdle like thick, dark brown band of glandular tissue called *clitellum* or *cingulum*.
- There are neither external grooves on the *clitellum* nor rings of setae. Being thick it helps in burrowing, being glandular it secretes loose but elastic girdle during cocoon formation.
- It has also taxonomic importance and forms important landmark on the body. On the presence of *clitellum*, the body is divisible into three regions such as:
    (i) Pre-clitellar region from 1st to 13th segments,
    (ii) Clitellar region extending over 14th, 15th and 16th segments and
    (iii) Post-clitellar region from 17th to last segment.

Thus clitellum is a glandular organ which secretes mucus, albumen and an egg case or cocoon for the eggs.

External apertures: Besides these, the animal also shows a number of openings or apertures on the body are as follows:
1. **Mouth:** It is a crescentic aperture situated at the anterior end. The mouth is surrounded by the first segment of the body or *peristomium*.
2. **Anus:** Anus is a vertical slit-like aperture at the posterior end on the anal segment.
3. **Spermathecal openings:** These are four pairs of small elliptical openings situated ventro-laterally in the intersegmental grooves between 5/6, 6/7, 7/8 and 8/9 segments. Through these apertures spermatozoa are received from other worm during copulation.

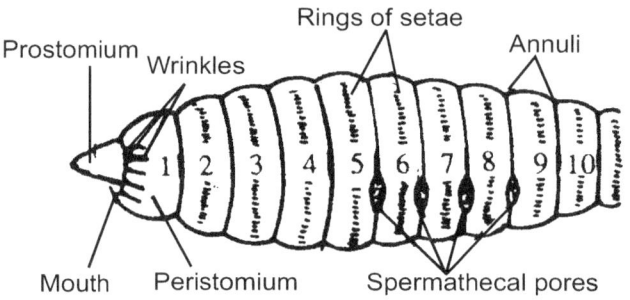

Fig. 4.2: *Pheretima*: Anterior region in lateral view

4. **Female genital pore:** It is a single aperture situated midventrally on the 14th segment.
5. **Male genital apertures:** These are a pair of apertures situated ventrolaterally on the 14th segment.
6. **Genital papillae:** These are two pairs of raised cup-shaped depressions situated ventrolaterally on the 17th and 19th segments. During copulation, the genital papillae function as suckers.
7. **Dorsal pores:** These are the minute openings lying along the mid-dorsal line one in each intersegmental groove from 12/13 segments posteriorly.
8. **Nephridiopores:** These are large number of small opening of integumentary nephridia scattered all over the body except the first six segments.

Body Wall

The integument or body wall is the external protective covering. It is thin, elastic, smooth and moist with pinkish brown in colour and without any exoskeleton. Histological structure of the body wall shows the following layers from outside (Fig. 4.3).

1. Cuticle
2. Epidermis
3. Muscle layer and
4. Parietal peritoneum

1. Cuticle: The delicate body wall is covered externally by a thin, non-cellular, transparent double layer membrane called *cuticle*. It is secreted by the underlying layer called *epidermis* or *hypodermis*. It uniformly covers the entire body of worm. The cuticle is made up of a collagenous protein and polysaccharide and small quantity of gelatin. It is perforated by numerous pores through which open the epidermal mucous glands and nephridia. The cuticle protects animal from physical and chemical injuries.

2. Epidermis: It is a single layer of tall cells lying beneath the cuticle and resting on the thin connective layer called basement membrane.

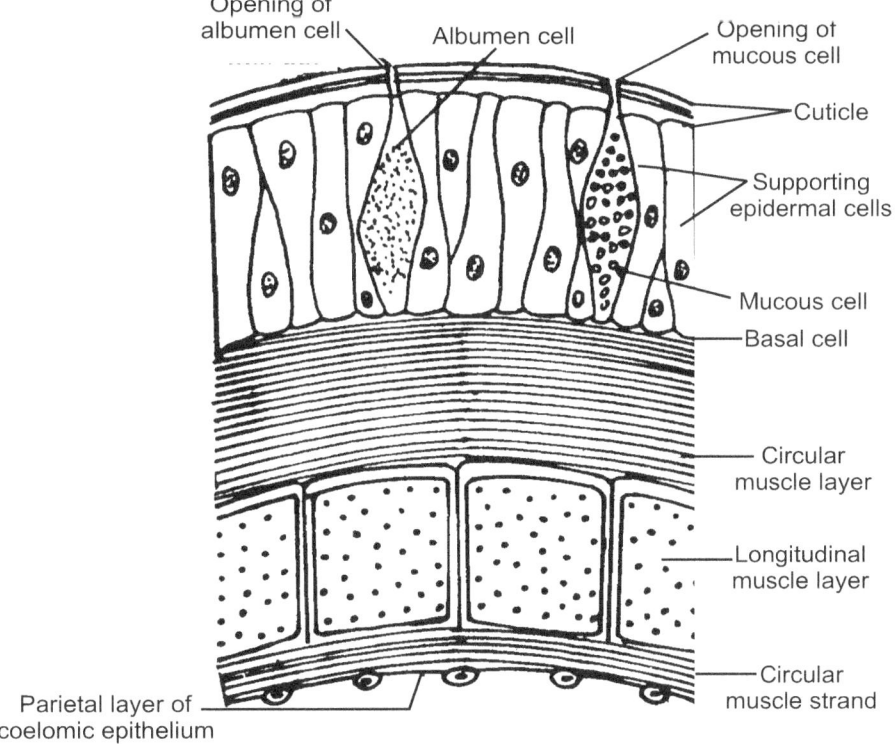

Fig. 4.3: *Pheretima*: T.S. of a portion of body wall

The epidermis consists of the following four types of cells:

(i) Gland cells: These are secretory cells which discharge their secretion on the surface of cuticle. These cells are characterised by granular cytoplasm and distinct nucleus at the base. The gland cells are of two types: mucous cells and albumen cells.

    (a) Mucous cells: These are numerous; large and ovoid in shape. Each cell has a broad rounded distal part containing mucus and narrow proximal part containing cytoplasm and nucleus. These cells secrete sticky substance called mucous which keeps the skin moist and slippery.

(b) **Albumen cells:** These are comparatively few, club shaped or columnar in shape with secretory granules uniformly distributed. Nucleus is situated at the proximal end of the cell. The albumen cells secrete proteinaceous substance forming cuticle.

(ii) **Supporting cells:** These cells are columnar in shape with clear cytoplasm and an oval nucleus in the middle of the each cell. These cells are closely placed and forming bulk of the epidermis. As the name suggets, they support the other cell of the epidermis.

(iii) **Basal cells:** These cells are small, rounded or conical or pyramidal in shape with a distinct nucleus in each cell. The basal cells are lying in the spaces between other cells, towards the base. Their function is probably to replace worn out glandular or supporting cells.

(iv) **Receptor cells:** They are sensory cells arranged in groups and restricted to certain areas. They are usually cylindrical cells with sensory processes on their free ends and basal ends are inervated by nerve fibres. These cells receive stimuli.

3. **Muscle layers:** The muscular layer lies below the epidermis and muscles are arranged in two layers, the outer thin circular muscle layer running in circular manner below the epidermis and inner longitudinal muscle layer running lengthwise in parallel bundles, separated by connective tissue. The muscle fibres are unstripped, long and spindle shaped. Among the circular muscle fibres pigment cells, connective tissue, nerve fibres and blood capillaries are also found. Alternate contraction and relaxation of these muscles help in locomotion. By the contraction of longitudinal muscles body of the worm elongates and shortening of the body takes place due to contraction of longitudinal muscles. Both the muscles are antagonistic because when one contracts other shows relaxation.

4. **Parietal peritoneum:** The inner most layer of the body wall is the somatic peritoneum or the parietal layer of coelomic epithelium, which also forms the outer lining of the coelomic cavity. It consists of a single layer of flat epithelial cells recognisable by their nuclei only.

Functions of the body wall

The body wall of earthworm performs many functions which are given below:
1. The body wall maintains the form of the body due to elastic nature.
2. It protects cuticle of the body from mechanical injury and desiccation. Thus, gives protection to the internal organs and fluids.
3. The gland cells of epidermis keep body wall slimy, moist and free from harmful micro organisms.
4. It helps in plastering the inner walls of burrows with the help of mucous it secretes.
5. It is without exoskeleton, but richly supplied with blood and remains always moist. It acts as the respiratory organ.
6. It helps in locomotion due to presence of muscle layers.
7. The setae are present in the body wall which help in locomotion.
8. The sensory epidermal cells help in the reception of external stimuli. Thus it acts as receptor organ.
9. The parietal layer of coelomic epithelium secretes coelomic fluid.
10. The body wall secretes albumen during cocoon formation which serves as food for the developing embryos in the cocoons.

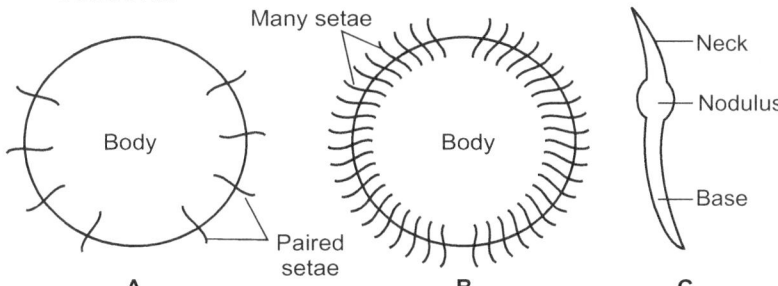

Fig. 4.4: A - Lumbricine arrangement. B - Perichaetine arrangement. C - A single seta

SETAE
- These are rod-like microscopic chitinuous structures embedded in the body wall.
  (Fig. 4.4).
- They are arranged in the form of ring in the middle of each segment except 1st, last and clitellum.
- This arrangement is called perichaetine arrangement. The number of setae per segment varies from 80 to 120.

- Each seta is an elongated S shaped $\left(\int \right)$ structure measuring about 0.25 mm long and 0.025 mm thick. It is made up of chitinuous and albuminous substances.
- It is distinguished into pointed distal end, blunt proximal end and a swelling called nodulus in the middle.
- Setae are worked by muscle bundles arranged in Y-shaped pattern attached to setigerous sacs.
- The setal sacs, secreting and lodging the setae, are merely the invaginations of the epidermis.
- Each setal sac consists of a neck, a body and a base.
- At the base of each sac are inserted two sets of muscles, a pair of *protractor muscles*, passing outwards to join the circular layer of muscles, and a single *retractor* muscle, passing inwards to join a thin sheet of circular muscles.
- Thus the forked arms of the Y form the protractors muscles and the stem forms the retractor muscles.
- The contraction of the protractor protrudes the seta out the skin while the contraction of retractor withdraws it into the body wall.
- Thus muscles control the movements of setae during locomotion.

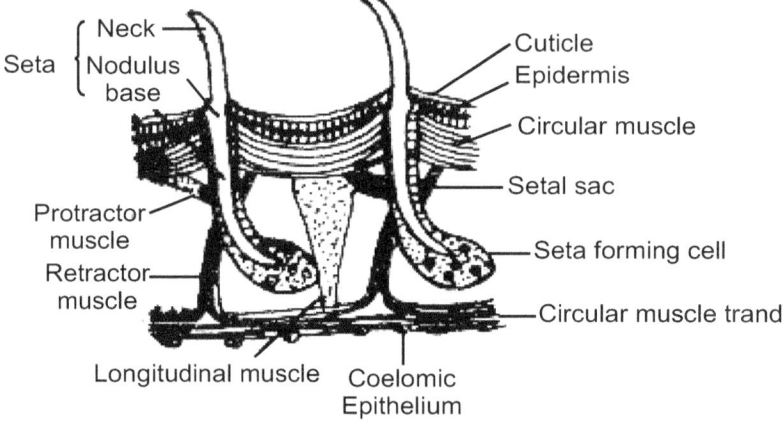

Fig. 4.5: *Pheretima*. Diagrammatic T.S. of a part of body-wall through a setal ring

- The functions of the setae is anchorage of the worm to the substratum and also to serve as fulcri to propel the body forwarded during locomotion.

Coelom

- Like all other annelids Earthworm shows true coelomic cavity or coelom. The coelom is a spacious cavity between the alimentary canal and the body wall. It is actually a tube within a tube, the outer tube is the body wall and the inner tube is the gut wall and the wide space between the two tubes is the coelom or body cavity.
- A true coelom is a cavity which is formed by the division of the mesoderm.
- During development the mesoderm divides into outer somatic (parietal) mesoderm and inner splanchnic mesoderm. The space in between these two is the coelom.
- The coelom or body cavity is internally linked by coelomic epithelium or peritoneum. It is bounded externally (i.e. lining of body wall) by the parietal peritoneum and internally (i.e. covering of alimentary canal) by visceral peritoneum. The coelomic cavity is filled with coelomic fluid which is milky white fluid.

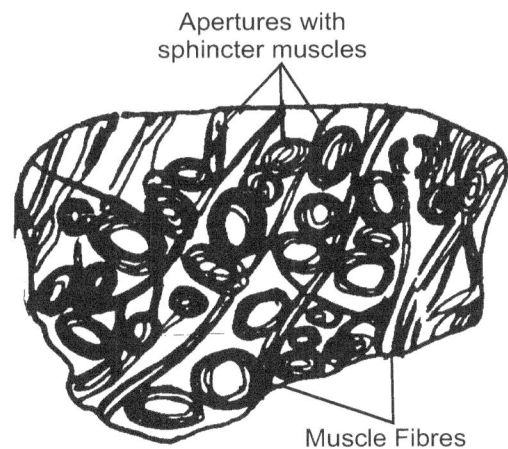

Fig. 4.6: *Pheretima*: A part of intersegmental septum

- In earthworm, the coelom is not continuous throughout the body but is subdivided into series of compartments by transverse muscular partitions called septa.
- The septa are inter-segmental in position. Each septum runs from gutwall to the body wall, where each becomes attached opposite in intersegmental groove.

- There are no septa in first four segments. After this the first septum is lying between segment 4th and 5th is thin and membranous.
- The next five septa between segments 5/6, 6/7, 7/8 and 8/9 to 10/11 are thick, muscular and cone like and non-obliquely backwards (or in the form of inverted cones) from the body wall to the gut wall. (Fig. 4.7).
- There is no septum between segment 9/10.
- The septa between 11/12, 12/13 and 13/14 are transverse and unperforated.
- All the septa behind 14th (14/15 onwards) segment are called *typical septa*. These are transverse and perforated septa.

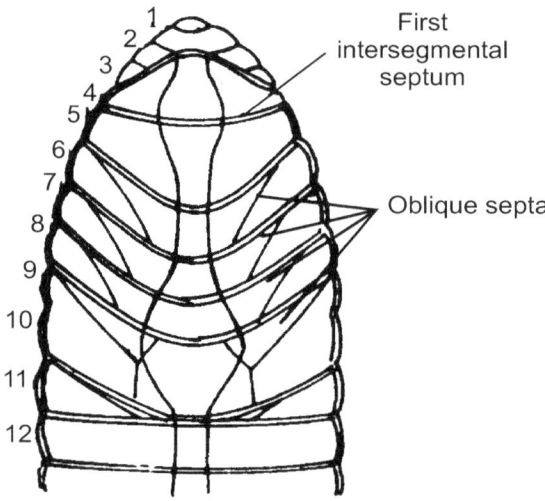

Fig. 4.7: *Pheretima*: Arrangement of septa in the anterior segments

- Each typical septum has 120 to 136 minute oval or circular apertures. The apertures are surrounded by thick sphinctered muscles.
- The spincters control the movement of coelomic fluid in the posterior segments from 14th to the last and vice versa.
- The closure of the sphincters, restricts coelomic fluid to any one or more compartments to make the segments rigid giving resistance to mechanical pressure.
- This helps in locomotion. The coelom opens to the exterior by the way of dorsal pores nephridipores and gonoducts.

Coelomic fluid and Corpuscles

The coelom or the body cavity is filled with coelomic fluid which contains about 99.9% of water. It is a colourless or milky white fluid made up of slightly alkaline matrix (pH-7.9). It contains numerous colourless nucleated cells or corpuscles with salt and some proteins.

There are the following four types of corpuscles. (Fig. 4.8).

1. The Granulocytes: These are numerous large nucleated, saucer shaped cells each showing deep concavity on one side and convexity on the other. The convex surface shows numerous folds. The nucleus is in the centre and the cytoplasm is full of granules. According to **Liebmann** (1942) the granulocytes are nutritive in function.

2. The Chloragogen cells: These cells are also called as amoeboid or yellow cells. They are numerous cells but small in size and show petaloid pseudopodia giving star-shaped appearance. They are supposed to be detached from the visceral peritoneum. They are phagocytic in function. They are also nutritive and excretory in function. These cells store food in the form of glycogen and fat droplets. These cells are excretory in function because they collect waste materials from coelomic fluid which are then eliminated when the coelomic fluid ejected through dorsal pores.

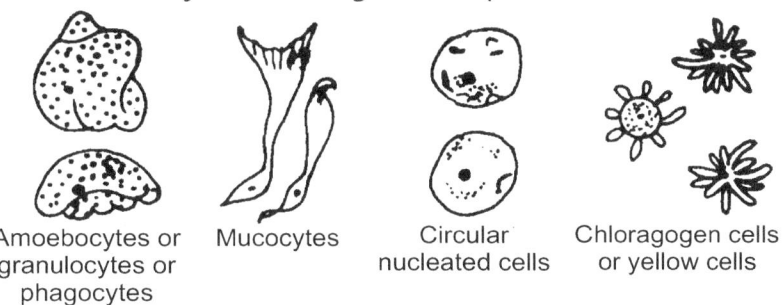

Amoebocytes or granulocytes or phagocytes   Mucocytes   Circular nucleated cells   Chloragogen cells or yellow cells

Fig. 4.8: *Pheretima*: **Coelomic corpuscles**

3. Leucocytes: These are flat circular cells with clear cytoplasm and nucleus. They show characteristic markings on the surface. The leucocytes are smaller than granulocytes. They are 10% of the total coelomic corpuscles. Their exact function is not known.

4. The Mucocytes: These are fan-shaped cells with nucleated cytoplasm at one end while the other end is expanded into fan-shaped body. They are modified phagocytes and phagocytic in function.

Functions of Coelomic Fluid

There are large number of pores on the dorsal side called dorsal pores through which coelomic fluid oozes out. The coelomic fluid performs the following functions:

1. The coelomic fluid forms a uniform environment for the internal organs.
2. It circulates digested food in the body by body contraction and relaxation.
3. The coelomic fluid helps in plastering the inner walls of burrows.
4. The coelomic fluid oozes out through dorsal pores and keeps the body surface moist, thus helping in respiration.
5. It destroys bacteria and harmful parasites which settle on the body surface of the animal.
6. It helps for collection and transportation of number of substances.
7. Alongwith the coelomic fluid some excretory material is also thrown out. The chloragogen cells along with excretory products pass out of the body.
8. It forms a protective covering around the internal organs and also reduces the friction between the internal organs.
9. It makes the body segments turgid exerting hydrostatic pressure thus helping in locomotion.
10. Above all it is a reservoir of water, preventing the desiccation of body tissues.

Locomotion

- The earthworm shows locomotion with the help of body muscles, the setae of the skin and the buccal chamber. It shows normally creeping movement.
- During locomotion coelomic fluid also plays an important role.
- When earthworm executes forward movement, the protractor muscles of the posterior part of the body contract causing the protrusion of the backwardly directed setae which firmly grip the substratum.
- At the same time the anterior part of the body becomes thinner and longer and is extended forwards as a result of contraction of the circular muscles and the relaxation of the longitudinal muscles.
- During this act, pressure on the coelomic fluid is exerted which results in elongation of the worm.
- The posterior part is stationary and the anterior part pushes forward.

- Now the buccal chamber is everted and it is fixed with the substratum as a sucker.
- The setae of anterior part also thrust out and firmly anchored in the soil.
- The posterior part of the body elongates and its setae are also withdrawn by the contraction of the retractor muscles.
- The wave of extension passed backwards throughout the body.
- By the contraction of longitudinal muscles and relaxation of circular muscles, the anterior part of the body shortens.
- The anterior part of the body is fixed in the substratum, consequently the posterior part is pulled forward towards the anterior end.
- The wave of contraction also passed backwards throughout the body, so that the posterior part of the body contracts its setae again protruded and anchored and the anterior part of the body is extended forward once again.
- Thus in earthworm, the locomotion is carried out by alternate waves of extension and contraction passing over the entire body from anterior end to posterior end assisted by setae and buccal chamber.
- At any one movement only one part of the worm is moving.
- During locomotion worm can cover a distance of about 25 cm in one minute.
- The coelomic fluid during locomotion plays a vital role of hydraulic skeleton.
- When muscles contract the coelomic fluid is compressed which provides stiffness to the body and helps in the extension of the longitudinal muscles.

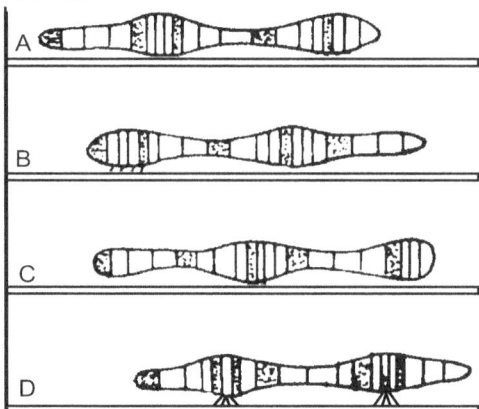

Fig. 4.9: *Pheretima*: Diagram to illustrate locomotion in an earthworm

- Backward movement is also seen in the earthworm just by reversing the direction of the setae.
- When animal is irritated, it shows violent, irregular and jerky movements. These movements help the animal to escape from the enemy.
- The rapid crawling movement is also performed by the animal over rough surface or through the soil.
- The animal moves with great difficulties on smooth or frictionless surface like glass on which setae cannot obtain a firm grip or anchoring.

4.3 Digestive System

Digestive system of earthworm consists of alimentary canal and associated glands which are embedded in the wall of the alimentary canal itself.

Alimentary canal: (Fig. 4.11) The alimentary canal is a long and straight tube. It extends from the mouth to the anus. It shows the following well defined regions:

1. Mouth
2. Buccal chamber
3. Pharynx
4. Oesophagus
5. Gizzard
6. Stomach
7. Intestine and
8. Anus

1. Mouth: The mouth is a crescentic opening lying ventral to the prostomium at the anterior edge of the prostomium.

2. Buccal chamber: The mouth leads to a short, thin walled protrusible buccal chamber which extends from first to the middle of third segment. It is connected to the body wall by muscle strands. Its inner lining remains folded. Earthworm constantly protrudes and retracts its buccal chamber and it acts as an organ of ingestion of food. The eversible buccal chamber also serves as an adaptation to burrowing habit as animal eats its way into the soil.

3. Pharynx: The buccal chamber is followed by a wider, pear shaped and thick walled muscular chamber, the pharynx. It extends from middle of the third segment to the end of 4th segment. It is marked dorsally from the buccal chamber by transverse groove lodging the cerebral ganglia or brain. It is dorsoventrally flattened structure connected to the body wall by muscle strands.

In T.S., the lumen of the pharynx is compressed dorsoventrally because of the presence of on its roof a orange thick pharyngeal mass or bulb containing salivary gland cells or *chromophil cells*, musculovascular tissue and internal living of ciliated epithelium.

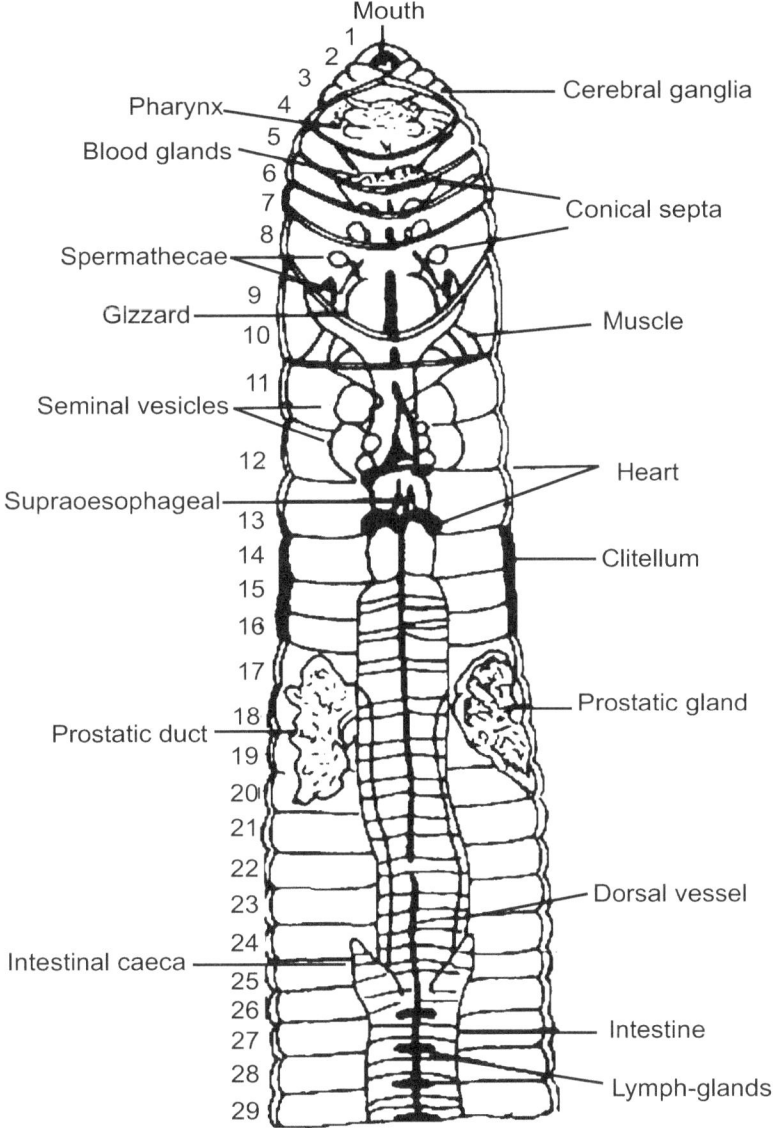

Fig. 4.10: *Pheretima*: General viscera

The lateral walls of pharynx are pushed inwards to form two lateral shelves. The lateral shelves divide the lumen of the pharynx into a dorsal *salivary chamber* and ventral *conducting chamber*. The pharyngeal mass produces a salivary secretion containing mucous and proteolytic digestive enzymes which are poured into the salivary chamber.

The lateral and ventral walls of the pharynx consists of scattered muscle fibres and dense connective tissue. From the pharyngeal walls runs outwards to the body wall numerous radial muscles. The contraction of the radial muscles dialate the pharyngeal cavity.

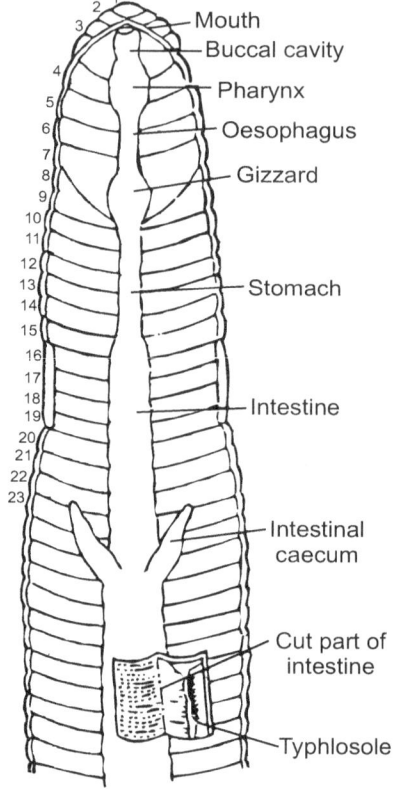

Fig. 4.11: *Pheretima*: **Alimentary canal**

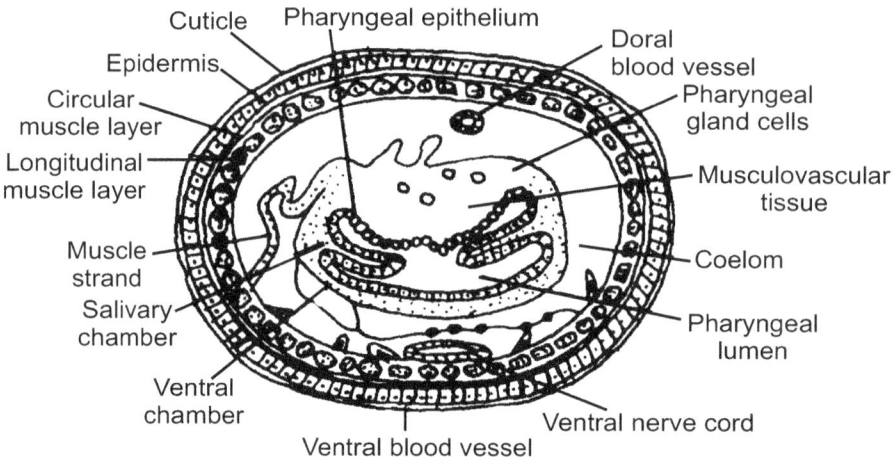

Fig. 4.12: *Pheretima*: **A T.S. through the pharyngeal region**

The pharynx functions as a suction pump (suctorial pump) in feeding. It secretes saliva which contains mucin and proteolytic enzymes. The mucin helps in lubrication of the food and proteolytic enzymes start digestion of proteins.

4. Oesophagus: Pharynx leads into oesophagus or gullet. The oesophagus is a short, narrow and thin walled tube anteriorly bent on itself and extends from 5th to 8th segment. Through this tube, the food coming from pharynx passes and enters the gizzard by peristalsis.

5. Gizzard: The oesophagus is modified into a prominent, oval, hard, thick walled, muscular structure called *gizzard*. It is lying in 8th and 9th segment. In T.S. it shows thick muscular wall made up only circular muscle layer. It is internally lined by a tough cuticle secreted by the underlying columnar epithelial cells.

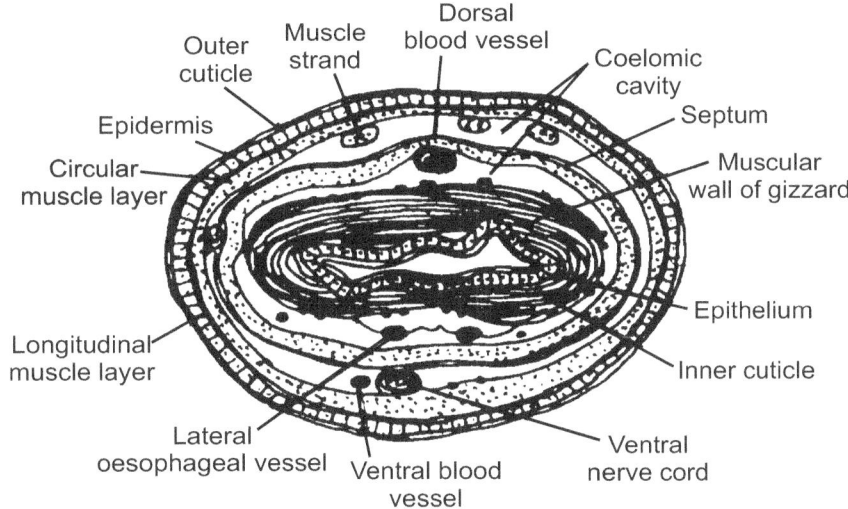

Fig. 4.13: *Pheretima*: A T.S. through the gizzard

The gizzard helps in mixing the food contents by contraction and relaxation of its circular muscles. It also helps in grinding humus into powder against the internal hard cuticle and with the coarse soil particles.

6. Stomach: The gizzard is followed by a short narrow tube called stomach. It is slightly wider than oesophagus and extends from 9th to 14th segments. The internal lining is transversely folded, highly vascular and glandular. It is provided with sphincter valves at both the ends hence called **stomach**. These sphincters control the passage of food. The stomach secretes proteolytic enzymes. In some species of earthworms (e.g. *Lumbricus*) calciferous glands are present which secrete calcium to neutralise acidity of the humus ingested. These glands help in excretion by removing excess of calcium and carbonate ions from food and passing them as calcite into the stomach to be eliminated with the mud through anus. There are two calciferous glands in *Pheretima*.

7. **Intestine:** The stomach leads into intestine which is a long, wide thin walled tube extended from the 15th segment to the last. It is highly vascular and glandular part, differentiated into following the three regions: (i) pretyphlosolar region, (ii) typhlosolar region and (iii) post-typhlosolar region.

(i) **Pretyphlosolar region:** This region which extends from the 15th to 26th segments. In 26th segment it bears a pair of short, conical anteriorly directed out growths called intestinal caeca. They extend anteriorly over three or four segment. The intestinal caeca secrete the enzyme amylase. Its wall is internally folded to form minute processes or villi and is highly vascular.

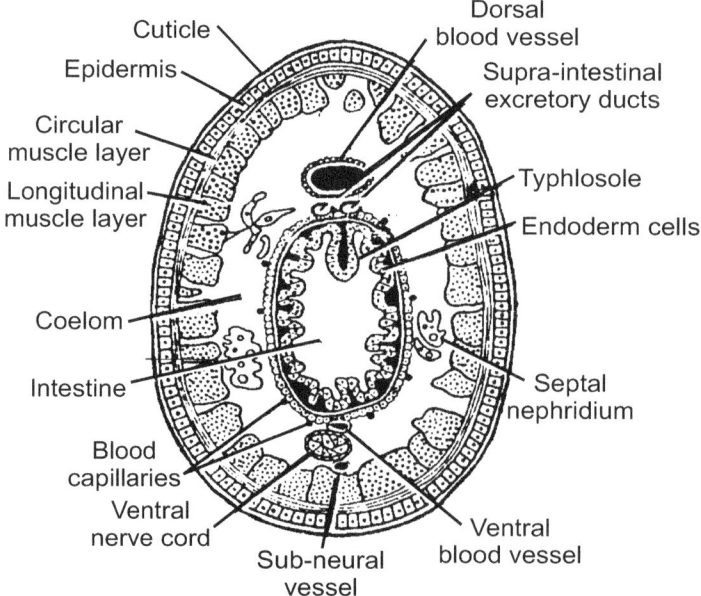

Fig. 4.14: *Pheretima* **: A T.S. through the typhlosolar region of the intestine**

(ii) Typhlosolar region: It is the longest, middle part of the intestine extending posteriorly from 27th segment except the last 25 segments. Internally, it shows large mid-dorsal tongue like fold called **typhlosole** projecting into the lumen of the intestine. Typhlosole increases the internal absorptive surface area.

(iii) Post-typhlosolar region: This region is also called rectum situated in the last twenty five segments. It has no typhlosole and opens to the exterior on the last segment by terminal anus.

In T.S., the intestine appears more or less oval in outline. Externally, it is surrounded by visceral peritoneum. The wall of the intestine is made up of thin outer longitudinal and inner circular muscle layers. The epithelial lining of the intestine is thrown into folds to increase the area of absorption. In typhlosolar region the mid-dorsal fold is enlarged to form a tongue like prominent structure called typhlosole. In the section external and internal blood plexuses are also seen. Dorsal blood vessel, supra-intestinal excretory ducts, ventral blood vessel and ventral nerve cord are also seen in the T.S. passing through the typhlosolar region.

The typhlosole performs many important functions. It contains numerous gland cells which secrete different types of enzymes required for digestion of food. Typholsole also increases surface area for digestion and passage of intestinal contents giving enough time for digestion and also for absorption of digestion products.

8. Anus: The anus is the terminal slit-like opening laced in the centre of the last or anal segment. It is guarded by a sphincter, controlling defaecation.

Food and Feeding Mechanism

- The food of the earthworm is decaying organic matter or humus present in the soil. Since the food contents or organic matter of humus present in the soils are insufficient, animal ingests comparatively large quantity of soil.
- Earthworms also feed directly upon leaves, grasses, seeds, algae and other vegetation. This food is generally gathered during night time when worms are very active.
- The food is ingested by protrusible action of buccal chamber and then sucked up into the mouth and pharynx by the sucking action of the muscular pharynx.

- Due to large quantities of soil, the gut therefore, is always full of soil. As the earthworm burrows in soil, the buccal chamber is protruded out and the cavity of the pharynx is expanded.
- Gradually, and very slowly the food along with the soil is drawn into the buccal chamber of sucking action of pharynx helps in drawing the food into the buccal chamber.

Physiology of Digestion:
- The organic matter ingested along with the soil contains mainly proteins, starch, fat and some sugar. These substances are digested by the various enzymes secreted in the stomach, intestinal caeca and intestine.
- Digestion starts in the pharynx. Here the food is mixed with saliva. The saliva contains mucin and proteolytic enzymes secreted by the pharyngeal glands. Mucin lubricates the food while proteolytic enzymes start the digestion of proteins. Thereafter the food is passed on the gizzard through oesophagus by peristalsis.
- In gizzard, the food is thoroughly mixed up, ground up into powder with the help of strong circular muscle and hard internal cuticle.
- While passing through stomach it again receives proteolytic enzymes which further enhance the digestion of proteins.
- In the intestine food is mixed with proteolytic, amylolytic and lipolytic enzymes acting on proteins, carbohydrates and fats converting them into amino acids, simple sugars, fatty acids and glycerol.
- It also secretes enzyme cellulase for digestion of cellulose of vegetable matter of the humus. Thus in the intestine, food is completely digested and absorbed. Typhlosole also helps in absorption of digested food.

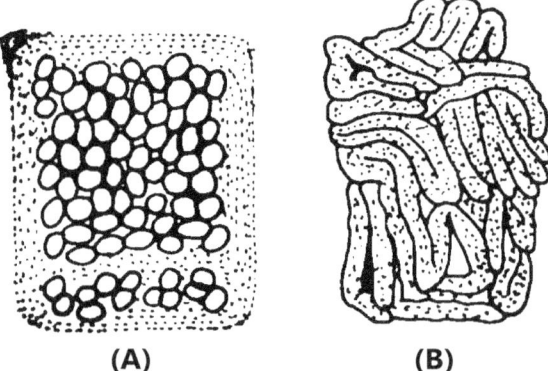

(A) (B)

Fig. 4.15: Castings of earthworms. A-*Pheretima*; B-*Eutyphoeus*

- In earthworms, the digestion of food is extracellular as in higher animals. The passage of food in the alimentary canal is caused by peristaltic movement of the gut wall caused by circular and longitudinal muscles.
- The digested food is absorbed by epithelial lining of the intestine and passed into the blood stream for distribution to various parts of the body.
- A part of the absorbed food enters the coelomic cavity and carried directly to those tissues bathed by coelomic fluid.

Egestion: The undigested matter is temporarily stored in the rectum. Along with the soil, it is then egested out through anus in the form of worm-castings, which are deposited on the surface of the ground near the mouth of their burrows. The castings of *Pheretima* consists of distinct, small and rounded pellets or balls. The worm castings greatly enrich the soil.

Respiration
- Although earthworm is a terrestrial animal but its respiration is more like that of simple aquatic animals. There are not special respiratory organs in the earthworm hence there is no respiratory system as such.
- However, animal shows cutaneous respiration. The gaseous exchange takes place through the moist and thin and highly vascularised skin. The blood of the earthworm contains haemoglobin in dissolved condition in plasma.
- Moisture is essential for gaseous exchange between the blood and the atmospheric air. Therefore, the epidermal glands keep skin always moist as well as the dorsal pore, ooze out the coelomic fluid also help in keeping skin moist.
- The skin is also maintained moist by the damp soil where the worm lives. If the skin is dried, gaseous exchange stops and the worm dies of asphyxia.

4.4 Blood Vascular System (Circulatory System)

The blood vascular system of earthworm is of closed type because the blood is circulated through the closed blood vessels.

The blood is red in colour due to the respiratory pigment haemoglobin is dissolved in plasma. It contains colourless blood corpuscles which are numerous and are suspended in plasma. The blood is always circulated within blood vessels and flows in a definite circuit. Near the pharynx, blood glands are present which produce haemoglobin and blood corpuscles. Haemoglobin has strong affinity with oxygen and it is dissolved in plasma hence blood of earthworm is efficient oxygen carrier.

The arrangement and the nature of blood vessels in the first 13 segments is different from that behind the 13th segment i.e. in the intestinal region (Fig. 4.16). Therefore, the blood vascular system can be conveniently described under two heads:

(A) The blood vascular system behind the 13th segment or in the intestinal region and

(B) The blood vascular system in the first thirteen segment (Fig. 4.17) or in pre-intestinal region.

The blood vascular system behind the 13th segment or in the intestinal region

It is convenient to consider first, the arrangement of blood vessels in the intestinal region because of less complexity. The blood vessels show metameric arrangement i.e. the blood vessels are same in all segments. In this region the vascular system consists of three longitudinal blood vessels running parallel to each other along with their branches.

They are:
1. Dorsal blood vessels.
2. Ventral blood vessels.
3. Subneural blood vessels.

1. Dorsal blood vessel: It is the largest blood vessels which runs mid-dorsally above the alimentary canal right from the anterior to the posterior end of the body. It has thick muscular and rhythmically contractile wall and a pair of valves in each segment just infront of the septum. The blood flows towards anterior region and valves prevent backflow. The dorsal vessel is mainly a collecting vessels in the intestinal region. It receives a pair commissural and dorsal intestinals in each segment.

(i) **Commissural vessels:** These are a pair of loop-like vessels running along the posterior surface of each septum. They collect blood from the subneural vessels, body wall, septa and nephridia. Each commissural on its way gives out a branch called septa intestinal supplying blood to the intestine. The commissural vessels opens on the dorsal surface of the dorsal vessels and at the point of opening the valves are present, to prevent black flow of the blood.

(ii) **Dorso-intestinals:** In each segment the two dorso-intestinals collect the blood from the intestine and open in the ventral surface of the dorsal vessel. At the point of opening a pair of valves prevent the backflow of the blood.

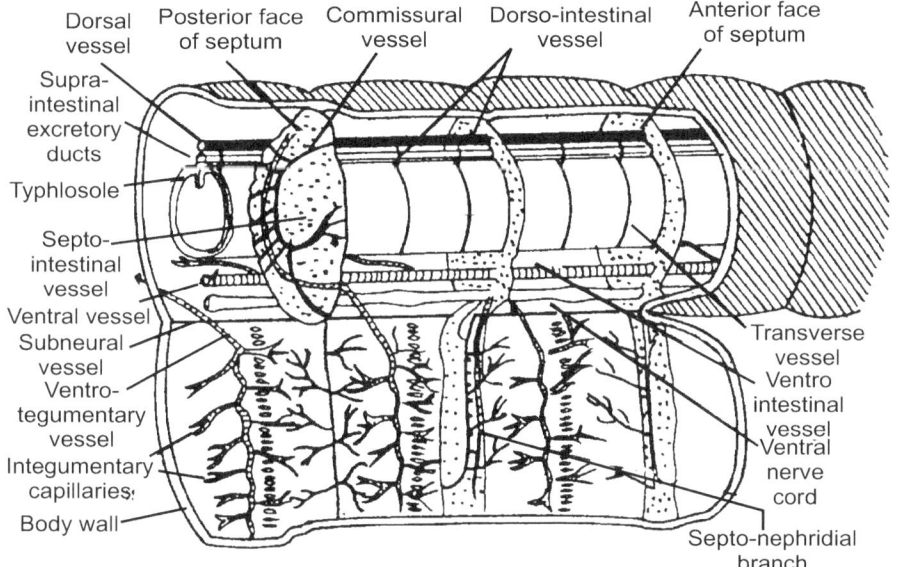

Fig. 4.16: *Pheretima*: Blood vascular system in the segments behind 13th. A part of body wall on the left side has been cut and reflected in order to expose the blood vessels in position

2. **Ventral blood vessel:** It is a large vessel running midventrally below the alimentary canal and like dorsal vessel it also extends from anterior to posterior end of the body. It is non-contractile and thin walled vessel, without valves in which the blood flows toward posterior region. It is a distributing vessel supplying blood to the alimentary canal and body wall. It gives off pair of ventro-tegumentaries and ventro-intestinals in each segment.

(i) **Ventro-tegumentary:** In each segment, the ventro-tegumentary originates from the ventral vessels on the anterior side of the inter segmental septum. It pierces through the septum to enter the succeeding segment. These vessels supply blood to the body wall, nerve cord and integumentary nephridia. Each ventro-tegumentary gives off a small branch i.e. septonephridial to septal nephridia.

(ii) **Ventro-intestinal:** In each segment, the ventral vessel gives off ventro-intestinal from it dorsal surface. It supplies blood to the intestine.

3. **Subneural blood vessels:** It is situated ventrally below the nerve cord. It is formed in the 14th segment by union of the two latero-oesophageals and then runs backwards right upto the last segment. In vessel, blood flows posteriorly. It is collecting vessel, which collects blood from ventral body wall and the nerve cord. The blood is send to the dorsal vessel through the commissural vessels. In this vessel, the blood flows from 14th segment backwards. It also gives out a pair of commissurals running along the posterior surface of the septum.

The intestinal blood plexus: The close network of blood capillaries in the wall of intestine forms the intestinal blood plexus. There are two types of intestinal blood plexus.

(i) **External blood plexus:** The capillaries of this are situated on the surface of intestine.

(ii) **Internal blood plexus:** The capillaries of internal blood plexus are situated between the circular muscle layer of intestine and its epithelial lining. The external plexus carries the blood into the internal blood plexus. The internal blood plexus absorbs the nutrients from the gut.

According to the arrangement of the blood capillaries, there are three regions of the intestine. The first region extends from 14th to 26th segment and consists of a close network of transverse capillaries. The second region extends from 26th segment to about twenty six segment in front of the anus and it is formed of longitudinal and oblique capillaries. The third region includes last 26 segments where the capillaries form an aroborescent tree like blood plexuses.

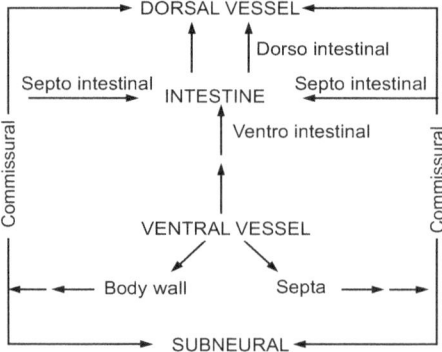

Fig. 4.17: *Pheretima.* **Course of blood circulation in intestinal region**

(B) The blood vascular system in first 13 segments

The arrangement and the nature of the blood vessels in the first 13 segments are considerably different from that in the intestinal region. Due to modification of the alimentary canal in the anterior region, the blood vascular system in this is also considerably modified. The main blood vessels of this region are: **(Fig. 4.18)**

1. Longitudinal blood vessels which include:
   (i) dorsal vessel,
   (ii) ventral vessel,
   (iii) latero-oesophageal vessels,
   (iv) supra-oesophageal vessels.
2. Four pairs of hearts and
3. Two pairs of anterior loops.

1. Longitudinal blood vessels: These blood vessels run dorsally, midventrally and lateral to the alimentary canal. Following are the main longitudinal blood vessels.

(i) Dorsal blood vessel: It is present on the dorsal side of the gut which runs on the middorsal line from 3rd to the last segment. It is thick muscular and contractile vessel provided with a pair of valves in each segment and flow of the blood is from posterior to the anterior. Dorsal blood vessel in this region in the main distributing vessel instead of being a collecting vessels as in the intestinal region. It supplies blood to the buccal chamber, pharynx, oesophagus, gizzard and spermathecae through paired short branches. These branches are present in 3rd, 4th, 5th and 8th segments. The major portion of the blood is however, drained into the ventral vessel through four pairs of hearts situated in the 7th, 9th, 12th and 13th segments.

(ii) Ventral blood vessel: It is present on the ventral side of the gut and extends anteriorly upto the second segment. It is distributing vessel in which blood flows towards the posterior direction. In each segment ventral blood vessel gives of a pair of ventro-tegumentary vessels. The ventro-tegumentaries distribute, blood to the body wall, septal nephridia, spermathecae, testis-sac, seminal vesicles, ovaries, oviducts etc. The ventro-intestinals are absent in this region. The ventral blood vessel in non-contractile and thin walled vessel without valves.

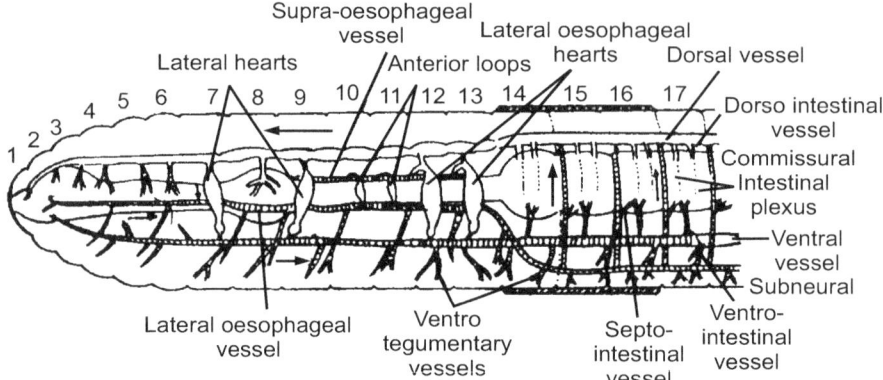

Fig. 4.18: *Pheretima*: The blood vascular system in the anterior 13 segments in the body

(iii) **Latero-oesophageals:** There are pair of large vessels situated on the ventro-lateral side on the gut from 2nd to 13th segments. They join in the 14th segment below the nerve cord to form the subneural vessel which extends posteriorly upto the last segment. The latero oesophageals extends anteriorly upto 2nd segment. In these vessels blood flows towards the posterior direction. They are towards the posterior direction. They are collecting vessels which receive blood from the body wall through a pair of efferent tegumentaries running parallel to different tegumentaries in each segment. They also collect blood from the buccal chamber, pharynx, oesophagus, gonads and nephridia but not from gizzard, through separate paired vessels. In the segments 10 to 13 the vessels are closely attached to the wall of the stomach and communicate with ring vessels.

(iv) **Supra-oesophageal**

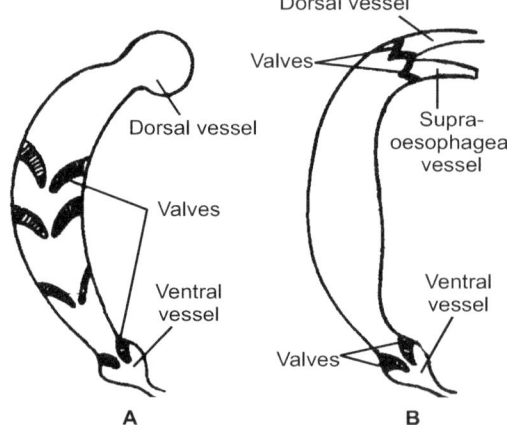

Fig. 4.19: *Pheretima*: A-Lateral heart; B-Latero-oesophageal heart

It is a short unpaired vessel present between 9th to 13th segment dorsal to the stomach which was formaly considered as a part of oesophagus. It is collecting as well as distributing vessel. In 10th and 11th segment it receives blood from latero oesophageals through the anterior loops. In 12th and 13th segment, the dorsal vessel and this vessel together send the blood to the ventral vessel through latero-oesophageal hearts. It collects blood from the gizzard by small branches and from the stomach through numerous ring vessels, which are 12 in each segment running through the wall of the stomach.

2. The Hearts: In the first 13 segments the dorsal and the ventral vessel communicates with each other with the help of muscular and pulsatile organs called the hearts. There are four pairs of hearts. The anterior pairs of heart in 7th and 9th segment are called lateral hearts and other two pairs in 12th and 13th segment are called latero oesophageal hearts (Fig. 4.18). The latero oesophageal hearts are connected dorsally with supra oesophageal and the dorsal vessel. The hearts are connected dorsally with supra oesophageal and the dorsal vessel. The hearts are enlarged, arched, hollow and muscular contractile structures. They are internally provided with valves. There are three pairs of valves in the latero oesophageal hearts and four pairs of valves in the lateral hearts. These valves prevent back flow of the blood. Being muscular and pulsatile they pump blood and keep it in circulation under pressure. Since they are provided with valves, they maintain the blood in one direction preventing backflow. The lateral hearts only carry blood from dorsal and ventral vessel. The latero oesophageal hearts besides, connecting the dorsal vessel to the ventral vessel also connect the supra oesophageal vessel with the ventral vessel through short connectives. They carry blood from the dorsal and supra oesophageal vessel to the ventral vessel.

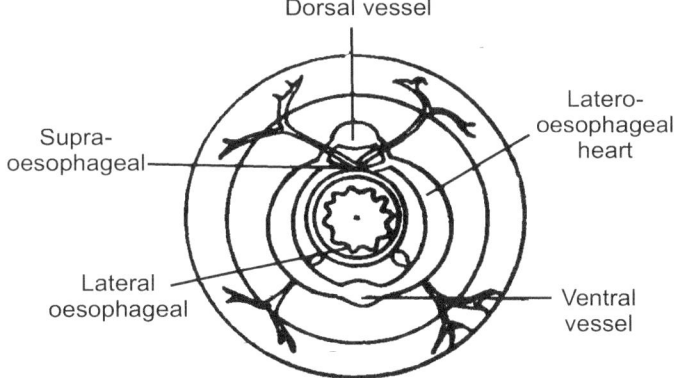

Fig. 4.20: *Pheretima*: T. S. through latero-oesophageal hearts

3. **Anterior loops:** In addition to 4 pairs of hearts, there are two pairs of loop-like vessels, one each in the 10th and 11th segment. They join the lateral-oesophageal to supra oesophageal vessel. The blood is collected from the stomach through numerous ring vessels to supra-oesophageal. These vessels or loops are non-muscular and non-pulsatile. They are called anterior loops. There are no valves and blood flows dorsally through the anterior loops.

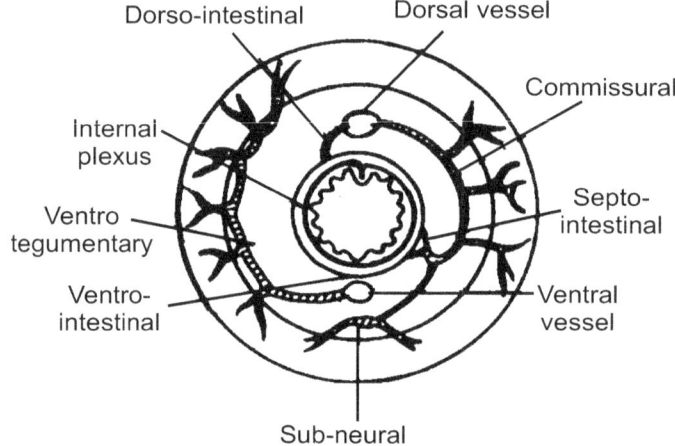

Fig. 4.21: *Pheretima*: T. S. through a segment on the left and through a segment on the right

The course of blood circulation in the first 13 segments is given below:

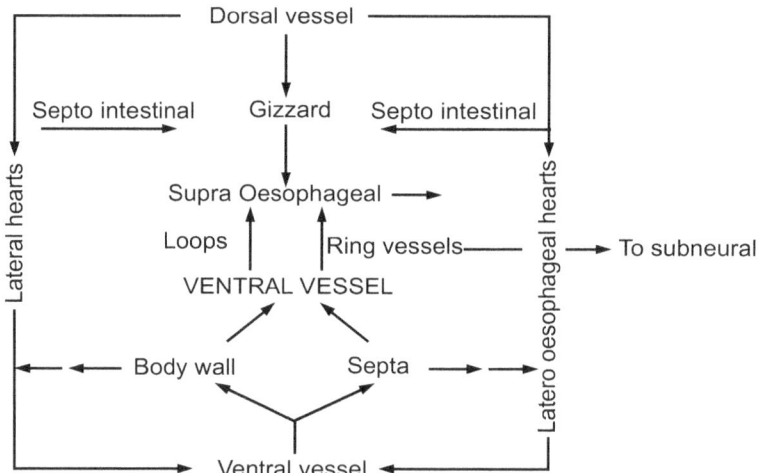

Fig. 4.22: *Pheretima*: Course of blood circulation in preintestinal region

4.5 Excretory System

- The liquid nitrogenous waste materials are formed in the body due to the metabolic activities. The separation, collection and elimination of liquid nitrogenous materials from the body is called Excretion. The system of organs which is concerned with excretion is called excretory system.
- The excretory system consists of metamerically arranged, coiled, microscopic tubules called nephridia. The excretory system is also called as nephridial system. Nephridia are present in all segments except the first three.
- Each nephridium is supplied with blood capillary plexus and bathed in the coelomic fluid from both of which they extract the waste materials.
- The greater part of the excretory fluid is poured into the alimentary canal through a system of canals and ducts. A small part of the excretory fluid is discharged outside, through the openings of nephridia called nephridiopores.

Thus, depending on the nature there are two types of nephridia:

(i) **Enteronephric nephridia:** These nephridia discharge their excretory fluid directly into the alimentary canal i.e. in enteron. In the intestine large amount of water is absorbed from the excretory fluid. This is an adaptation for conservation of water.

(ii) **Exonephric nephridia:** These are the nephridia which discharge excretory fluid directly on the surface of body wall through the nephridiopores.

According to the position of nephridia in the body of the animal and difference in their structures, the following types of nephridia are classified:

(1) Pharyngeal nephridia
(2) Integumentary nephridia and
(3) Septal nephridia.

1. Pharyngeal nephridia: They are situated around the pharynx and oesophagus hence the name. They are arranged in three paired bunches on either side in the 4th, 5th and 6th segments. They are very much similar to that of septal nephridia but there is no nephrostome. The slender ducts of these nephridia unite to form three pairs of long ducts, one pair of each segment. The pair of ducts arising from the 6th segment is longest and opens in the buccal chamber. The paired ducts from 4th and 5th segments open into the pharynx. Large number of cell masses called blood glands are present amongst these nephridia. These nephridia are without nephrostomes. Since they open into the alimentary canal, they are also called enteronephric nephridia and they help the alimentary canal in conservation of water.

2. **Integumentary nephridia:** They are found irregularly scattered on the innerside of the body wall or integument hence the name. They are situated in all segments except the first six segments. These nephridia are the smallest nephridia and devoid of nephrostomes. They are V-shaped with one arm slightly longer than the other. The number of nephridia in each segment varies from 200 to 250 but in the clitellar region i.e. in segment number 14th, 15th and 16th they are about 2000 to 2500 per segment forming a "forest of nephridia." They open directly to the outside on the surface of the body wall through minute openings called nephridiopores. Hence, these are called exonephric nephridia.

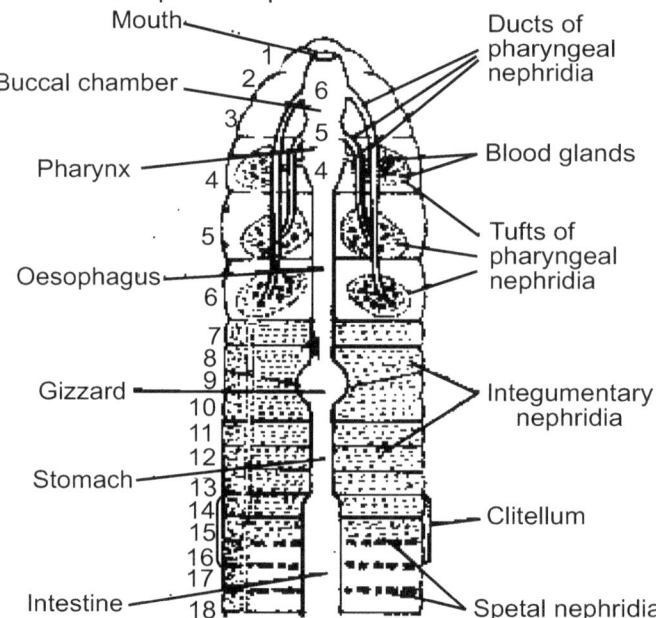

Fig. 4.23: *Pheretima*: **Different types of nephridia and general plan of their distribution**

3. Septal nephridia: (Fig. 4.24). The septal nephridia are the largest and attached to both the faces of each intersegmental septum behind the 15th segment. Each septum bears four concentric rows of nephridia, two on its anterior and two on its posterior face. Each row has 20 to 25 nephridia so each septum or coelonic compartment contains 80 to 100 septal nephridia. All the nephridia are freely suspended in coelomic fluid.

Structure of septal nephridium: Each septal nephridium is large and consists of four parts such as:

(i) Funnel or nephrostome (ii) Short neck
(iii) Body of the nephridium (iv) Terminal duct.

(i) **The Nephrostome:** The funnel or nephrostome is anterior free funnel shaped structure made up of a large hood-like upper lip of 8 or 9 ciliated marginal cells and small lower lip consisting of 4 to 5 compact cells. Between these is enclosed a central cell perforated by a crescentic opening of the mouth leading internally into long continuous central canal.

(ii) **Neck:** The mouth or funnel leads into a short narrow ciliated tubule i.e. neck. It joins nephrostome with the body.

(iii) **Body:** The body of the nephridium consists of a short straight lobe and a long spirally twisted loop, which is about twice the length of the straight lobe. The spirally twisted loop consists of a proximal limb and distal limb spirally twisted around each other.

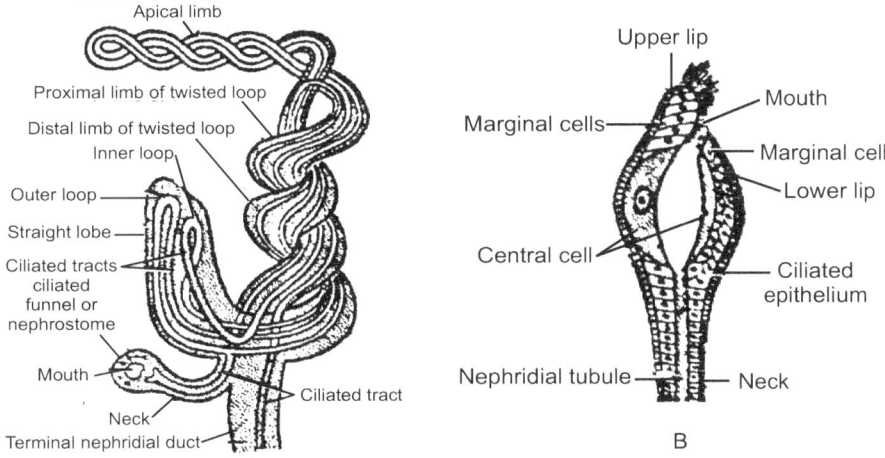

Fig. 4.24: *Pheretima*: **A septal nephridium**

The number of twists varies from 9 to 13. At the base of the nepridium, the straight lobe continues into the distal limb. The proximal limb receives on one hand a nephrostome, on the other hand it gives out a terminal duct. All the parts of a nephridium contain ciliated canals. There are four canals running parallel to one another in straight lobe, three in the proximal and the distal limb, two in the apical region, while the neck and the terminal duct have single canal.

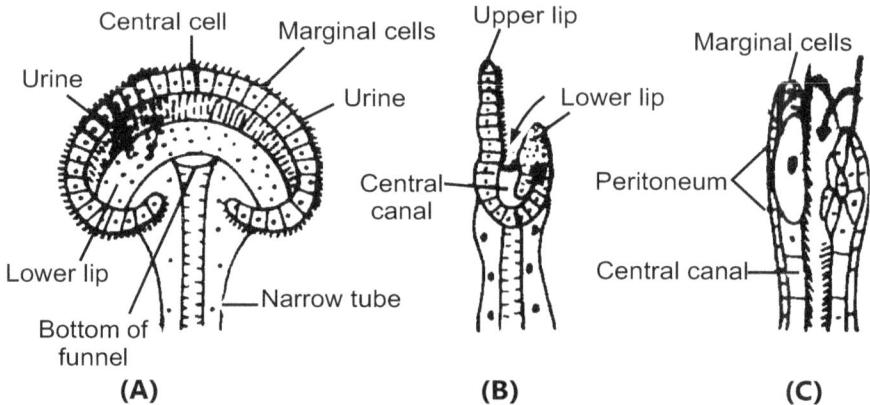

Fig. 4.25: A-Nephrostome of earthworm; B and C-L.S. of nephrostome

(iv) Terminal duct: It is a short and straight tube. The central canal of the terminal duct is ciliated. The nephridium hang freely in the coelomic fluid but are attached only by terminal ducts.

Throughout the length and within the nephridium runs a central canal right from the mouth to the terminal duct. The cells lining the central canal are glandular. In the body of nephridium the central canal gets twisted forming three coils in each limb of the spirally twisted loop and four coils in the short lobe. The cilia help in driving the waste products further.

The terminal ducts of all septal nephridia of each septum open into a pair of septal excretory canals which run along the posterior surface of each septum and inturn open into a pair of supra intestinal from 15th to the last segment. The supra-intestinal excretory ducts open into excretory ducts running dorsal to the intestine the lumen of the intestine at the level of each intersegmental septum. The excretory products pass from the blood and coelomic fluid to the exterior via septal nephridia → septal excretory canals → supra intestinal excretory ducts → lumen of the intestine and anus.

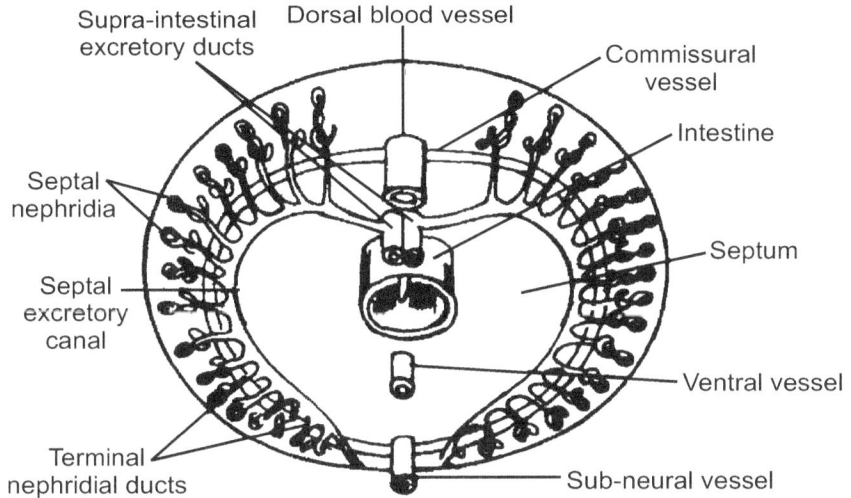

Fig. 4.26: *Pheretima*: **The arrangement of septal nephridial system in relation to the intestine**

Physiology of Excretion
- The nephridia are richly supplied with the blood vessels. They absorb the nitrogenous waste matter from coelomic fluid as well as surrounding blood capillaries.
- The nitrogenous waste products from different organs diffuse into coelomic fluid. Then these waste materials are absorbed by septal nephridia through nephrostome or through the body of nephridia by simple diffusion.
- As the fluid passes through central canal, selective reabsorption takes place. The cells lining the canal or glands cells extract the excess of water, the essential salts and other useful substances and the remaining fluid forms 'urine'.
- The urine of earthworm contains various excretory products such as, urea, ammonia, creatinine but there is no uric acid in the urine.
- The elimination of the urine out of the body is either through nephridiopores or indirectly through intestine along with the faecal matter. The urine is usually hypotonic from both the blood and coelomic fluid. However, the concentration of the urine depends upon the environmental condition.
- Thus nephridia perform the function of excretion, regulation of salts and water balance of body fluids and removal of break down products of haemoglobin.

- In the septal nephridia the third ciliated canal shows an accumulation of dark-brown granules. Most probably these are the products of the breakdown of haemoglobin which are disposed by the nephridia.
- Some authors also suggest that the dark brown granules are concerned with active secretion of urine.

Chloragogen cells
- The nephridia are not the only organs of excretion in earthworm. A large number of yellow cells or chloragogen cells are found surrounding the intestine and the dorsal blood vessel.
- Histologically, they are derived from the peritoneum or coelomic epithelium of the alimentary canal. These cells also perform the function of excretion. They absorb and store nitrogenous waste material from the blood and coelomic fluid.
- When the cells are full of waste products, they get detached, disintegrate and are ultimately discharged through dorsal pores along with coelomic fluid.
- Although there are difference of opinions regarding the exact nature and function of these cells, yet they seem to perform the function of excretion.
- These cells take up waste products from the blood capillaries of the gut and deposit them as yellow granules (guanine) in their cytoplasm.
- These cells fully laden with waste products detach from gutwall, drop into coelomic fluid and are eliminated out through septal nephridia or the dorsal pores.
- Some authors consider these cells as degenerated chloragogen cells which are eventually destroyed by phagocytic coelomocytes.
- Another view suggests that these cells serve as a storehouse for reserve food in the form of glycogen and fat which they manufacture from the fatty acids. Chloragogen cells are also said to be concerned with deamination of proteins, formation of ammonia and synthesis of urea.

4.6 Reproductive System

The earthworm reproduces sexually. The animal is monoecious or hermaphrodite i.e. both male and female sex organs are situated in one and the same individual. The gonads are mesodermal in origin and are restricted to the anterior one-fourth of the body and situated in definite segments (Fig. 4.31).

4.6.1 Male Reproductive System

The male reproductive system consists of testes, testis sacs, seminal vesicle, vasa deferentia, prostate glands and accessory glands (Figs. 4.27-4.30).

1. Testes: There are two pairs of testes situated in testis sacs in 10th and 11th segments. They are white minute lobed structures lying beneath the alimentary canal and close to the mid ventral line on either side of the nerve cord. Each testis is made up of compact narrow base from which 4 to 8 small finger like processes arise. Spermatogenesis proceeds upto the spermatogonia stage in the testis. The spermatogonia or sperm mother cells are packed in the matrix of a minute testis. Each testis is attached to the anterior wall of the testis sac.

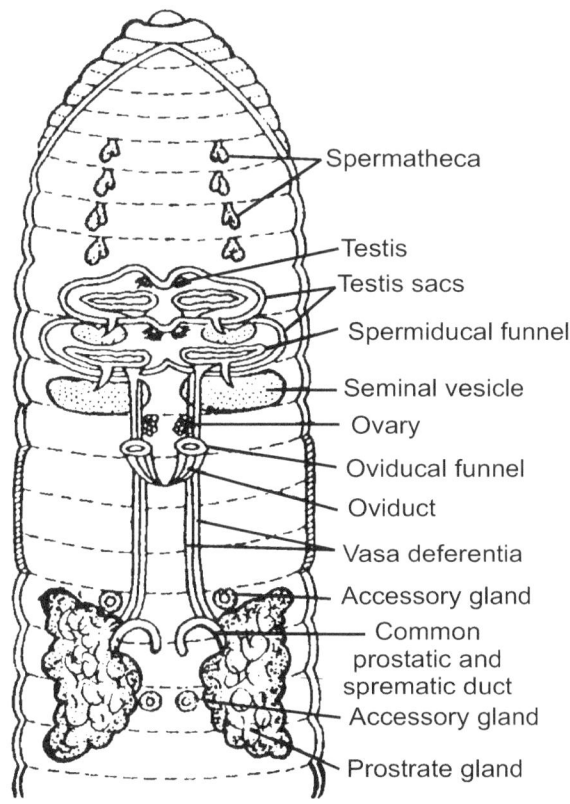

Fig. 4.27: *Pheretima*: **Reproductive system**

2. Testis sacs: There are pair of sac like structures situated in 10th and 11th segment which are filled with the fluid. They are considered as closed off portions of the coelom. The testis sac of 11th segment is larger than that of 10th segment. Each testis sac encloses a pair of testis and a pair of ciliated spermiducal funnels one on each side of their respective segments. Each testis sac communicates posteriorly with a pair of seminal vesicle. The testis-sac of 11th segment are larger because they also enclose seminal vesicles of that segment.

3. **Seminal vesicles:** These are two pairs of sac like bodies situated on one pair of the 11th and one pair of 12th segment. The one pair lying in 11th segment is enclosed in the testis-sac of the segment while the 2nd pair of seminal vesicle is free in 12th segment. The seminal vesicles are regarded as outgrowth of the septa. The testis-sac of 10th segment communicates with the seminal vesicles of the 11th segment and the testis sac of the 11th segment with the seminal vesicles of the 11th segment. The seminal vesicles secrete their secretion which gives nourishment to the developing sperms. From the testis the spermatogonia are dropped into the testis sacs from where they enter the seminal vesicles. In the seminal vesicles they undergo maturation division to form spermatozoa. The spermatozoa find their way back into the testis sac by the lashing movements of their tails.

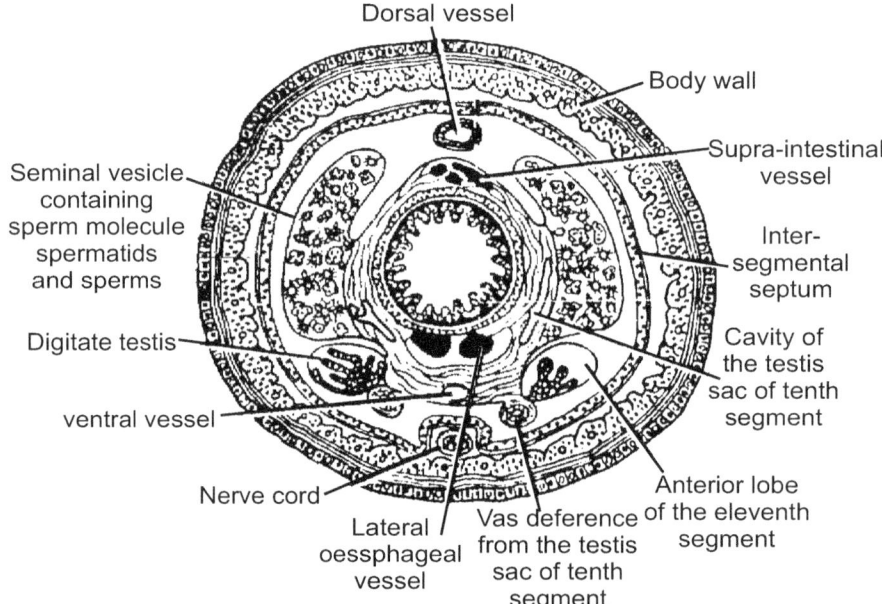

Fig. 4.28: *Pheretima*: T.S. passing through the testis sacs, testes and seminal vesicles in the anterior region of 11th segment

4. Spermiducal funnels: There are two pairs of ciliated spermiducal funnels, one pair situated in each testis sac. Large masses of sperms are usually attached to the margins of the funnel.

5. Vasa deferentia: The spermiducal funnels continues behind as the vasa deferentia. The two vasa deferentia run backward upto the 18th segment. They are thin wall, ducts lying one pair of either side of the nerve cord. They are internally ciliated throughout. The two vasa deferentia on each side then run laterally parallel to the nerve cord upto 18th segment where are incorporated into the common prostatic duct. The cilia help in the movement of spermatozoa towards the male genital opening.

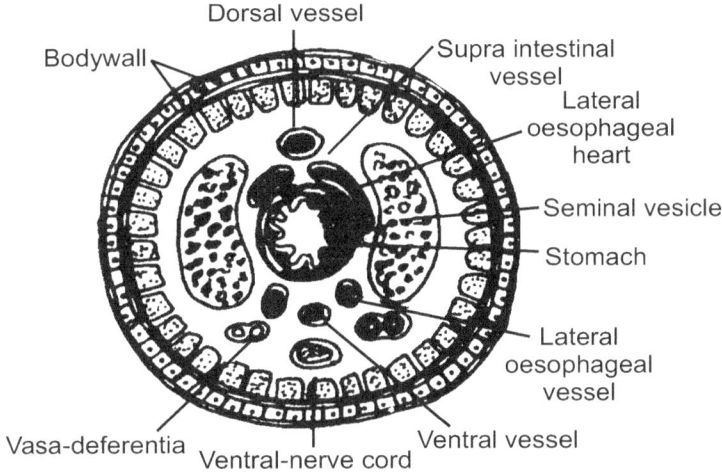

Fig. 4.29: *Pheretima*: T.S. of 12th segment of body

6. Prostate gland: These are a pair of pinkish, flat, irregular, lobulated solid glands. They are present in 17th to 20th or 21th segments situated one on each side of the alimentary canal.

Each prostate gland consists of a large glandular and a small non-glandular portion. Each prostate gland gives out a prostate duct which is enclosed (but not fused) in a common connective tissue sheath, along with two vasa deferentia, to form hook shaped common prostatic duct.

The two common prostatic ducts open outside by a pair of male genital apertures on the ventrolateral sides of the 18th segment. The secretion of the prostate gland probably serves to activate the sperms.

7. Accessory glands: There are two pairs of accessory or copulatory glands situated internal to the genital papillae in the 17th and 19th segments. They are white fluffy masses consisting group of glandular cells which open outside on the genital papillae by numerous minute pores. The secretion of the accessory glands probably helps in copulation.

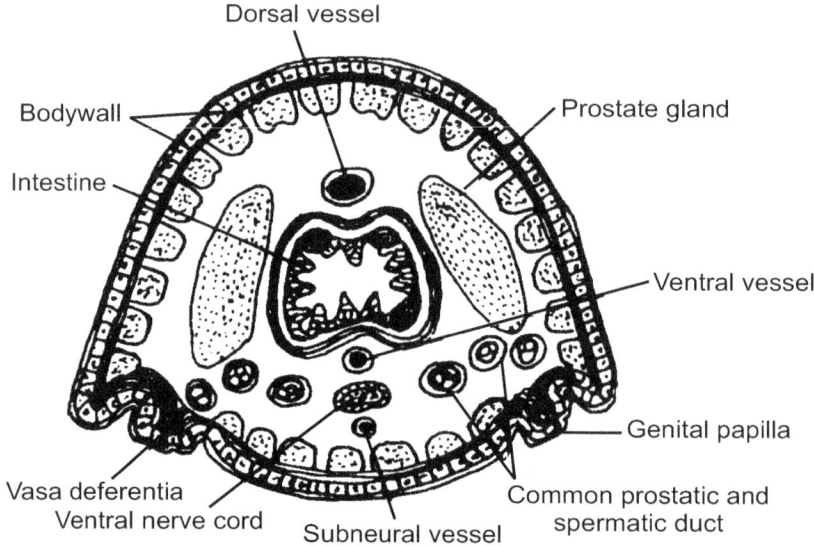

Fig. 4.30: *Pheretima*: T.S. of 18th segment of body passing through prostate glands and genital papillae

4.6.2 Female Reproductive System

The female reproductive organs consists of:
(i) Pair of ovaries,
(ii) Oviducal funnels,
(iii) Pair of oviducts and
(iv) Four pairs of spermathecae

1. Ovaries: (Fig. 4.31). The ovaries are a pair of essential female reproductive organs situated in the 13th segment. The ovaries are white finger like masses attached to the posterior surface of septum. $12/13^{th}$ segment lying on the either side of the nerve cord below the alimentary canal. Each ovary has eight to nine finger like processes which contain ova in various stages of development. The mature ova are present towards the free ends and are released into the coelom of the 13th segment. Each mature ovum shows distinct nucleus, yolk granules and is covered by egg membrane.

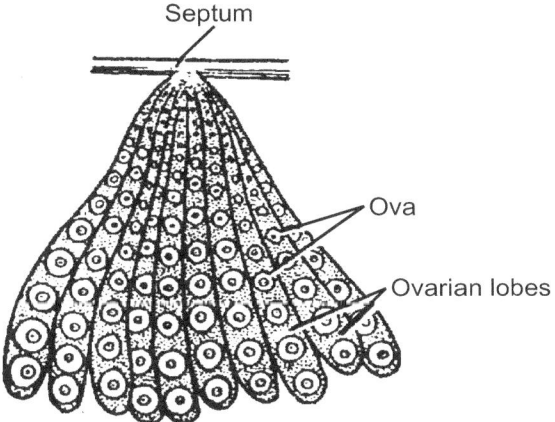

Fig. 4.31: *Pheretima*: Ovary

2. Oviducal funnels: A large saucer-shaped pair of oviducal funnels are present in 13th segment situated close to the ovaries. They are with folded and ciliated margins. The oviducal funnels run posteriorly into a short conical and ciliated tubes called oviducts.

3. Oviducts: There are pair of short V-shaped ducts situated in the 13th segment. They run posteriorly and after piercing the septum of 13/14 segments, converge to meet in the mid-ventral line below the nerve cord and then open ventrally and medially outside on the 14th segment by a common female genital aperture. The mature ova are dropped into coelomic fluid of 13th segment by the rupture of follicular membrane. They enter the oviducal funnels due to the ciliary movement of the latter passdown the oviducts and eventually passout through female genital aperture, at the time of cocoon formation.

4. Spermathecae: (Fig. 4.32). There are four pairs of spermathecae which are the accessory organs useful for receiving the sperms from the other individual during copulation, hence, included in the female reproductive system. The 4 pairs of spermathecae are situated in the segments 6, 7, 8 and 9 and they open to the outside by four pairs of separate spermathecal pores, situated, ventrolaterally in the grooves between 5/6, 6/7, 7/8, 8/9 segments respectively. Each spermatheca has a broad, pear shaped body, the ampulla and a short narrow neck, which gives off a narrow elongated blind caecum or diverticulum before opening to the exterior.

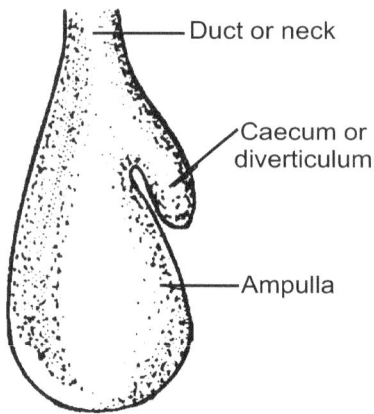

Fig. 4.32: *Pheretima*: Spermatheca

The diverticulum stores sperms during copulation while ampulla provides sperm nourishing fluid. The function of spermathecae is to store sperms during copulation from other earthworm, to keep the sperms viable for a long time by nourishing fluid it contains and also to squeeze out the sperms at the time of cocoon formation.

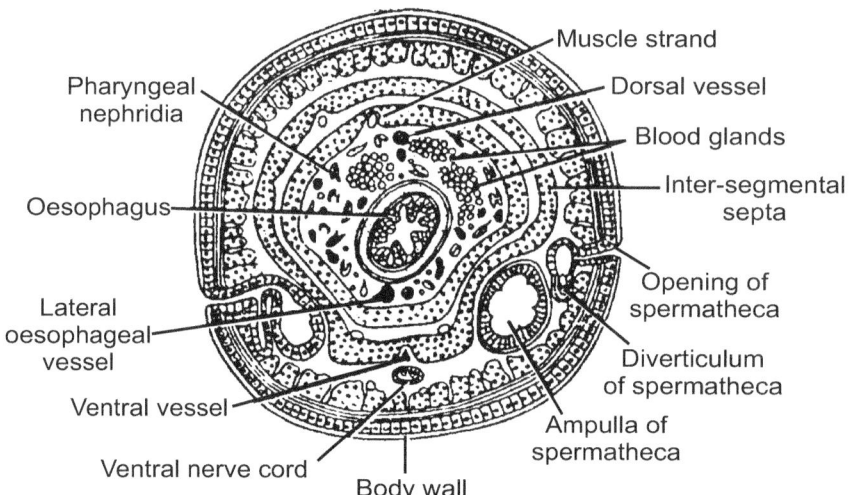

Fig. 4.33: *Pheretima*: T.S. passing through the region of spermathecae

Copulation and Fertilization

- Earthworm is bisexual or hermaphrodite animal, still self fertilization does not occur.

- The animal cannot fertilize its own eggs because it is protandrous. It means its testes ripen earlier than ovaries. Thus self-fertilization is avoided.
- In earthworm there is always cross fertilization accompanied by copulation after which eggs are laid in a cocoon.
- Copulation takes place when testes are matured. Copulation takes place usually late at night or at dawn in rainy season, on the surface of soil. The process in which the spermatozoa of one worm are transferred to another is called copulation.
- However, copulation has not been observed in *Pheretima posthuma* so far, though it is seen in allied species. It probably takes place underground. There are external sex organs for transfer of sperms.
- During copulation, two earthworms come close together in head to tail position in such a way that the spermathecal openings of one worm lies opposite to the male genital openings of the other.
- The copulants are held together by their ventral surfaces by the sticky secretion of the clitellum and accessory glands. The male genital openings are then raised into the papillae. The papillae are inserted into the spermathecal openings of the other successively from behind forward one after the other.
- Copulation lasts for about an hour during which mutual exchange of sperms and prostatic fluid takes place filling up all four pairs of spermathecae. After reciprocal insemination, the worms separate. This is called reciprocal or cross fertilization. Fertilization is external, taking place in a transparent bag like structure called cocoon.

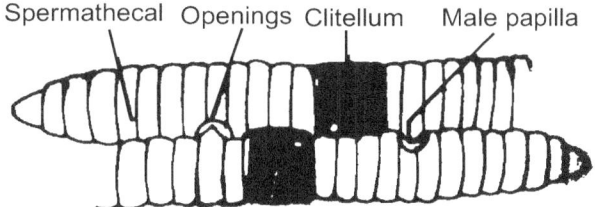

Fig. 4.34: *Pheretima*: Copulation

Cocoon Formation

- Cocoon formation takes place after copulation and when the ovaries mature. Cocoon is a product of clitellum.
- After copulation the clitellar glands become active and secrete a secretion around the clitellum. It forms a loose but elastic girdle around the clitellum.

- The mature ova or eggs are then deposited on the innerwall of the girdle along with albumin and some mucus through female genital opening of 14th segment.
- The worm then wriggles backwards so that the girdle containing eggs is pushed forward.
- As the girdle passes over the spermathecal openings (i.e. 6th to 9th segments) the spermatozoa stored during copulation are squeezed out into the girdle. As the worm withdraws completely, the girdle is released from its anterior end.
- Because of the elasticity of girdle, the two ends of the girdle are closed and it forms an oval or spherical membranous bag containing ova and sperms. This closed girdle is known as cocoon or egg case.
- Fertilization occurs after the cocoon has been deposited. The cocoon of *Pheretima* is small and oval body, light yellow in colour, which is deposited in a moist place.
- Usually, the cocoons are laid during monsoon. In this season there is plenty of moisture and the temperature in suitable for the development.
- However, the cocoons may be laid (in gardens, etc.) in any season under favourable conditions. Many cocoons may be formed in succession after each mating, so that all sperms, stored in the spermathecae are not passed out at once.
- Fertilization of the eggs and entire development thereafter takes place inside the cocoon.

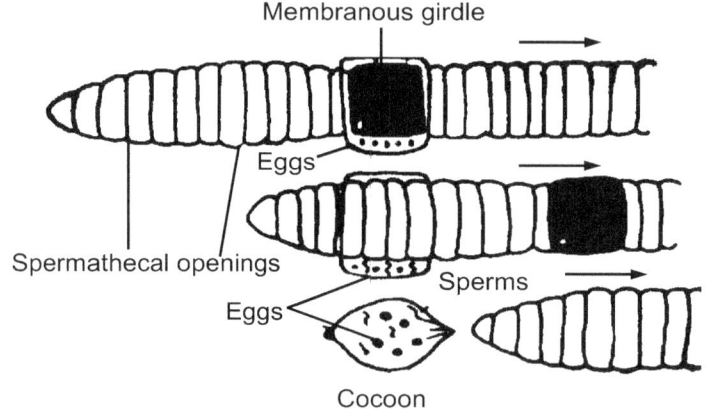

Fig. 4.35: *Pheretima*: Cocoon formation

Cocoon: A cocoon is an egg case containing both eggs and sperms of two different individuals. It is somewhat elongated or oval in shape with olive or light yellow in colour. It looks like a bead of glass and measuring about 2 mm in size. Since there are many eggs in the cocoon most of them are fertilized. After completion of development only single worm hatches out and other eggs are used as a food during development of the worm. Regarding the importance of the cocoon it contains both sperms and egg hence facilitates fertilization.

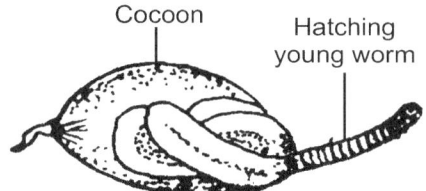

Fig. 4.36: *Pheretima*: Young worm hatching from a cocoon

Cocoon protects the eggs and developing embryos from adverse environmental condition. The undeveloped eggs are also provided as food material to the developing embryo.

Development

- Development starts after fertilization of eggs by sperms in the cocoon. Cleavage is holoblastic and unequal and development is direct because there is no free larval stage.

- A hollow blastula is formed which is converted into blastula by invagination. The mesoblast cells from the mesoderm divide and form two mesoblastic bands, which give rise to the coelomic epithelia lining.

- During the development unfertilized eggs serve as food material. The fully grown worm crawls out of the cocoon in about 2 or 3 weeks.

- The young worm does not receive parental care and it resembles the adult at the time of hatching, except size and absence of clitellum.

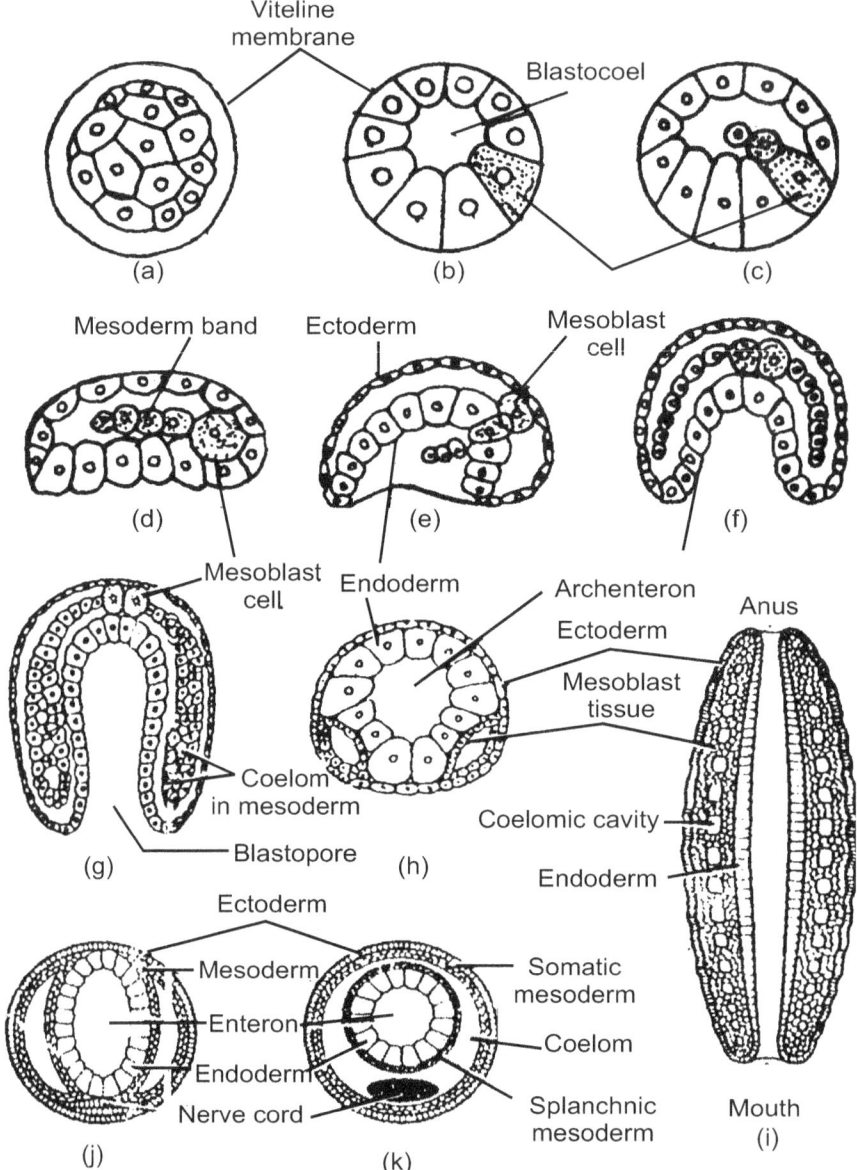

Fig. 4.37: Development of an *Pheretima*: (a) Blastula; **(b)** T.S. blastula with mesoblast cell; **(c)** T.S. blastula with growth of mesoblast; **(d)** L.S. of early gastrula; **(e)** Lateral with gastrula showing invagination; **(f)** T.S. gastrula; **(g)** L.S. early embryo; **(h)** T.S. early embryo; **(i)** L.S. late embryo after the formation of mouth and anus; **(j)** T.S. late embryo and **(k)** Later embryo in T.S.

4.7 Nervous System and Sense Organs

There is well developed nervous system of the earthworm which is centralised and ganglionated type.

It consists of three parts:

1. Central nervous system,
2. Peripheral nervous system, and
3. Sympathetic nervous system.

1. Central Nervous System: It consists of cerebral ganglia, pharyngeal connectives, sub-pharyngeal ganglia and ventral nerve cord (Fig. 4.38). Thus the central nervous system forms two parts, (a) the nerve ring and (b) the ventral nerve cord.

(A) Nerve Ring

(a) Supra pharyngeal ganglia: The nerve ring is formed by a pair of closely united white pear shaped, cerebral or supra pharyngeal ganglia called **Brain**. They are situated dorsally in the middle of the 3rd segment in the depression between the buccal cavity and the pharynx. Each cerebral ganglion gives eight to ten nerves to the prostomium, wall of the buccal chamber and the pharynx, the brain has control over the major body activities.
It acts as inhibitory centre, as worm will go on wriggling without stopping on its removal.

(b) Subpharyngeal ganglia: These are pair of ganglia present below the pharynx in the fourth segment. These are also connected ganglia situated on the ventral side. They act as stimulating centres as their removal impairs spontaneous movements.

(c) Circum-pharyngeal or peripharyngeal connectives: These are pair of thread like structures running around the pharynx and joining the supra-pharyngeal ganglia with the subpharyngeal ganglia to form the nerve ring.

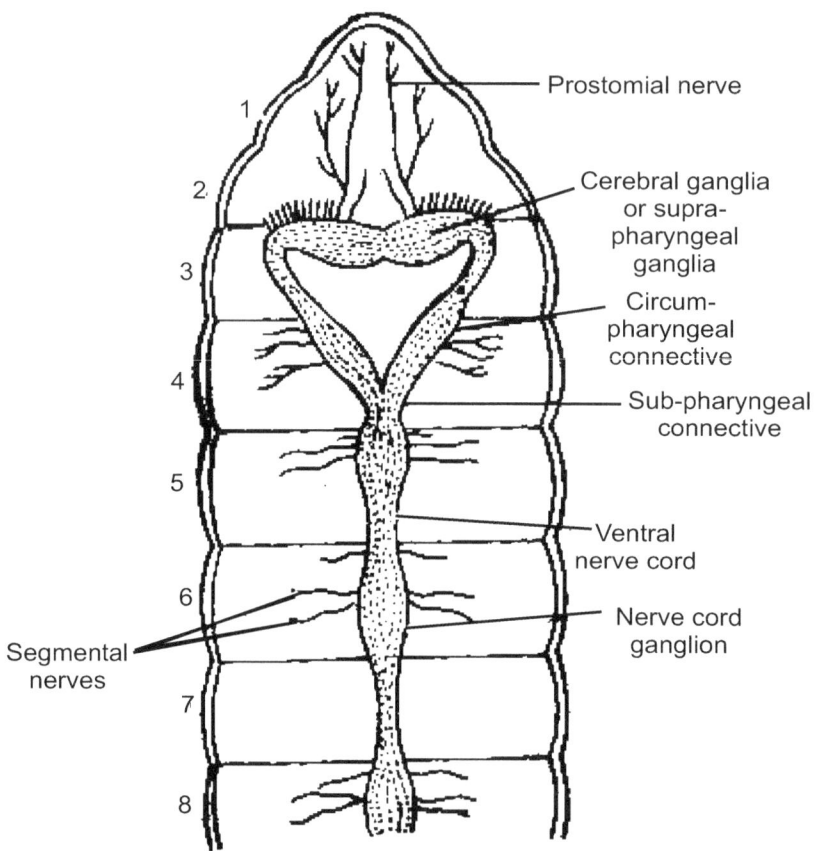

Fig. 4.38: *Pheretima*: Nervous system in dorsal view

(B) Ventral Nerve Cord
- The ventral nerve cord extends from the subpharygeal ganglia to the posterior end of the body. It is formed by the fusion of two longitudinal nerve cords.
- The double, solid nerve cord is covered by a common connective tissue sheath.
- The ventral nerve cord runs, mid-ventrally, beneath the alimentary canal, from sub-pharyngeal ganglia in the 4th segment right upto the last segment.
- In each segment (except first three) the nerve has swellings called **ganglia**.
- The successive ganglia are connected by the nerve fibres called **commissures**.

- In each segment from the 5th segment to the last segment segmental ganglia are present.
- A segmental ganglion also represents the fusion of a pair of ganglia, one belonging to each half of the ventral nerve cord.
- From each ganglion three pairs of nerves are given out, a pair in front of the row of setae and two pairs behind.

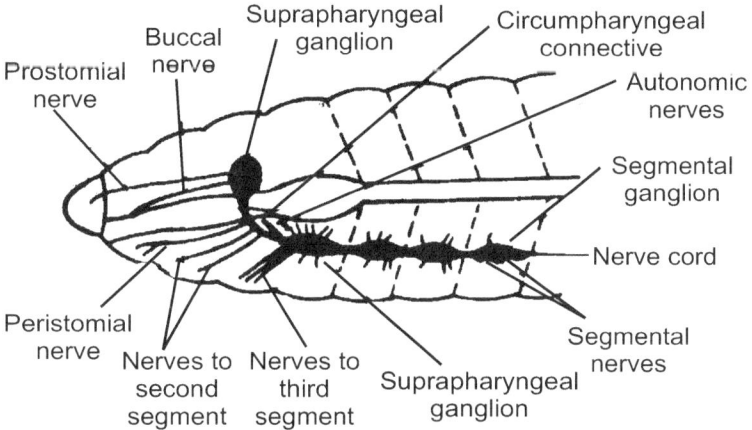

Fig. 4.39: *Pheretima*: Anterior end in lateral view to show the disposition of nerve ring and nerve cord

- Although the ventral nerve cord externally appears single in a transverse section it distinctly shows a double solid cord surrounded by a fibrous capsule or epineuriumin.
- A vertical dorsal region four giant nerve fibres are present.
- One median, one submedian and two lateral giant fibres extend through the entire length of the ventral nerve cord.
- They give off branches in each segment keeping all the segments under control and co-ordination.
- They conduct impulses in both directions and much faster than the ordinary nerve fibres.
- Their rate of conduction of impulses is 60 to 150 feet per second.
- Their function is quick conduction of impulses, end to end contraction, sudden coiling and twisting of the body and rapid withdrawl from abnoxious stimuli.
- The tissue of neuraglia forming the substance of nerve cord includes both nerve cells and nerve fibres embedded in it.

- The nerve cells though more numerous in the ganglia occur diffusely along with the nerve fibres throughout the central nervous system.
- The middle and upper parts of ventral nerve cord consists chiefly of nerve fibres while lower and outer parts contain nerve cells.

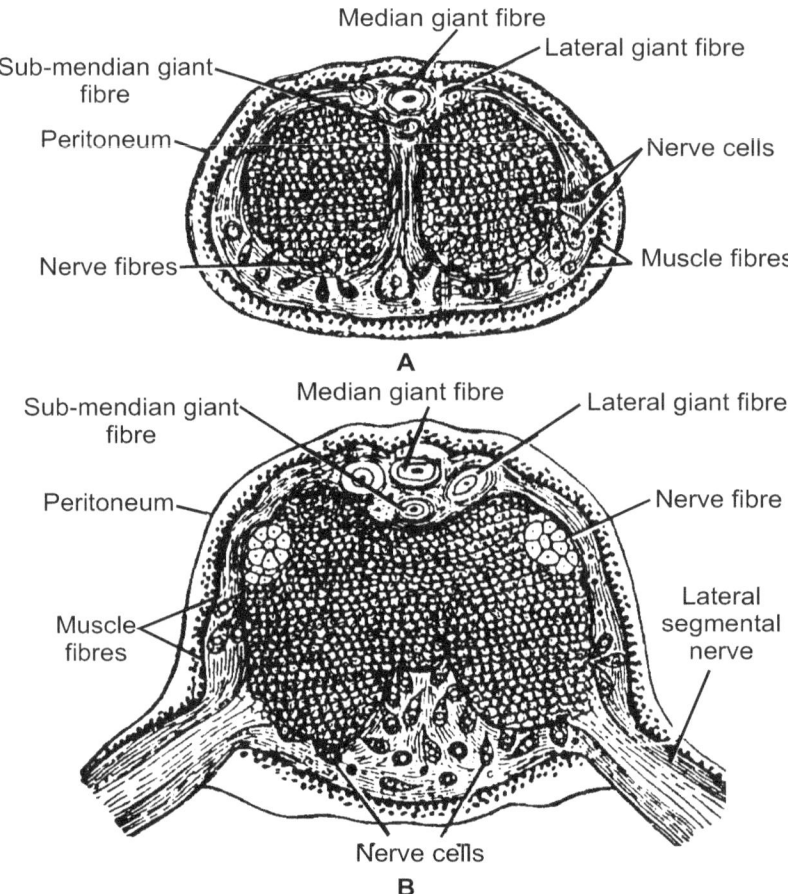

Fig. 4.40: *Pheretima*. A-Section of ventral nerve cord; B-Section of ventral nerve cord at the region of the origin of segmental nerves

2. Peripheral Nervous System

The nerves given out from the central nervous system to the different parts of body is called peripheral nervous system.

(i) Each cerebral or supra pharyngeal ganglion gives off 8 to 10 nerves which innervate the prostomium, buccal chamber and pharynx.

(ii) The circumpharyngeal connectives give out two pairs of nerves going to the organs in 2nd, 3rd and 4th segments.

(iii) In each segment, each segmental ganglion of ventral nerve cord gives off three pairs of lateral nerves, one pair infront of two pairs behind the row of setae, which lead to gut wall, body wall and other internal organs of their segment.

Each nerve is a mixed nerve containing both sensory and motor fibres.

3. Sympathetic Nervous System

It consists of an extensive nerve plexus spread beneath the epidermis and on the alimentary canal and connected with the circumpharyngeal connectives.

Working of Nervous System

- All the activities of the earthworm are under the control of the nervous system. These activities are simple or interconnected reflex actions. Each nerve consists of both afferent and efferent fibres. The afferent fibre starts from receptor organ in the epidermis and terminate in the ventral cord in fine branches.
- Near the branches, in the ventral nerve cord, and forming a synapse with them, arise similar branches of the efferent fibres, which run outward and terminate in the muscles.
- This circuit is nothing but a reflex arc along which the nerve impulses are transmitted.
- The stimuli or sensory impulses are conducted from the receptors by the afferent or sensory fibres of the ventral nerve cord, from where they are transmitted to the motor neuron through sympathetic connection.
- The motor neuron transmits the impulse to the effector organ like muscle or gland which bring about the responses.
- Very often the adjustor neuron may be located between sensory and motor neurons within one segment or its process may extend over to more than one segment co-ordinating the activities of those segments.
- The giant nerve fibres come into play only when the co-ordination between all the body segments is required, such as, end to end contraction and relaxation of the body and sudden coiling of the worm.

SENSE ORGANS

There are no eyes, palps and tentacles in the earthworm, but it shows well developed receptors or sense organs. These sense organs are simple consist of a single or group of specialised ectodermal cells. *Pheretima posthuma* has the following three types of sense organs or receptors (Fig. 4.41).

1. Epidermal receptors,
2. Buccal receptors and
3. Photo receptors.

1. Epidermal receptors: [Fig. 4.41 (A)]: These receptors are abundant and distributed all over the epidermis. They are more numerous on the lateral sides and ventral surface of the body. Each receptor shows slightly elevated cuticle which covers a group of tall, slender and columnar receptor cells. These cells bear small hair-like processes at their outer ends and their inner ends are connected with nerve fibres. These cells are surrounded by simple supporting epidermal cells. There are spaces between these cells hence they are separated from each other and the nuclei of these cells are at different levels. There are also few basal cells placed internally. The epidermal receptors are tactile in function. They are also concerned with changes in temperature and respond to chemical stimuli. Worms are extremely sensitive to touch and mechanical vibrations. Abnoxious and irritating chemical vapours in the air also cause them to withdraw immediately in the burrow.

2. Buccal receptors: [Fig. 4.41 (B)]: These receptors are located only in the epithelium of the buccal chamber. The cells of these receptors are very much similar to epidermal receptors except that they posses broader outer ends, better developed sensory hair and more deeply situated nuclei. These receptors are gustatory and olfactory (related to taste and smell). They also respond to chemical stimuli. (Chemoreceptor).

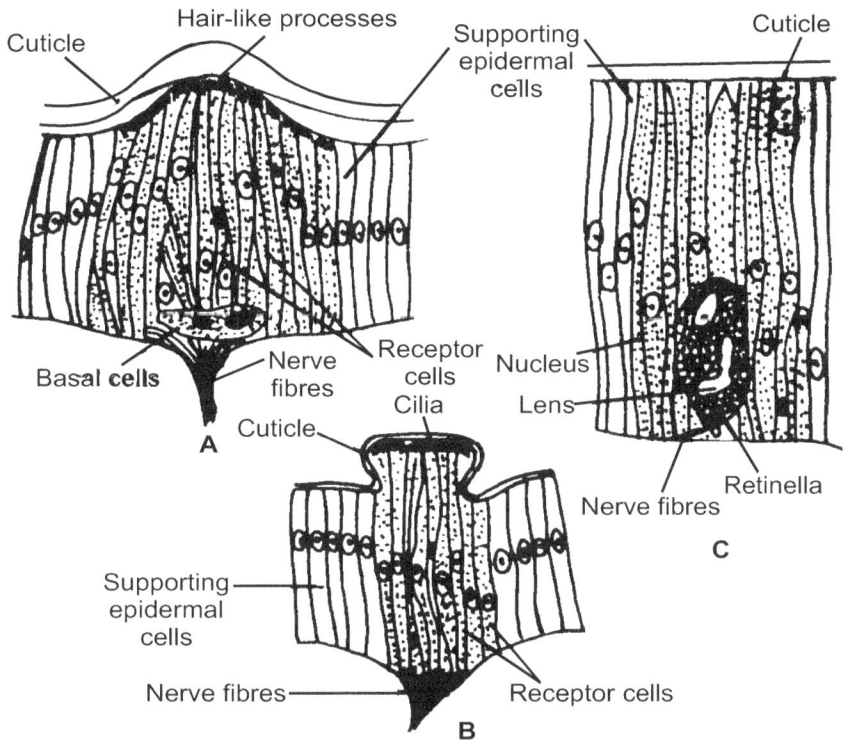

Fig. 4.41: *Pheretima*: Sense organs A-An epidermal receptor; B-A buccal receptor, C-A photoreceptor

3. Photo receptors: [Fig. 4.41 (C)]: These are photo (light) sensitive organs located only on the dorsal surface. They are more numerous on the prostomium but their number gradually decreases towards the posterior end. There are no photoreceptors in clitellum. Each receptor consists of a single ovoid cell, with a nucleus and clear cytoplasm containing a network of neurofibrillae and a small transparent L-shaped lens or optic organelle. They enable the worm to judge the intensity and duration of light. The worms generally avoid intense day light and hence remain into a burrow.

4.8 Economic Importance of Earthworm

Earthworms are of great economic importance to man, particularly to the farmers. Though they are small and simple worms but directly or indirectly useful to man in the following ways:

1. As bait and food: Earthworms are used as a bait for fishing. They are also used as the best food material for fish in aquaria and laboratory animals. In many parts of world uncivilized people consume earthworms as a food material. Many predator animals like birds, frogs, snakes, centipedes also feed on earthworms.

2. In agriculture: Earthworms are of great importance to agriculture. Hence, they are good friends of farmers and gardeners as they are continuously ploughing and manuring the soil. Due to their burrowing and swallowing habit the fertility of the soil increases by many ways. Their burrows permit the penetration of air and moisture in the porous soil. This improves the drainage of water and make easier the downward growth of the roots. The earthworms make soil into fine state useful for cultivation. The leaves in the burrow and the castings of worm make soil more fertile. The excretory products and other secretions of the worm also enrich the soil by adding nitrogenous material which is essential for the growth of the plants. They also reduce acidity and alkalinity of the soil and thus provide optimum conditions for plant growth. Due to burrowing and churning of soil, deeper soil is brought to the surface and castings and the organic matter is mixed to the lower levels of soil.

3. Medicinal use: In past earthworms were used as medicines. The medicines prepared from earthworms were used to cure stones in urinary bladder, jaundice, pyorrhea, piles, rheumatism or gout, diarrohea, sexual impotency. Nowadays also earthworms are still being used in fancy medicine in China, Japan and India.

4. Used in laboratories: Earthworm is the best dissecting invertebrate animal material. Because they are easily available and with convenient size. Thus in most of the zoological and research laboratories it is used as a representative type of Annelida. It is also good animal material for general and comparative physiology study.

Sometimes these worms also prove harmful as their burrows may cause loss of water by seepage from ditches in irrigated lands. The earthworms also serve as intermediate host in transmission of some parasites such as gapeworm, gapeworm of chicken and the lung nematode of pigs. Some parasites carry virus, bacteria causing hog or swine influenza. Some species act as a pest of plant damaging roots and stems. Some earthworms also damage greens of golf courses.

Summary

- Earthworm is annelida animal.
- It is burrowing animal.
- Body is segmented containing 100 to 120 segments.
- Earthworm is bisexual or hermaphrodite animal.
- Rod like chitinous structures present in the body wall useful for locomotion.
- Digestive system consists of alimentary canal and associated glands.
- Blood vascular system is of closed type and blood is circulated through closed blood vessels.
- Nephridia are the excretory organs and they are namely pharyngeal, integumentary and septal nephridia.
- Nervous system of earthworm consists of central nervous system, peripheral nervous system and sympathetic nervous system.
- Male reproductive system of the earthworm consists of testes, testis sacs, seminal vesicle, vasa diferentia, prostate glands and accessory glands.
- Female reproductive system consists of pair of ovaries, pair of oviducts and four pairs of spermathecae.
- Earthworms are of great economic importance to man, particularly to the farmers. They are used in medicine, in agriculture and in laboratories.

Review Questions

1. Describe the structure of body-wall of *Pheretima posthuma*. How it helps in respiration?
2. Give an account of the coelom and coelomic fluid of *Pheretima* and give its functions.
3. Give an account of the alimentary canal of *Pheretima* and its mode of feeding.
4. Describe the detailed structure of septal nephridium of *Pheretima*. How it differs from the other type of nephridia of the same worm?
5. Describe the nervous system of the *Pheretima*.
6. Describe the circulatory system of *Pheretima* in the anterior thirteen segments.

7. Describe the circulatory system of *Pheretima* in intestinal region.

8. Give an account of the reproductive system of *Pheretima* and add a note on cocoon formation.

9. "Earthworms are farmers friend". Discuss.

10. Write short notes on
    (1) Coelomic fluid cells
    (2) Locomotion in *Pheretima*
    (3) Typhlosole
    (4) Pharyngeal nephridia
    (5) Spermatheca
    (6) Cocoon formation in *Pheretima*
    (7) Economic importance of *Pheretima*
    (8) Sense organs in *Pheretima*
    (9) Coelom in *Pheretima*
    (10) Hearts and anterior loops.

11. Draw neat labelled diagrams only
    (a) T.S. of a part of body wall through setal ring.
    (b) T.S. through pharyngeal region.
    (c) T.S. through the gizzard.
    (d) T.S. through typhlosolar region.
    (e) Septal nephridium.

University Questions

1. Give an account of excretory system of earthworm. Add a note on physiology of excretion.

2. Define Setae in *Pheretima*.

www.ingramcontent.com/pod-product-compliance
Lightning Source LLC
Chambersburg PA
CBHW082036230426
43670CB00016B/2673